EVERYTHING RETIREMENT

EVERYTHING RETIREMENT

A Holistic Approach to Your Future

Cheryl Waites Spellman, EdD, MSW, LMSW
Lester Guy Spellman, MBA

ASCEND PUBLISHING, 2025

While every precaution has been taken in the preparation of this book, the publisher assumes no responsibility for errors or omissions, or for damages resulting from the use of the information contained herein.

EVERYTHING RETIREMENT:
A HOLISIC APPROACH TO YOUR FUTURE

First edition: September 1, 2025.

Copyright © 2025 Cheryl Waites Spellman and Lester G. Spellman Jr.

Paperback ISBN: 979-8-9992795-3-8

Hardcover ISBN: 979-8-9992795-4-5

eBook ISBN: 979-8-9992795-2-1

Written by Cheryl Waites Spellman and Lester G. Spellman Jr.

Explore the Everything Retirement platform - Books, Courses and Community

Continue your journey with support, resources and inspiration for your next chapter.

Scan the QR Code or visit EverythingRetirement.org

CONTENTS

Introduction 1

Part I Holistic Retirement Planning 9
Chapter One: Redefining Retirement: Charting a
Meaningful Next Chapter 11
Chapter Two: Embark on Your Path to Retirement Planning 33
Chapter Three: Creating Your Vision for Retirement............. 53

Part II Achieving Financial Security and
Satisfaction in Retirement........................... 67
Chapter Four: Saving for Retirement: Finances and Estate Planning 69
Chapter Five: Financial Satisfaction: Challenges and Strategies 109
Chapter Six: Artful Planning: Developing Your Financial Plan......135

Part III Thriving in Retirement......................... 163
Chapter Seven: Anchoring Retirement in Purpose and Meaning... 165
Chapter Eight: Cultivating Good Health for a Vibrant Retirement . 189
Chapter Nine: Fostering Emotional Wellness in Retirement....... 233
Chapter Ten: Family, Friends, and Communities: Building Social
    Networks for a Rewarding Retirement...................... 257
Chapter Eleven: Retirement Living: Options for Every Lifestyle ... 295

Part IV Your Holistic Retirement Plan.................... 343
Chapter Twelve: Putting It All Together: Action Plan
for Thriving in Retirement 345

Concluding Thoughts 384
Resources 388
About the Authors 389

INTRODUCTION

Everything Retirement: A Holistic Approach to Your Future is designed to empower you—whether you're a Baby Boomer, a member of Generation X, a Millennial, or a current or future retiree from any background—as you prepare for retirement. It offers comprehensive guidance on developing a holistic retirement plan that encompasses essential areas such as having a retirement vision, the importance of purpose and meaning, planning for financial security and satisfaction, cultivating good health and health care access, how to maintain emotional wellness, cultivating family, friends, and organizations as support networks, and options for retirement living.

With practical, step-by-step guidance, this book equips you with the tools to navigate the complexities of retirement effectively. You will discover actionable tips for not only managing the transition but also embracing it with confidence and excitement.

By integrating stories from real-life individuals with expert insights, *Everything Retirement* aims to inspire you to envision and plan for a retirement filled with passion and purpose. You will learn how to leverage your skills, nurture your relationships, and create a fulfilling lifestyle that aligns with your values and aspirations.

As you delve into the comprehensive content within these pages, you will find invaluable resources to help you take charge of your retirement journey. Whether retirement is decades away, you are actively planning for it, or you are already enjoying being retired, this book is your essential companion for living your best life. Embrace the opportunity to create a fulfilling and meaningful retirement filled with possibilities.

As the complexity of retirement planning increases, it requires active engagement and a nuanced perspective. This book examines the evolving demographics and addresses the challenges and opportunities associated with this significant life stage. *Everything Retirement* encourages readers to incorporate their unique cultural background or identity into their retirement planning in meaningful ways. It also includes insights tailored for each generation—Baby Boomer, Generation X, Millennial, and more. These considerations contribute to making informed decisions about retirement.

ABOUT THE AUTHORS

Everything Retirement is the result of years of personal and professional experience. Together, our backgrounds include healthy aging, community development, and financial management. United by a vision of a purposeful, secure, and fulfilling retirement, we created this book with the mission to help you thrive in the retirement chapter of your life.

Cheryl's Story

In the late 1980s, my mother retired with great enthusiasm. As a divorced single parent who successfully raised and supported two daughters, she was prepared to embark on a new chapter of her life, one filled with travel and leisure. She had prudently capitalized on the substantial equity in her home by selling it and was also fortunate to receive a generous pension, comprehensive health insurance coverage, and Social Security benefits. Consequently, she moved to another state, choosing to settle in the southern US region where she continues to live today. Throughout her retirement, she has traveled, pursued various hobbies and interests, and spent considerable time with friends and family.

Over three decades later, and three months into my retirement, I found myself participating in a pottery class, appreciating both the challenge and tranquility of creating a well-crafted pot. I found myself among three other retired women who were thoroughly enjoying their lives. The positive energy in the room was reassuring.

In my former work life, I'd been a gerontologist, researcher, practitioner, and educator, so I understood from a professional standpoint the challenges of aging. Yet, there I was with a smile on my face with others who all felt contentment in retirement. I felt compelled to ask my classmates, "What do you think creates a successful retirement?" We all agreed that preparation, both financially and mentally, was the secret—in addition to staying active and being positive about the possibilities of one's new life phase.

Lester Shares Some of His Story

I was raised in a middle-class suburban household, the son of a business company executive and a social worker. At the age of 52, my father passed away, leaving behind my mother, my married sister, and me, at the time a high school student. My father, a Certified Life Underwriter and insurance company executive, had extensive experience counseling families on funeral plans, estate planning, and retirement planning. His death highlighted the importance of his profession to me.

Subsequently, my mother retired from her position with a state agency to care for me. I quickly became aware of the detailed plans that had been established many years earlier to ensure our financial security. This included a thorough cataloging of assets, debts, and actionable steps, which ultimately provided a financially stable retirement for my mother, who lived until the age of 95.

Roughly two decades after the passing of my mother and following the COVID-19 epidemic, I decided to retire. As I reviewed my savings, assets, and health insurance coverage, among other things, I concluded that I was well prepared. Despite my colleagues' pleas for me to stay in my career, I was looking forward to the next chapter of my life. Now, I'm writing a new, exciting chapter and enjoying adventures of my choosing. And I am loving it.

FINANCES TO LIVING MEANINGFULLY

We are now enjoying our retirements thanks to our planning and vision for this stage of life. Friends and colleagues who haven't yet retired often ask us, "How do you like being retired?" or "What do you do all day?" When we respond, "It's wonderful," and "We stay busy with travel, family, and pursuing our hobbies," we receive comments and questions such as:

"I can't wait to retire. Any suggestions on what I need to know?"

"I have a 401(k) that I contribute to monthly. What else should I be doing?"

"Oh, I will never retire—I like to work, I like to keep busy."

"What do you do all day with your time? Are you bored?"

"I'm afraid that I can't financially afford to retire. I will have to work until I am 80."

"Why did you retire so young? You're too young to be retired."

These comments led us to realize that while some people are excited and looking forward to retirement, many others feel apprehensive about this significant transition. Unfortunately, stereotypes and misconceptions about retirement often cloud the ability to see the rewarding and positive experiences that lie ahead.

Introduction

When we ask individuals about their vision and plans for retirement, many reveal that they have a financial plan in place but little beyond that. In fact, while they know they must save for retirement, they may not have fully considered important aspects such as health care planning, their overall wellness, and the transition from a work-focused identity to a retirement lifestyle that aligns with their interests.

Questions about how to stay meaningfully engaged, what social supports and services they may require, and what their preferred living arrangements will be in their new chapter of life often remain unaddressed. Consequently, their vision and plans can lack comprehensiveness, leaving them unprepared for the various dimensions of retirement living. Taking the time to delve into these considerations can empower individuals to approach retirement with confidence and clarity, ensuring a fulfilling and enriching experience.

To address these concerns and misconceptions, it's essential to engage in comprehensive retirement planning that extends beyond just financial considerations. As you prepare for this next chapter of your life, remember that planning for retirement involves much more than managing your assets; it includes preparing for changes in health, daily activities, life goals, and family dynamics, as well as identifying the resources you may need.

Think about your emotional and spiritual well-being and what your living arrangements will look like in retirement. Have you considered how changes in your health may affect your daily activities and overall lifestyle? What life goals do you wish to pursue, and how will family dynamics play a role in your retirement experience? By giving consideration now to these important topics and acting proactively on your ideas, you can ensure that your retirement is not only financially secure but also fulfilling and aligned with your personal goals and values. Embrace this opportunity to shape a future that resonates with who you are and what you want to achieve.

CHERYL AND LESTER'S ADVICE

We both came to understand that retirement planning requires certain key elements, all of which are discussed in this book. They are:

- **Early and Thoughtful Planning.** The importance of planning for retirement well in advance, considering both financial and lifestyle aspects.
- **Financial Security.** The value of securing financial stability through careful management of savings, assets, and health insurance.
- **Proactive Health Management.** This is being prepared and proactive in managing health, daily activities, and life goals as well as health insurance and access to quality health care.
- **Embrace Change.** The significance of welcoming new phases in life with enthusiasm and readiness.
- **Active and Engaged Lifestyle.** Staying active and involved in various activities, hobbies, and social interactions post-retirement.
- **Positive Outlook.** Maintaining a positive attitude towards retirement and the opportunities it brings.

A HOLISTIC APPROACH TO RETIREMENT

Everything Retirement is the overarching framework that guides you through our "Holistic Retirement Planning Guide." This comprehensive strategy helps you create a vision for the future by defining your motivations, aspirations, and goals. It also ensures you address all essential areas of retirement planning.

The framework is as follows:

1. Establish a Clear Vision
- Reflect on your individual goals, values, and dreams for retirement.
- Consider what fulfillment means to you and how you want to spend your days.

2. Develop a Comprehensive Plan
- Identify lifestyle preferences, and the necessary resources and actions needed to bring your vision to life.
- Prepare to assess your financial needs, including savings strategies, potential income sources, healthcare considerations, and all other essentials for a fulfilling retirement.

3. Set Realistic Goals
- Break your vision down into achievable, measurable goals that can guide your progress.
- Ensure that each goal aligns with your overall retirement vision.

4. Create a Timeline
- Establish a timeline for reaching your goals, outlining when you would like to achieve them.
- Include milestones along the way to help track your progress and celebrate successes.

5. Prepare for Success
- Engage in thorough planning to equip yourself for your retirement aspirations.
- Remain flexible, allowing for adjustments to your plan as circumstances evolve.

6. Utilize Guidance and Resources
- Refer to the resources provided in this book for insights on creating your vision and plan.
- Leverage available tools and resources to help you in your planning process.

HOW TO USE THIS BOOK

This book is divided into four parts, each addressing aspects of retirement that require planning. Part I, "Holistic Retirement Planning," discusses how retirement planning has changed and why a holistic approach is needed today. This section addresses the normal fears and anxieties about retirement and encourages the reader to embrace change while guiding you to develop a vision for your retirement—the first step on your path.

Part II," Achieving Financial Security and Satisfaction in Retirement," is a comprehensive guide to financial planning, including saving, investment, property, and matters of intergenerational wealth transfer—wills, trusts, and estates. This section introduces the concept of financial satisfaction and provides guidance on evaluating your current and future resources.

Finally, Part III, "Thriving in Retirement," offers advice on every topic to ensure a fulfilling retirement. It begins with the importance of having purpose and meaning and then goes on to address health matters, fostering emotional wellness, ensuring a community of support surrounds you, and how to evaluate a variety of retirement living options. Then, Part IV provides you with all the worksheets you need to bring your plan together.

The book is filled with advice, tips and resources on each topic, together with worksheets for you to complete to help you formalize your thinking. Read the book for self-help, and know that by rolling up your sleeves and using the worksheets will really bring your retirement planning to the next level.

We hope that through this book, you will see that retirement is nothing to be afraid of. Instead, you will come to realize that it can be a wonderful time of new opportunities and growth. That's what we have found, and our wish for you is that you will find it, too.

PART

I

HOLISTIC RETIREMENT PLANNING

CHAPTER ONE

REDEFINING RETIREMENT:
Charting a Meaningful Next Chapter

Often when you think you're at the end of something,
you're at the beginning of something else.
—FRED ROGERS (AKA MR. ROGERS)

Life is a balance of holding on and letting go.
—RUMI

Retirement is defined as the phase of life in which an individual transitions from full-time employment or a career to a period of reduced work-related responsibilities or complete disengagement from professional duties. The transition phase, as well as full retirement, enables individuals to pursue personal interests, leisure activities, and new opportunities for growth and fulfillment.

Many individuals neglect to develop a thorough plan for this stage of life. While some view retirement planning with enthusiasm, others experience uncertainty about how to go about it. This may be due to common stereotypes and misconceptions about retirement as well as a lack of awareness regarding the opportunities available during this phase.

It seems that when people talk about retiring, they are often primarily focused on the financial aspects. Although finances are quite important, if someone wants to ensure a well-rounded retirement experience, planning should be more comprehensive than that. It requires an approach that addresses other key considerations, such as health care, life goals, purpose, social support networks, emotional well-being, and living arrangements, in other words, a holistic approach. Many don't think ahead about these factors; instead, retirement planning for many may be vague or not addressed at all. The retirement landscape has significantly changed due to social, demographic, and medical advancements. Therefore, a holistic approach to retirement planning is now essential.

SOCIETAL CHANGES

The period following WWII ushered in significant societal shifts in the United States. Divorce and birth control became acceptable, with the result that today, 50% of marriages end in divorce, and many individuals have elected not to have children. Single-individual households are on the rise.

In addition, in the past, the main way most people provided for their retirement was to work for many years for an organization that provided them with a defined-benefit plan and to buy and ultimately pay for their home. This shifted considerably in 1978 when the Internal Revenue Code was amended to allow individuals to defer taxation on income invested in a retirement account. Thus, 401(k)s, named for that section of the Tax Code, were born. Now that people could save for retirement, they were expected to, and more and more companies did away with defined-benefit plans in favor of "matching" employee contributions to company 401(k)s.

Formerly, retired parents relied on their children for assistance. Although the industrialization era began the trend of individuals moving around for employment, this has continued. Now, children may live far from their parents and may not be able to offer support to them due to their need to focus on their own careers. Those in retirement must seek out other services to support them.

Other societal shifts that seemed to arrive with the Boomer generation included strides in psychology and holistic approaches to health and well-being that included mental health. More than ever before, people focused on personal purpose and life meaning. At the same time, options for medical care, health insurance, and long-term care became more complex.

MEDICAL ADVANCES AND LONGEVITY

Another reason more comprehensive retirement planning is needed today is because the retirement years often last longer than they have in the past. Thanks to significant advancements in science, medicine, and technology, many individuals are living 20 to 30 years beyond the traditional retirement age of 65. Moreover, the number of centenarians worldwide is increasing. As a result, people must prepare for long lifespans but without fear or worry.

Increases in longevity raise important questions about retirement: What exactly is retirement, and what does it look like? Why is 65 considered the traditional retirement age, and is that the right age for someone to retire? How should someone spend these additional years? Can they be filled with enjoyable experiences, personal growth, and purpose, or will the fear of long years of boredom, isolation, and loneliness prove accurate? This book explores these questions.

Laura Carstensen and the Stanford Longevity Center discuss the concept of "century living," which emphasizes the importance of creating a life plan for a full century with thoughtful strategies for each stage of life. This approach encourages individuals to develop meaningful lives filled with belonging, purpose, and value at every stage, ensuring a rewarding experience throughout retirement.

A remarkable example of someone who embraced this concept is former US President Jimmy Carter, who lived to be 100 years old. After leaving the White House, he dedicated his later years to service and advocacy. Carter remained actively engaged in promoting humanitarian causes, advocating for peace, and supporting various charitable organizations, particularly Habitat for Humanity. His life serves as a testament to how purpose-driven engagement during retirement can lead to a fulfilling existence, enabling you to make a lasting impact while enjoying the benefits of a longer life.

Another remarkable centenarian, Gertrude Weaver, was recognized as the oldest verified American when she passed away at the age of 116 in 2015. She shared her secrets to longevity, which included kindness and positive thinking.

Additionally, Carmen Herrera, the Cuban-American abstract painter born on May 31, 1915, is still alive as of 2025 and currently resides in New York City. Herrera is celebrated for her vibrant geometric paintings and has made significant contributions to contemporary art, gaining recognition later in her career. Her longevity and continued creativity serve as a powerful reminder of how purpose and engagement can enhance our lives, especially in the context of increasing lifespan and the vibrant, diverse community of centenarians shaping our perceptions of aging.

Embracing the prospect of longer lives means that each phase, including your retirement years, can be rich with opportunities for growth and engagement. It is imperative to rethink retirement and engage in comprehensive, holistic planning for your retirement years that represents a multifaceted approach to ensure financial security, access to health care, overall wellness, social support, an active lifestyle, and age-friendly living environments for the duration. By focusing on these elements, you can effectively prepare for the extended years ahead and cultivate a purposeful and fulfilling life and, much like Carter, Weaver, and Herrera, navigate each chapter with intention and joy.

Chapter 1. Redefining Retirement: Charting a Meaningful Next Chapter

EMBRACING OUR DIVERSITY

Much like the United States population, adults aged 65 and older are becoming increasingly diverse. This group now represents a vibrant tapestry of various racial and cultural backgrounds, ethnicities, disabilities, socioeconomic statuses, gender identities, religions, and sexual orientations. The demographic composition of the United States is projected to undergo considerable change over the next 15 years. Factors such as immigration, evolving family structures, birth rates, longevity, and advancements in health care drive these changes, reinventing the landscape for our retirees. The projected changes are highlighted in the next table.

Demographic Projections of US Racial and Ethnic Diversity

YEAR	WHITE	BLACK OR AFRICAN AMERICAN	LATINX OR HISPANIC	ASIAN	NATIVE AMERICAN OR ALASKA NATIVE	NATIVE HAWAIIAN OR OTHER PACIFIC ISLANDER	TWO OR MORE RACES
2025	61%	22%	19%	10%	2%	1.5%	5%
2030	58%	21%	24%	11%	2%	1.5%	6%
2035	57%	20%	26%	12%	2%	1.5%	7%
2040	55%	19%	28%	13%	2%	1.5%	8%

Figure 1: Demographic Projections for the United States (Vespa, Medina, and Armstrong 2018).

RACIAL AND CULTURAL COMMUNITIES

Reflecting on the racial and ethnic diversity of the United States, let's celebrate the unique strengths these communities bring and recognize the value of diverse experiences which contribute to a retirement experience that supports everyone in their journey. Changing demographics underscore the need for comprehensive retirement planning resources tailored to individual cultural and other circumstances.

Members of racial and ethnic communities often face challenges rooted in historical discrimination, legal inequalities, and healthcare disparities that can impact their retirement planning. For example, limited access to quality healthcare over their lifetime may lead to greater health issues in retirement, making it essential to factor in these disparities when preparing financially and medically for the future. Additionally, these communities should carefully consider retirement living arrangements and long-term care options to ensure they meet their specific needs and cultural preferences.

On the other hand, by leveraging the resilience and strengths of racial and ethnic groups and incorporating them into holistic retirement planning, individuals can still approach this period in their lives with confidence. Emotional well-being is fostered by community membership and support. Additionally, established community organizations and faith groups can offer valuable services, advocacy, other resources, and social opportunities that facilitate a more engaged retirement, helping individuals feel a genuine sense of belonging. Many cultural groups that experienced limited access to mainstream health care maintained their traditional knowledge of natural healing methods, which can be gentle adjuncts to health care and well-being care.

Communities that have historically faced challenges have developed resilience and adaptability, empowering their members to navigate the complexities of retirement planning. Drawing on their rich experiences in overcoming obstacles, they can thrive despite adversity.

LGBTQ+

As the LGBTQ+ community plans for retirement, its members must embrace the diversity within the community while acknowledging the unique challenges they may face. Issues of discrimination and health care disparities can influence the retirement journey. The landmark Supreme Court ruling in Obergefell v. Hodges in 2015 granted same-sex couples the right to marry and access essential legal benefits. However, discrimination can still occur in health care settings, which may complicate LGBTQ+ individuals' ability to receive the inclusive and compassionate care in retirement they deserve.

Many older LGBTQ+ individuals have also encountered economic obstacles stemming from past workplace discrimination, leading to gaps in social safety nets and retirement benefits. Moreover, social isolation is a significant concern for many, particularly for those who have lost partners or familial connections, thereby impacting mental health and overall well-being.

Despite these challenges, there are strengths within the LGBTQ+ community that can be harnessed in retirement planning. By embracing their identity and fostering connections with others, LGBTQ+ individuals can create a fulfilling retirement for themselves. It can be a time of advocating for inclusive policies and support systems not only to improve their own quality of life as they age but also to contribute to a more equitable future for others. The life experiences of LGBTQ+ individuals, coupled with the resilience those experiences created, are powerful assets in navigating the next chapter of retirement, one filled with purpose, joy, and connection.

Transgender or nonbinary individuals planning for retirement—in addition to the challenges faced by the LGBTQ+ community as a whole—can experience even greater levels of healthcare discrimination, including restricted access to gender-affirming care that can leave their health needs unmet. In addition, legal obstacles, such as obtaining accurate identification documents, complicate access to essential services. Social isolation and stigma may also affect the mental health and emotional well-being of these individuals.

A strong community of advocates is working to create change. By standing together and advocating for supportive measures, transgender and nonbinary individuals can help ensure a dignified and comfortable retirement for themselves and others in their community. Embracing who they are and leveraging the resilience born of their life experiences empowers the members of this community to navigate these challenges and allows them to thrive in this exciting new chapter of life.

PERSONS WITH DISABILITIES

Those living with disabilities may face some unique challenges when planning for retirement. They may have experienced discrimination, inadequate accommodations, limited job opportunities, or reduced working hours, all of which can lead to lower earnings and retirement savings. Additionally, managing living costs—such as medical expenses and the need for adaptive equipment—can further restrict their ability to save. Securing accessible and affordable housing and transportation is essential for maintaining the financial stability of persons with disabilities both before retirement and after.

It's important to remember that as a person living with a disability you are not alone in this journey. Embracing your strengths, such as resilience, determination, and resourcefulness, can empower you to overcome these challenges. By actively addressing these issues and seeking out supportive measures—whether through community resources, advocacy, or connections with others facing similar circumstances—you can work towards achieving a secure and comfortable retirement.

The global population of older people is growing and, in the United

States, is becoming more diverse. With the expectation of longer lifespans, many issues and opportunities will arise as individuals retire. It is important to plan carefully, stay informed, and be open to evolving concepts of retirement. No matter your age, it is best to start preparing for this transition now. Take proactive steps to create a vision and comprehensive plan, one that incorporates considerations regarding your race, ethnicity, gender, gender identity, disability or generational cohort.

By actively addressing these issues and seeking out supportive measures—whether through community resources, advocacy, or connections with others facing similar circumstances—you can work towards achieving a secure and comfortable retirement.

THE IMPACT OF GENERATIONAL COHORTS ON RETIREMENT

Generational identity plays a crucial role in helping us understand how the era in which we grew up has shaped our worldview and our place within it. The significant events, cultural shifts, and technological developments during our formative years contribute to our values, beliefs, and perspectives. In this book, we use generational identity as a valuable lens to provide important context for retirement planning, which may differ across generations. From Baby Boomers to Generation Z, every cohort must navigate its own set of obstacles and opportunities as they prepare for a secure and fulfilling retirement.

Retirement planning is a necessity for every generation, whether the individuals in it are already retired, close to retirement, or decades away. This book adds a dimension to retirement planning by helping the members of various generational cohorts think about retirement framed within the context of their cohort's concerns and needs. Baby Boomers ("Boomers"), Generation X ("Gen Xers"), Millennials ("Generation Y"), and Generation Z ("Gen Z"). Additionally, the book also provides context for "Cuspers"—individuals born on the cusp of two generations and those who identify as part of "Microgenerations," which are distinct smaller groups within a generational cohort. By exploring your generational cohort alongside others, you can gain not only information on your cohort but also a broader perspective on retirement planning.

The Generational Cohorts

GENERATION	TIME PERIOD WHEN BORN
The Greatest Generation	1901–1927
The Silent Generation	1928–1945
Baby Boom Generation or Boomers	1946–1964
Generation X or Gen X	1965–1980
Millennial or Generation Y	1981–1996
Generation Z or Gen Z	1997–2012
Generation Alpha	2012–Present

BABY BOOMERS: *REDEFINING RETIREMENT*

Let's begin by focusing on Baby Boomers, those born between 1946 and 1964. This generation is at the forefront of shaping new paths for retirement, with many older Baby Boomers approaching their '80s. As pioneers, they are redefining what retirement means and moving beyond traditional expectations. Coming of age during the Civil Rights and Women's Movements and the Vietnam War, many Baby Boomers challenged societal norms and expectations, which led to increased advocacy for equality and rights. The Civil Rights Movement fought against racial discrimination and inequality, while the women's movement focused on issues such as gender equality, reproductive rights, and workplace participation. As a result, many women from the Baby Boomer generation were able to enter the workforce in greater numbers than previous generations, significantly transforming workplace dynamics and having lasting impacts on the economy. This shift has contributed to ongoing discussions about gender roles, pay equity, and workplace inclusivity, making Baby Boomers a crucial influence on the social and economic landscape in the United States.

Now, as the members of this cohort stand firmly in what was once considered the "golden years," they undoubtedly have found that their experiences reflect a broad spectrum of lifestyles, financial situations, saving habits, and retirement plans. The many who are already retired may be focusing on family and pursuing personal hobbies, passions, and interests. Conversely, those in this generation who have yet to retire may be feeling apprehensive about this transition and grappling with the desire to remain engaged in the workforce amid fears of the social disengagement that can accompany retirement. A 2009 Pew Research survey revealed that many Boomers believe old age doesn't begin until age 72, underscoring the desire to remain active and vibrant.

Prominent Baby Boomers, such as Oprah Winfrey, Geena Davis, Dolly Parton, and Sally Ride, exemplify the diversity and varied contributions of this generation. Influential political figures like Bill Clinton and George W. Bush are in this cohort, along with legal trailblazers such as Sonia Sotomayor and Condoleezza Rice, further showcasing this rich tapestry of Boomer achievements. Voices of justice in this cohort include Ruth Bader Ginsburg and prominent Native American figure Ben Nighthorse Campbell. They highlight the remarkable accomplishments of Baby Boomers in advocacy and representation.

In the arts, the creative work of Bruce Springsteen, Madonna, Stevie Wonder, and Denzel Washington continues to inspire. Additionally, icons like Arnold Schwarzenegger, John Travolta, Eddie Murphy, and Cher have made significant impacts in film and entertainment, while musicians such as Gloria Estefan, Garth Brooks, and Randy Travis have shaped the music landscape in meaningful ways. Cultural figures like Liza Minnelli, Cornel West, Michelle Yeoh, and Yo-Yo Ma reflect the richness and diversity within the Baby Boomer generation.

Entrepreneurs like Steve Jobs, Steve Wozniak, and Bill Gates have transformed the technology and business landscape with their innovation and vision. Together, the Baby Boomers demonstrate how this generation continues to make a lasting impact through their varied experiences and contributions.

As the Baby Boomers prepare for and manage their retirement, it's important to recognize the strong values that they possess, including a commitment to hard work, optimism, family, and consumerism. These values play a significant role in how they approach retirement planning. While many of them are happily living their next chapter, and others may be well-prepared for it, there may still be others who might face challenges requiring thoughtful consideration. With this group's life expectancy now significantly longer than that of previous generations, it's essential that they evaluate their income and health care needs as part of their retirement strategy.

If you are already retired, reflecting on your and your cohort's values can help you lead a fulfilling retirement. Your hard work can guide you in managing resources effectively, while your optimism can help you embrace new opportunities and adapt to changes. Cherishing family connections allows you to nurture relationships that bring joy and support, ensuring your retirement is enriched with meaningful interactions. Understanding the role of consumerism can also help you prioritize spending on experiences that enhance your quality of life.

By trusting in your experiences and the values you hold dear, you can navigate this exciting new phase of life with confidence and purpose, creating a fulfilling retirement that aligns with your aspirations and enriches your well-being.

Chapter 1. Redefining Retirement: Charting a Meaningful Next Chapter

NAVIGATING RETIREMENT WITH CONFIDENCE AS A GEN XER

As the members of Generation X approach retirement over the next few years, it's vital to recognize the diversity and richness within this group. Born between 1965 and 1980, prominent figures such as Barack Obama, Holly Robinson Peete, Sofia Vergara, Ken Jeong, and Michelle Rodriguez exemplify the varied backgrounds and contributions of this generation. While they may have access to resources and opportunities that not everyone has, their successes can serve as inspiration for anyone navigating their own retirement journey.

Many Gen Xers possess strengths that will aid them in planning for a fulfilling retirement. Their unique resilience and adaptability have been shaped, in part, by navigating economic challenges, such as the recessions of the 1970s, '80s, and '90s. This has instilled in them a pragmatic approach to finances, encouraging their ability to budget effectively and seek innovative solutions. Additionally, having faced rising education costs, many of them have developed strong problem-solving skills and determination. Although some may still carry student loan debt, this experience can motivate them to prioritize financial literacy and informed decision-making in their retirement planning. Finally, given that it is such a diverse cohort, Gen Xers reflect this in their varied perspectives and skills, which help them to foster valuable connections and enrich their social networks.

As you, a Generation X member, assess your retirement goals and lifestyle expectations, remember that your ability to embrace change, seek out support networks, and engage with community resources will empower you as you create a meaningful retirement. Reflect on what you truly value and how you can align your plans with your passions. By leveraging your strengths and remaining proactive, you can turn the challenges of retirement into opportunities for personal growth and fulfillment, ensuring that the next chapter of life is vibrant and rewarding.

MILLENNIALS PREPARING FOR THE FUTURE OF RETIREMENT

Millennials (Generation Y), born roughly between 1981 and the late '90s, are a cohort that came of age in a rapidly changing world, one marked by technological advancements, economic shifts, and social changes. This generation is not only diverse but also incredibly influential. Prominent figures like Beyoncé Knowles-Carter, LeBron James, and Mark Zuckerberg represent the immense talent within the Millennial generation. Artists such as Taylor Swift, Lady Gaga, Rihanna, and Ariana Grande advocate for important social issues, including mental health awareness and LGBTQ+ rights.

Additionally, Jessica Alba has transitioned from actor to successful entrepreneur and advocate for health and sustainability with her company, The Honest Company. Business leaders like John Zimmer, cofounder of Lyft, have also made significant contributions to innovation and social change. Influencer and entrepreneur Michelle Phan has empowered a generation through beauty and lifestyle content while promoting self-expression and empowerment.

In sports, champions like Serena Williams and Michael Phelps continue to inspire many, while comedian Trevor Noah raises awareness on global matters. Rappers like Kendrick Lamar engage in social justice discussions, and political leaders like Alexandria Ocasio-Cortez (AOC) and Pete Buttigieg contribute to contemporary conversations.

Together, these individuals showcase the diverse experiences and strengths of the Millennial generation, inspiring future generations to embrace their identities and make a positive impact.

As you, a Millennial, approach retirement—though it may seem distant—it's never too early to start planning for your future, as this significant chapter will be here sooner than you think. The financial crisis of 2008 greatly influenced many Millennials, in particular, due to the unique challenges of entering the workforce during and after such a difficult economic period.

Chapter 1. Redefining Retirement: Charting a Meaningful Next Chapter

HOW GEN ZERS CAN EMPOWER THEIR FUTURES

Generation Z (Gen Z), born roughly between the late '90s and 2010s, is the youngest generation in the workforce as of this writing. Prominent figures like poet Amanda Gorman, singer Billie Eilish, and musician Olivia Rodrigo exemplify the creativity and passion of this cohort. Gen Z influencers and advocates, including Asia Jackson, Greta Thunberg, Malala Yousafzai, and political activist David Hogg, underscore the importance of activism and social change.

Notable figures in entertainment and sports—like Kylie Jenner, Jenny Ortega, Khaby Lame, Simone Biles, Caitlin Clark, Chloe Kim, and Naomi Osaka—showcase the diverse talents within this cohort. Musicians like Lil Nas X and Maddie Marlow from Maddie & Tae contribute to the vibrant musical landscape of Gen Z, while Emma Chamberlain highlights the powerful role social media plays in shaping conversations around lifestyle and mental health.

The sooner you start thinking about your future, the better off you will be. As you do so, remember that understanding financial literacy, cultivating social networks, and focusing on your health and life purpose are essential. While you can't predict exactly what lies ahead, actively preparing for retirement can set you up for success. You have decades to develop a retirement vision that aligns with your values and aspirations. By considering your goals and seeking out resources now, you'll be better equipped to embrace the opportunities that await you in this important chapter of life. The earlier you start, the more choices you will create for yourself.

MICROGENERATIONS AND CUSPERS

A microgeneration refers to a smaller generational group typically spanning a narrower range of birth years, who share unique experiences that distinguish them from broader generations. Such microgenerations may be subsets of larger generations or straddle two generations as "Cuspers." For example, "Generation Jones" refers to a subgroup of Baby Boomers born between 1955 and 1965. Microgenerations help to better capture the unique experiences and cultural contexts of people who do not fully fit within the broader generational definitions. While the exact years and names may vary depending on the source, these labels have gained popularity as a way to understand the nuances within generational cohorts, as in the table that follows.

Cuspers are individuals born at the tail end of one generation and the beginning of another. They are "on the cusp" between two generational groups. Cuspers may identify with or share the traits of both their border cohorts without necessarily identifying with either or being defined as part of a distinct group. Cuspers are about the overlap between generations. For example, the term "Xennials" is often used to describe a Cusper microgeneration born between 1977 and 1985, whose members experienced an analog childhood but adapted to the digital revolution in their adolescence or early adulthood. (Within the Cusper generation of Xennials is a microgeneration known as the "Carter Babies.") Zillenials are Cuspers that straddle the Millennial and Gen Z generations. Like larger cohorts, members of a microgeneration share specific historical, cultural, or technological experiences that set them apart from both their broader generational groups, as the table that follows shows.

Chapter 1. Redefining Retirement: Charting a Meaningful Next Chapter

Microgenerations and Cuspers

GENERATION JONES (1955–1965)

General Attributes: Microgeneration within Baby Boomers

Characterized by their skepticism and pragmatism, Generation Jones grew up during the 1960s and '70s, experiencing the optimism of the post-war boom, followed by the disillusionment of the 1970s. They are known for their work ethic but also for feeling a sense of unfulfilled expectations ("keeping up with the Joneses").

XENNIALS (1977–1985)

General Attributes: On the cusp of Generation X and Millennials

Seen as having the skepticism of Gen X, who are known for their critical thinking and independence, combined with the optimism and tech savviness of Millennials, who embrace technology and innovation. Xennials are often described as having an analog childhood and a digital young adulthood, experiencing significant events such as the rise of personal computers and the Internet. They are almost exclusively the children of baby boomers.

CARTER BABIES (1977–1981)

General Attributes: Microgeneration of Xennials

This microgeneration was born during the presidency of Jimmy Carter and came of age during the Reagan era. They were too young to fully take part in the counterculture movements of the 1960s and 1970s but were heavily influenced by the economic and cultural shifts of the 1980s. Carter Babies are a subset of Xennials, specifically born during the presidency of Jimmy Carter. They share many traits with Xennials but have distinct experiences from the late 1970s and early 1980s.

ZILLENNIALS (1993–1998)

General Attributes: On the cusp of Millennials and Generation Z

Too young to fully relate to early Millennials who remember a world before widespread Internet access but too old to be fully considered part of Gen Z, who are true digital natives. They were babies and children when 9/11 struck and did not know life before airport security screenings, rampant domestic terrorism, and other frightening threats.

Baby Boomers, Gen Xers, Millennials, and Gen Zers exhibit diverse attitudes toward work, retirement, life stages, financial priorities, health, social support, and community. Similarly, individuals in the Cusper and Microgeneration groups have their own unique perspectives. Generation Alpha, next after Gen Z, is still young, and their life experiences, behaviors, and viewpoints are continuing to evolve. It is important to recognize that generational identity and cohorts are not meant to confine someone; they are just one aspect of a complex identity that includes age, gender identity, culture, ethnicity, religion, socioeconomic status, profession, community, significant events, shared history, among other factors.

As we progress further into the 21st century, how generations make choices on the pathways to retirement will continue to emerge and develop. Retirement, as a phase in the lifespan, is evolving and influenced by a range of factors, including one's generational cohort and the broader world context. It is imperative to have a clear vision of what is important, understand your context, address challenges, and prepare for this life stage. Being self-aware, intentional, and informed and having a well-defined plan and vision are essential for navigating this transition successfully.

DIFFERENT GENERATIONAL CONCERNS

Data from the US Census Bureau reveals that approximately 56 million individuals in the United States were aged 65 and older in 2020. By 2030, this number is expected to climb to around 73 million, meaning nearly one in five Americans will be at least 65 years old. This increase in the older population reflects the demographics of the Baby Boom generation, who have now aged into retirement, and enhancements in life expectancy. This trend is likely to continue with subsequent generations. As a result, there is a growing need for holistic retirement planning to meet the needs of both current and future populations.

A significant number of Baby Boomers have already retired and transitioned into the retirement stage. Their experiences have helped shape an evolving understanding of what retirement can be, bringing a unique perspective to this life stage. For example, Barbara Corcoran, a prominent real estate mogul and television personality on *Shark Tank*, sold her company and embraced retirement by focusing on entrepreneurship, investing, and mentoring others. Another notable Boomer, former NFL quarterback Joe Namath, years after his football and subsequent acting careers to engage in philanthropy and advocate for seniors' health issues in his retirement. Additionally, Salma Hayek, is a semi-retired actor and producer who now focuses on producing, philanthropy, and her family while still remaining active in the industry.

Numerous current retirees speak with express joy in their newfound freedom and share their unique insights about and experience of life after full-time work. They exemplify how retirement can be a time for exploration, creativity, and personal fulfillment.

THE HOLISTIC RETIREMENT PLANNING FRAMEWORK

Given the social and demographic changes and concerns that those considering retirement are faced with, it is clear that focusing on the financial aspects of retirement is no longer enough. A more holistic approach will ensure that those in retirement will be as engaged and secure as possible in what may be the long retirement years.

The process starts with identifying your passions, interests, and purpose to create a clear vision for retirement. The chapters that follow guide you to develop these as well as a comprehensive plan that covers financial security, healthy living, emotional wellness, supportive networks, and retirement living options. The planning process is dynamic and evolves with your changing needs and priorities. The 10-step process is as follows:

Steps for Holistic Retirement Planning

1. Begin by addressing concerns and fears, which leads to embracing change
2. Create a vision for retirement
3. Plan for financial security and satisfaction
4. Thrive through purpose and meaning in retirement
5. Cultivate good health practices and a healthy lifestyle
6. Maximize health insurance coverage and benefits
7. Foster emotional wellness
8. Build your social support networks
9. Discover your ideal retirement living options
10. Put it all together

Whether retirement is imminent or even decades away, it is essential to plan for a balanced and fulfilling transition to this new phase of life. This book is based on the Holistic Retirement Planning framework; it provides valuable insights and suggestions designed to help you navigate the complexities and pleasures of retirement. It will help you develop a thorough plan that encompasses financial security, emotional well-being, healthy living, and supportive networks. Included in the chapters that follow are detailed information, resources, and actionable steps for effective retirement planning. Plan your future effectively.

TAKEAWAYS FROM REDEFINING RETIREMENT

Thanks to societal and economic changes in conjunction with medical advances, retirement planning is not what it used to be. The key points from this chapter include:

Retirement is not one-size-fits-all.

Today, the wisest course is to plan for a long retirement since people are living longer than ever before.

Your retirement journey is unique, so good planning will reflect your individuality, including your ethnicity, culture, and generation. The best planning will incorporate your personal passions, interests, and sense of purpose. Embrace this opportunity to define what fulfillment and happiness mean for you.

By planning thoughtfully and taking a holistic approach, you can create a clear vision for your retirement years that fills your retirement with purpose, excitement, and well-being.

CHAPTER TWO

EMBARK ON YOUR PATH TO RETIREMENT PLANNING

Fears about retirement stem from uncertainty; embracing change can transform anxiety into excitement.
—SUZE ORMAN

The future depends on what you do today.
—MAHATMA GANDHI

Retirement is a blank sheet of paper. It is a chance to redesign your life into something new and different.
—PATRICK FOLEY

The first task anyone must undertake when facing retirement is to consider what fears or anxieties about retiring may be on their mind. The end of traditional work is one of life's major transitions. Naturally, people have concerns and worries about what will happen next. A critical component of retirement planning is to look squarely at these fears, so they don't influence other planning decisions. Many ease into retirement gradually. One way to do this is to think about what retirement means to you.

MANAGING THE EXCITEMENT AND ANXIETY OF RETIREMENT

As someone contemplates retirement, it's normal to feel a mix of excitement and anxiety. Then, when this significant transition grows closer, those emotions may intensify. Older people might be thrilled at the prospect of entering a relaxed and fulfilling next chapter after decades of hard work. They have earned this. No more morning alarms, commutes, or the pressures of clocking in. Say goodbye to late-night work, endless meetings, deadlines, and navigating office politics, and leave behind the stress of dealing with difficult coworkers or managers.

Furthermore, as people envision this new phase of life, they can imagine spending more time on activities they love, pursuing hobbies, traveling, and focusing on self-care and relaxation. This time is also a chance to enjoy deeper connections with family, such as your grandchildren and friends. The possibilities ahead are exciting and numerous.

However, it is also completely normal to feel anxiety or fear about retiring. Entering retirement involves a transition from full-time employment, which can raise concerns about financial security, identity, and health. Someone might grapple with questions of identity and purpose, pondering, "Who will I be?" and "What will I do?" In addition, as someone facing retirement looks forward, they may worry about such matters as what is the best age to retire, how to ensure financial resources will be enough, whether access to quality health care will be available, and whether meaningful ways to spend your time can be found. These uncertainties are natural. If they acknowledge these feelings and know that they are not alone as they navigate the journey toward retirement, they will be better able to embrace the excitement of more freedom and prepare themselves to address the concerns with a proactive approach.

The advice to work through fears about retirement does not mean to imply that there are no challenges ahead. Retirement is like any other phase in life: there will be challenges. And usually, fears and anxieties center around them. Next is a frank discussion of these challenges. By putting them on the table, you will be better able to manage the fears they bring up.

TRANSITIONING FROM EMPLOYMENT TO RETIREMENT

Leaving a full-time job can be challenging, as it provides financial stability, identity, purpose, routine, and structure. Retirement often disrupts these aspects, leading to common adjustment challenges, which are listed and discussed in the following list.

ADJUSTMENT CHALLENGES

Challenges

Loss of Identity and Purpose

Many derive a sense of self from their work. Retirement can lead to feelings of emptiness or lack of purpose.

Loss of Structure

Work gives daily routines. Without it, some struggle to fill their time, leading to boredom or restlessness.

Social Isolation

Work also provides social connections. Leaving work can cause feelings of loneliness and disconnection.

Financial Concerns

Worries about running out of money, unexpected expenses, or inflation, especially if social security and savings just cover basic needs.

Mental Health Impact

Adjusting to retirement can cause stress, anxiety, or depression, especially if feeling disconnected or insignificant.

Physical Health Adjustments

Less activity without the routine of work can negatively impact physical health.

Overwhelming Choices and Uncertainty

Some may feel overwhelmed by the many options and changes that come with retirement.

As you prepare to transition to the next chapter, understand these challenges and what they might mean to you so you can confront any apprehensions you may have about retirement.

COMMON FEARS ABOUT RETIRING

The following table presents commonly reported fears and anxiety regarding retirement. Do any or all of them resonate with you?

Fears That Provoke Anxiety

Maintaining Financial Security
- Running out of money
- Losing significant retirement assets on the stock market, 401K, etc.
- Rising inflation and/or a recession
- Dependence on the future stability of Social Security

Identity and Purpose
- Struggling with the transition from work to retirement
- Dealing with feelings of loss regarding old identity
- Not having a clear new identity

- Losing a sense of purpose that has disappeared
- Not knowing how to uncover or develop a new purpose
- Finding a renewed sense of purpose will be difficult
- Limited or no engagement in meaningful activities (volunteering, part-time work) outside of full-time employment
- How to fill time after leaving the workforce
- Difficulty in identifying your purpose during the transition

Health and Wellness Management
- Contending with dementia, Alzheimer's, or other cognitive decline
- Managing health crises and illnesses
- Handling rising healthcare costs and understanding Medicare and insurance coverage
- Difficulty accessing quality healthcare or losing access altogether
- Needing long-term care and how to access it
- Managing complex health issues, medications, and medical records

Relationships and Support
- Changes in relationships with family and friends
- Adjusting to more time with a spouse or partner
- Losing a spouse, loved ones, or close friends
- Feeling like a burden on family
- Family relationships becoming strained or problematic
- Losing contact with work friends
- Being single and lacking a strong support system
- Feeling socially isolated or withdrawing
- Experiencing loneliness and inability to stay engaged
- Losing touch with family, friends, social groups, and community

- Feeling depressed, anxious, or disconnected
- Not wanting to socialize outside of home

Independence and Physical/Mental Decline
- Undergoing physical or mental decline
- Losing the ability to live independently
- Coping with medical conditions
- Needing caregiving or long-term care services
- Navigating support systems to get and keep necessary services
- Difficulty managing important documents or identification
- Failing to manage financial affairs effectively
- Doing end-of-life planning

Not surprisingly, many of the fears reported by people regarding retirement reflect the challenges presented in the section "Transitioning from Employment to Retirement." The next section helps you identify your fears and worries.

CONFRONTING YOUR RETIREMENT CONCERNS

Now, let us address your specific fears about retirement with the self-assessment worksheet that follows. Answer the worksheet questions by using the 1-to-5 scale provided to self-evaluate the degree of your fears and concerns about specific retirement topics. The purpose of this exercise is to have more awareness about your fears, enabling you to address them more effectively.

RETIREMENT CONCERN LEVEL WORKSHEET

Use this Scale to answer the questions below:

How concerned are you about the following:

5 = Most fearful (I am very fearful),
4 = Somewhat fearful (I have some fear or concern),
3 = Neutral (I am neither fearful, concerned, nor unconcerned),
2 = Partially at ease (mildly comfortable),
1 = At ease (entirely comfortable).

____ Savings, having enough money and financial security in retirement
____ Being able to develop an identity not tied to previous work or career
____ Finding a sense of purpose
____ The Loss of routine and structure
____ Any possible mental health impact of retirement
____ The possibility of physical health adjustments
____ Feeling overwhelmed by choices and uncertainty
____ Changing Relationships with Family and Friends
____ Maintaining and Managing Health and Wellness
____ Remaining engaged with others and preventing loneliness and social isolation
____ Maintaining your independence
____ Other Concern _____

Briefly list the concerns that you scored at 4 or above.

_____
_____
_____
_____
_____

Outlined below are strategies to address any concerns or apprehensions you may have about retirement. Please review these suggestions while bearing in mind that there may be added actions not included here that you could consider. Feel free to include any such added suggestions.

RESEARCH TO EXPAND YOUR KNOWLEDGE WILL ADDRESS FEARS

When planning for retirement, it's natural for people to ask questions and do some research. Talking to people can help point you in many valuable directions. The best thing about arming yourself with information is that it can help calm your fears by giving you a sense of control.
Here are some suggestions for what information to gather:

Seek guidance from a qualified financial advisor or planner to get expert insights on achieving financial stability and retirement planning. Such advice can alleviate concerns about your financial future and offer valuable perspective.

- Seek advice from retired friends and family members about how they handled their transition to retirement. They can offer useful information, enhance your understanding of retirement, and reduce concerns associated with ending full-time employment.
- Engage in discussion, planning, and counseling with your spouse or partner about the transition to retirement or the next chapter, which can facilitate a shared vision for retirement and a smooth transition.
- Consult health care professionals about your current health status, schedule regular health and dental checkups, and discuss wellness strategies for healthy aging. In this way, you

are also learning how to navigate the health care system and promote your overall health.

- Investigate various retirement living locations and options, which will allow you time to understand the choices available and help you align your desired lifestyle with available living arrangements.

- Obtain information, insight into potential resources, and advice from online resources and webinars provided by the AARP (American Association of Retired Persons), Social Security Administration, Centers for Medicare & Medicaid Services, Department of Veterans Affairs, National Institute on Aging, U.S. Department of Health and Human Services, and U.S. Department of Aging.

- Seek information and guidance from the AAA (Area Agencies on Aging) in your local community, health insurance providers, and long-term health care providers and from your local health department. Among these and other potential local resources you will find support services for physical health and the prevention of loneliness and social isolation.

- Consult with your employer's human resources department to get information about retirement benefits, counseling services, financial planning help, retirement eligibility, training and workshops, transition programs, and online resources. This will aid you in maximizing earned benefits and preparing for retirement.

- Finally, seek guidance from a professional counselor, therapist, or coach to help in managing the transition to retirement and any associated fears or anxieties. Being supported in this way helps to address feelings of being overwhelmed and other concerns related to this significant life change.

YOUR STRATEGIES TO ADDRESS RETIREMENT ANXIETY

If you are still experiencing retirement anxiety, create a beginning strategy to address each fear or concern you named in the "Retirement Concern Level" worksheet, beginning with the fears you have marked with the highest numbers—fours and fives. State the fear or concern and what action you will take to address it.

- _____
- _____
- _____
- _____
- _____
- _____
- _____
- _____
- _____
- _____

RETIREMENT AS A GRADUAL PROCESS CAN ALSO CALM FEARS

Retirement doesn't have to be all-or-nothing. A powerful way to relieve fears about it is to transition into it gradually. This can make the process smoother and more enjoyable. One way to do this is to explore options such as reducing your work hours, switching to part-time, or starting your own venture on the side. Part-time work can give you confidence and provide a sense of purpose, supplement your income, and keep you socially engaged.

Even before full retirement, think about how you might open yourself to new experiences or start to establish relationships for retirement when work connections are gone. If possible, you could consider taking a sabbatical or extended vacation to allow yourself to adapt to a slower pace and test your retirement budget. Start to be proactive in exploring new hobbies, interests, and social connections. These can enrich you today and later in retirement and help you discover passions you may not have considered before.

Make it a point to become more engaged with your community—whether through volunteering, joining local clubs, or taking part in classes—to cultivate new friendships and a sense of belonging. Here are some ideas for pre-retirement preparation:

- Explore hobbies or interests you would like to pursue now and when you retire. Start this before you retire so you'll stay engaged.

- Enroll in courses, join community groups, attend neighborhood events, or take part in social clubs or activities related to interests that you may wish to continue during retirement. This will help in discovering a purpose and staying engaged.

- Take a vacation to a place of interest. It will give you an understanding of how much more there is to learn and experience.

- Establish and support relationships with new and old friends and expand your social network, including individuals outside of your workplace or profession. This will help you remain connected and engaged within your community.

- Utilize modern technology to keep connections with friends and loved ones and continue learning to be current and informed.

- Explore opportunities to engage with your community, whether through volunteering or other service, joining local clubs, or participating in local political processes. This will help you learn more about your community, stay engaged, and find purpose.

A gradual transition over several years not only eases the shift into post-career life but considerably eases fears as you put some activities and connections in place before retirement, which allows you to enjoy your exciting new chapter fully.

EMBRACING CHANGE

First, acknowledge your retirement fears. Addressing these concerns is crucial to enjoying a fulfilling retirement. In so doing, it frees you up to focus on the opportunities ahead. Michael's journey is an example of this.

MICHAEL'S TRANSITION:
ACCEPTING CHANGE AND MOVING FORWARD

I'm a married 54-year-old Chinese American who retired just a couple of months ago. So far, it's going well. I spent my career at an international financial services company where I was a principal engineer, which provided me with job satisfaction, a supportive boss, and a strong sense of purpose that aligned with the company's mission. However, a series of events led to a shift in my trajectory.

About two years ago, I sustained a back injury that put me on short-term disability. When I returned to work, I found that my boss had retired, and I was now reporting to a new manager who had formed a team. The misalignment of our missions and working styles resulted in a significant drop in my job satisfaction. Additionally, a long-time colleague, a valued team member who was 67, decided to retire, prompting me to consider my future seriously. It was during this time that the idea of retirement transformed from a distant thought into a real option, leading me to assess both my financial and health care needs and begin to implement my path to retirement. My wife, who is still working and has not yet retired, supports this transition as I explore new possibilities.

When my employer presented me with a retirement package two months ago, I felt ready to embrace this new phase of life. Reflecting on it, my primary concern regarding retirement was securing my financial stability for the future. Although I had saved enough to manage everyday expenses (family monthly fixed costs) I still wanted to make sure that I had sufficient funds for unforeseen circumstances and medical emergencies. Additionally, I aspired to travel more extensively and participate in activities that were not feasible while working full-time.

Now, after two months of retirement, my worries have mostly subsided. I've established a fulfilling routine that includes working around the house, exercising, playing pickleball, and even doing woodworking projects—I'm currently working on a desk for my son! Surprisingly, I don't miss my identity as a principal engineer. Instead, I find joy in my daily activities and the time I have to dedicate to my interests. I'm excited about several international trips we have planned for later this year.

My two sons, both in their twenties, are forging their own paths, and I cherish the opportunity to support them while I navigate my own evolving journey. While traditional Chinese culture often expects the younger generation to care for their parents, I don't hold this expectation for my sons, who were born in the United States and don't strictly follow those norms. My wife and I believe in supporting ourselves and the older generation and setting a positive example for our sons as they build their futures. As I redefine my life, I am eager to embrace new opportunities, pursue my interests, and solidify my long-term goals.

MICHAEL'S ADVICE

My advice is to start working toward financial independence as early as possible. Begin by developing a solid financial plan that aligns with your goals. In addition, focus on building a social network and exploring hobbies and interests that bring you joy. These connections and activities will help you manage stress, both while you're working and after you retire. Stay open-minded and embrace new ideas; flexibility is key to adapting to change. By planning and cultivating this mindset, you'll find that your retirement experience will be much more fulfilling and rewarding.

JAMES'S NEXT CHAPTER: *MY JOURNEY TO RETIREMENT*

As I approach my 61st birthday this year, I recognize the significance of the next chapter—retirement—that lies ahead. As a Baby Boomer with dual citizenship in the United States and Canada, I've spent over 25 years working with an American multinational financial services company, currently serving as a senior AVP infrastructure engineer. With retirement on the horizon in just a couple of years, I am actively focusing on my investments to build the resources I need for sustainable financial security. I didn't start my retirement planning early, which makes my current efforts even more important.

While I have concerns about having enough money to support myself and my family, I find comfort in knowing that my adult children and grandchildren are thriving in Canada. My main priority is to create dependable income streams to ensure I won't run out of money during retirement. I also worry about health care, particularly for my mother, who is almost 80. She retired years ago and moved to the United States from Canada after my dad passed away. Her presence nearby motivates me.

Once I retire, I plan to repurpose myself by becoming an entrepreneur. I am working towards establishing an interior design business with my partner, which would be something my mother would enjoy, too. This venture will allow me to be a consultant, let my partner be more hands-on, and keep my mother engaged. It will also generate extra income for our retirements. I'm actively working on this plan because I believe it offers a valuable opportunity.

Regarding my life goals and finding purpose after leaving full-time employment, I feel confident and excited about what lies ahead. I am a goal-oriented person who thrives on learning new things and embracing adventure. For example, I have a strong desire to learn how to fly a plane. The opportunity to continue growing inspires me as I look forward to this new chapter!

JAMES' ADVICE

My advice for everyone is to be consistent with your financial planning. Start investing when you're young and stick with it. The earlier you begin, the more you'll see your investments grow—time truly becomes your best friend in building wealth!

GETTING STARTED WITH YOUR RETIREMENT PLAN

The questionnaire that follows can help you get started on the journey of planning your retirement. Take some time to think about and answer the questions. Circle the lettered questions that apply to you and fill in the spaces provided.

REFLECTION QUESTIONNAIRE

1. What are your current plans for retirement?
    a. I have no written or well-thought-out plans for retirement.
    b. I am currently saving for retirement through a 401(k), 403(b), or pension, but no other plan is in place.
    c. I have a comprehensive, holistic retirement plan that includes health and living arrangements beyond a financial security plan.
    d. Other _____
    _____
2. I'm *most* concerned about (circle the top five)?
    a. Transitioning to retirement will be like jumping off a cliff into the unknown or a new landscape.
    b. Running out of money after I retire—that I will outlive my

       savings and retirement funds
- c. Declining values or loss of my retirement funds due to a stock market downturn.
- d. Rising inflation, or a recession, or other economic problems affecting the value of my retirement funds
- e. Losing my work identity, no longer being defined by my job
- f. Filling up my time after leaving the workforce
- g. Finding my new purpose
- h. Being a burden on my family
- i. Declining physically and mentally as I age
- j. The escalating cost of health care
- k. Managing an illness or health crisis
- l. Having access to quality health care and the efficacy of Medicare and health insurance coverage
- m. Experiencing loneliness and being socially isolated
- n. Feeling disconnected from family, friends, and/or community
- o. Losing my independence
- p. Other _____

_____

3. What gets you excited about the prospect of retirement (circle the top five)?
    - a. Moving forward because the joy in work is no longer there
    - b. No more morning alarm clocks, wake-up routines, commutes, and meetings
    - c. Spending more time with my children and/or grandchildren
    - d. Doing more fun activities with family and friends
    - e. Having more time to discover and pursue my interests and passions
    - f. Pursuing a new and different career
    - g. Spending more time doing what I love
    - h. Opening my own business

i. Returning to school or taking continuing education courses
   j. Evolving and learning new skills, i.e., a new language, playing an instrument, or pottery
   k. Being able to do more volunteering and community involvement
   l. Devoting more time for physical activities, i.e., walking, swimming, yoga, or tai chi
   m. Traveling and exploring
   n. Having more time to relax and just be
   o. Other _____
   _____

4. At what age do you want to retire? How many years do you have until you reach this target age?
   _____
   _____
   _____

5. The reasons for my retirement will be due to (please select at least two):
   a. Work no longer brings me joy
   b. Being able financially to do so
   c. My partner, family, and friends have all retired.
   d. My desire to pursue another career.
   e. Health (health/illness triggers retirement)
   f. Caregiving (must leave full-time work to care for a family member)
   g. Unemployment, a job loss, and difficulty finding new employment means it might be time to retire
   h. Early retirement was always the goal
   i. Reaching mandatory retirement age
   j. Having reached my goal retirement age (not the age required by my employer)

k. Other _____

_____

6. To what generational cohort do you belong (based on your date of birth)? Check one.

   Baby Boomer (1946–1964) _____

   Gen X (1965–1980) _____

   Millennial (1981–1995) _____

   Gen Z (1996–2010) _____

   Microgeneration, which one _____

   _____

   Cusper (between generations), which two _____

   _____

7. How might demographic factors such as diversity and generational cohort influence your retirement vision and plan? Provide a brief statement.

   _____
   _____
   _____

8. List 5 resources, people, mindsets, or other factors that you will need to thrive in your retirement years.

   1. _____
   2. _____
   3. _____
   4. _____
   5. _____

Keep this questionnaire and review it as you move through your retirement journey. Updating your responses periodically will help you to understand how your thoughts and ideas may change and to address any concerns about retirement. Such self-reflection will improve your confidence and prove to be valuable in your planning process.

TAKEAWAYS FROM EMBARK ON YOUR PATH TO RETIREMENT PLANNING

The prospect of retirement brings up both anxiety and excitement in more people, the takeaways from this chapter discuss how to manage these feelings to prepare you to embrace change:

Planning for retirement may seem daunting, and it does come with common challenges. It's best not to worry about them because you can learn how to manage them over time.

Thinking about retirement can bring up many fears and anxieties. Some are experienced by many; others may be unique to you.

Acknowledging your fears is the first step to managing them and freeing yourself to feel excited about what retirement might bring. Gathering information helps with this process.

If possible, alleviate worry about retiring by doing research, making it a gradual process, and "trying on" some of the activities you hope to engage in once you have retired.

Shift your outlook from anxiety to one of embracing change.

It's never too early to start planning for retirement.

With your fears addressed, you can reshape your retirement into a fulfilling and meaningful chapter of your life. Enjoy the journey, and remember that this is your time to thrive. The next chapter will show you how to create a vision of how to do that.

CHAPTER THREE

CREATING YOUR VISION FOR RETIREMENT

There is a whole new kind of life ahead, full of experiences just waiting to happen. Some call it "retirement." I call it bliss.
—BETTY SULLIVAN

Don't retire from something, retire to something—embrace the possibilities.
—HARRY EMERSON FOSDICK

Betty Sullivan's quote perfectly encapsulates the joy and excitement retirement can bring, encouraging you to embrace this time as an opportunity for blissful living. Your journey toward a meaningful retirement begins with envisioning what that next chapter looks like and creating a solid plan to turn your vision into reality. As Harry Emerson Fosdick wisely said, "Embrace the possibilities."

As you think about your retirement timeline, it's important to consider several key factors: the status of your health, the continuity of your current job, potential upcoming changes to your pension or retirement benefits, family caregiving responsibilities, personal preferences, and financial readiness. Each of these aspects significantly impacts your retirement decisions. By thoughtfully addressing these factors and planning ahead, you empower yourself to craft a fulfilling and enriching retirement experience that truly reflects your aspirations and lifestyle.

Remember, retirement age can vary significantly among individuals, influenced by industry standards and personal circumstances. While some may eagerly anticipate retiring at 65, others might imagine working for as long as they can, which may be well into their seventies or even eighties. Some people may retire as early as age 62 when they can access their Social Security—albeit at a reduced rate—while others find satisfaction in continuing their careers or doing other work beyond age 65 or 66. It's important to consider that retirement timing can be shaped by a variety of factors, so it is wise to think about different possible scenarios. Keeping in mind that there are multiple pathways to retirement, it is possible to find the one that aligns with your goals.

PATHWAYS TO RETIREMENT

Individuals who are beginning to think about their transition to retirement should first realize that the traditional notion of retiring from full-time employment in a single, irreversible step is becoming less common. Today, retirement pathways can vary from person to person. In some industries or organizations, a specific mandatory "retirement age" may dictate when you are expected to leave your job—often around age 65. However, for many, retirement age can be more flexible. Retiring earlier than what has been the traditional age may be shaped by personal circumstances such as health issues, caregiving responsibilities, or even corporate downsizing. Life events like unemployment, job loss, or difficulty finding a new position may also influence your decision to retire sooner than planned. Some individuals even aspire to an early retirement to explore a second career or pursue interests that align with their passions.

Continuing to work beyond the traditional age depends on your employer or your ability to create a new form of employment, for example, engaging in consulting or setting up a business. Today, web-based businesses and online meeting platforms allow many who are out of the traditional workforce to continue working from home.

Societal factors can also play a significant role in your retirement decision. For example, the COVID-19 pandemic triggered what many are calling the "Great Retirement," leading a substantial number of Baby Boomers to leave the workforce earlier than expected. According to the Pew Research Center, nearly 30 million Baby Boomers retired during this time, allowing them to reassess their priorities and embrace new phases of life. Many realized they could achieve greater fulfillment by stepping away from their jobs.

Regardless of individual circumstances, it is imperative to develop a vision and plan for retirement. Although this vision and plan may evolve over time, starting the process early is advisable. The age range of between 40 and 50 is an optimal period to consider your post-retirement lifestyle and evaluate your financial standing thoroughly. As retirement approaches in your 60s, preparation becomes even more critical. Establishing a clear vision and understanding the key considerations of your plan will ensure a smooth transition into the next phase of life.

As you consider your own path to retirement, reflect on the factors that resonate with you and shape your vision for this exciting new chapter.

A RETIREMENT VISION BASED ON WHAT IS IMPORTANT TO YOU

Creating a vision of the next chapter of your life is the first step and a key strategy for achieving your retirement dreams. Your vision should resonate with your values and ideals, your passions, and your purpose in life. It should promote your overall well-being and generate energy and enthusiasm. To begin crafting your vision, let's begin with some reflection.

WHAT MATTERS TO YOU?

This exercise will help you relax so you can tap into what is important to you and makes you happy. Take a minute to find a comfortable seated position. Set a timer for 10 minutes. Now close your eyes, take a few deep cleansing breaths, relax your entire body, and breathe. Hold this position for about 10 minutes while you think about two or three activities, interests, or hobbies that bring you joy. Visualize yourself actively taking part in each one. After the 10 minutes, slowly open your eyes and jot down a few notes or impressions about what you have just experienced.

Now that you are in a state of positivity and joy. You have now set the stage to explore in more detail.

The next step is to think about yourself in a deeper way by contemplating your principles and values as well as all the areas that matter most to you, such as family, friends, home, community, work, volunteering, health, quality of life, faith, spiritual connections, personal growth, leisure, and happiness. Allow yourself the freedom to dream and concentrate on your own wishes rather than thinking about what is realistic or conforming to the expectations of others. Remember, this is an exploration as you answer the reflection questions in the worksheet that follows.

REFLECTION QUESTIONS

What principles do you hold dear? Consider values such as honesty, kindness, or being of service.

_____
_____

What matters are of significance to you? Think about family and other relationships, personal growth, spiritual connections, or other topics, such as societal or political issues.

_____
_____

What are your secret passions and dreams?

_____
_____

What are your talents? What is special about you?

_____
_____

What would bring more joy and happiness into your life?

_____
_____

How do you envision the nature of your relationships with significant others, family members, and friends now and when you retire?

_____
_____

What qualities that might be helpful when you retire would you like to develop now?

_____
_____

Which skills or talents do you wish to use upon retirement?

_____
_____

What legacy would you like to leave behind?
_____
_____

Now, review your answers to the worksheet questions. Your responses highlight your life themes and goals and what is important to you. Incorporate these as you craft your vision of your retirement and desired future sense of purpose.

FORMING A VISION THAT REFLECTS YOUR UNIQUENESS

There is no one-size-fits-all approach to retirement. Diverse cultural backgrounds can shape distinct attitudes towards aging, retirement, family structures, and social support systems. As you develop your retirement vision, embrace your diversity by acknowledging and respecting your culture's nuances according to what is comfortable for you. Everyone is unique, and today, a retirement plan that addresses your individuality can be arranged simply by acknowledging and attending to your racial, ethnic, and cultural background or strengths and challenges as a member of the LGBTQ+ community or someone living with disabilities.

Similarly, another aspect of what makes you who you are is your generation, so it is important to acknowledge the unique perspective of you and your peers as you look ahead to the next chapter. As you consider your retirement plans, it is important to give voice to that perspective in order to maximize your well-being.

Society's attitude toward retirement has started to be influenced by the diverse needs and perspectives of individuals and communities. Recognizing these needs ensures that retirement planning can be more inclusive and ensure that it resonates with everyone. A significant issue that many marginalized communities face—including racial and ethnic groups, gender-diverse individuals and other LGBTQ+ community members, and people with disabilities—is how frequently their members have experienced income disparities, which affect their ability to save for retirement and buy insurance. Many also are limited in their access to quality health care. As society addresses these economic inequities and places a value on financial security for all, then it can ensure that everyone will retire with dignity.

GENERATIONAL COHORTS AND FORMING A VISION

Whether you are a Baby Boomer in your 60s or 70s, a Gen Xer in your 40s or 50s, or a Millennial in your 30s or 40s, creating a clear vision for retirement is essential.

Baby Boomers are likely focused on completing preparations, managing risks, and making crucial decisions that will affect the rest of their lives. Gen Xers and Millennials still have time to engage in proactive planning, set realistic goals, and build retirement savings that align with their financial and lifestyle expectations. Those who belong to a Microgeneration or are a Cusper can look to the strengths of both generational groups to which they are related to create a comprehensive retirement vision.

When planning for retirement, understand the unique challenges and aspirations of your cohort so they can inform the development of your vision. Then, tailor your retirement strategies to accommodate how health considerations, financial security, and lifestyle preferences, among other factors, impact your cohort. By recognizing the specific challenges and opportunities unique to your generation, you can better prepare for a thriving, financially secure, and fulfilling retirement.

Establishing your vision for retirement will guide your planning process and ensure that you consider what you truly want for your retirement years. Think about your aspirations related to travel, hobbies, family engagement, and community involvement. This vision will serve as a foundation for achieving your multiple retirement goals.

DAVID: "GET READY FOR THE BEST JOB YET."

Growing up in the Midwest, role models from an earlier generation surrounded me—individuals who worked at the local mill, established their families, raised their children, and retired around the age of 65. They enjoyed good benefits, pensions, and union support. As I matured, I ventured away from this community to attend college and eventually settled in the Northeast, where I pursued a career in communications and marketing with a multinational technology company.

At 62, my company offered me a retirement package. My wife, who worked in Human Resources for the same company, also considered the offer. After thoughtful deliberation, we decided it was best for me to accept the package while she continued her career for another five years. Our years of financial preparation—contributing to pensions, 401(k) plans, and personal savings—had positioned us well for our transition to retirement.

As my wife's retirement date approached, we began considering where we wanted to live after both of us retired. We decided to move to a warmer climate and a new state and started searching for a new home and community. Reflecting on the retired men from my old neighborhood who seemed to relish their retirement years, I eagerly anticipated this new chapter in my life.

DAVID'S ADVICE

For some individuals, work becomes a significant part of their identity, making the concept of retirement feel challenging. However, this chapter of life can be immensely fulfilling. David is an example of how someone can shape their vision for retirement. David's strong foundation for a positive vision of retirement stems from years of dedicated financial preparation and the inspiring examples set by his role models. With this groundwork in place, David felt empowered to embrace the opportunities that retirement would bring, looking forward to the freedom of this new chapter in his life.

It's crucial to start planning for retirement as early as possible. Participate in your employer's retirement savings plan and explore additional avenues for saving. Cultivating hobbies and interests outside of work and beginning to enjoy them before you retire can create a smoother transition. With this proactive approach, you can ensure a rewarding retirement experience aligned with your vision and values.

HOW TO DEVELOP A VISION STATEMENT

To get started, combine the life themes, interests, and goals that you explored in this chapter. This will help you to create your personal vision statement. Next, read some of the samples provided below of brief retirement vision statements. Once you have the early stages of a vision, try some of the techniques for clarifying your ideas. Finally, write your vision statement. Vision statements are fluid. Go back to them and refine them frequently during your planning process, when you retire, and in retirement.

EXAMPLES OF VISION STATEMENTS

The retirement vision statements that follow are meant to be examples and to give you ideas for your own.

I want to create a retirement filled with exploration, creativity, and joy, where I continually learn, share wisdom, and savor cherished moments with loved ones, all while fostering a legacy of positivity and resilience for future generations.

When I embark on a retirement adventure, I want it to enrich my life with unforgettable journeys and lifelong memories. My retirement will be defined by exploration and cultural immersion, where I traverse the globe, experience varied landscapes and diverse traditions, and forge connections with people worldwide.

Retirement, for me, will be about entering a time of reinvention and contribution. I plan to embrace new roles as a mentor, volunteer, or entrepreneur, using my skills and experiences to make a meaningful impact in my community and beyond while continuously learning and growing both personally and in competency.

My plan for retirement is that it will be my gateway to deepening my lifelong passions as I dedicate time to immersing myself in hobbies like painting, gardening, and literature. It will also be a time to cultivate creativity, find renewed purpose, and share my love of these pursuits with others, enriching my life with every brushstroke, bloom, and turned page.

In retirement, I envision living life to its fullest, embracing each day with gratitude and enthusiasm. I will prioritize my well-being, nurture relationships with loved ones, and explore new interests with a sense of adventure. It is to be a chapter dedicated to enjoying simple pleasures, creating lasting memories, and cherishing the beauty of every moment.

My vision for my retirement is a life filled with joy, adventure, and meaningful connections. I will embrace each day with gratitude, exploring new interests, nurturing relationships, and cherishing every moment. My retirement will be a time of growth, discovery, and giving back as I pursue passions, create lasting memories, and inspire others to live their best lives.

My personal retirement vision is to lead a well-balanced and harmonious life that allows me to follow my passions while also taking care of my physical, emotional, and spiritual health. I want to develop a lifestyle that helps me succeed in every area of my life now and in the future.

I intend to lead a purposeful and meaningful life, focusing on positively affecting others. I will prioritize relationships with loved ones and give time and resources to support those in need.

Preparing for retirement is a crucial step toward ensuring a fulfilling and secure future. To achieve this goal, it is essential to develop a clear vision of your desired retirement lifestyle and to align that vision with a comprehensive plan.

WAYS TO CLARIFY IDEAS INTO A RETIREMENT VISION

In the example above, when David decided to retire early, he and his wife's vision was to move to a new state with a warmer climate and cultivate a community there. Their vision also included pursuing their hobbies and interests. They were clear about their vision for retirement. This is your first opportunity to start piecing together what you've thought about so far about your interests, values, and life goals for your vision statement. As you develop your own vision and plan for retirement, your ideas may feel vague at first. That's okay; it's a start. Here are several tools that can help you clarify those ideas so you can shape them into your vision statement:

Vision Boards. Create a physical or digital vision board featuring images and quotes that represent your dreams and aspirations for retirement. This visual representation can shake out what you truly want.

Retirement Workshops and Seminars. Many organizations and financial institutions offer workshops on retirement planning, providing valuable insights and actionable steps to help you shape your future.

Journaling. Keeping a retirement journal allows you to reflect on and refine your thoughts, ideas, and goals for retirement. Writing can bring clarity and help you track your progress.

Retirement Planning Books. Consider reading books on retirement planning that offer insights and frameworks. They can inspire and guide you.

Life Planning Tools. Websites like MindTools provide frameworks for personal and professional life planning, which can also be applied to your retirement journey.

Networking with Peers. Talking with friends, family, or retirement groups can provide ideas, tips, valuable insights, and inspiration as you define your own retirement vision.

Using these tools will help you develop a clearer understanding of what you want your retirement to look like and create a fulfilling plan for the future.

YOUR PERSONAL VISION STATEMENT FOR RETIREMENT

Now, it is your turn to write down your vision statement. Keep in mind that it is not set in stone and will change over the years. Write a brief paragraph that encapsulates your retirement themes, goals, and purpose. Keep in mind that your next chapter could span 20, 30, or even more years after retirement.

_____
_____
_____
_____
_____

Chapter 3: Creating Your Vision for Retirement

Great Work!

The next two parts of the book, Part II, Achieving Financial Security and Satisfaction, and Part III, Thriving in Retirement, will teach you how to develop a retirement plan that's aligned with your vision. Each chapter in those sections has the potential to reshape your perspective and guide you closer to your ideal retirement. Before you continue, take a moment to reread your retirement vision. As you progress through the book, your vision is likely to evolve, and that's a natural part of the journey.

TAKEAWAYS FROM CREATING YOUR VISION FOR RETIREMENT

The following takeaways summarize the most important concepts related to creating your vision for a fulfilling retirement:

There are many pathways to retirement today, from retiring early to retiring at the traditional age of retirement to continuing to work while retired.

Having a vision for retirement lays the framework for your retirement plan. A good vision incorporates what matters to you in all areas of your life.

Take some quiet time, and with your eyes closed, imagine what truly gives you joy. Let this set the scene as you envision your retirement.

Today, the vision for your retirement plan must include considerations of what makes you unique, your race, ethnic or cultural origins, challenges, and the demographic and generation cohorts that you are a member of.

Even if your vision statement is unclear at first, use tools like a vision board or journaling to bring it into focus.

Remember, your vision statement is fluid. You will revisit and revise it throughout your retirement journey.

PART

II

ACHIEVING FINANCIAL SECURITY AND SATISFACTION IN RETIREMENT

CHAPTER FOUR

SAVING FOR RETIREMENT: FINANCES AND ESTATE PLANNING

It's not how much money you make, but how much money you keep, how hard it works for you, and how many generations you keep it for.
—ROBERT KIYOSAKI

Retirement is like a long vacation in Las Vegas. The goal is to enjoy it the fullest, but not so fully that you run out of money.
—JONATHAN CLEMENTS

If you look at what you have in life, you'll always have more. If you look at what you don't have in life, you'll never have enough.
—OPRAH WINFREY

Retirement, as discussed, brings a mix of excitement and concerns. Most people worry about financial matters and fear they will outlive their savings, will be unable to maintain their lifestyle, and the potential costs of medical care. Other common concerns include being able to afford their home and travel and even the possibility of needing to return to work. The future can seem uncertain, but there are ways to address these worries.

The next few chapters address the topics of financial security and financial satisfaction and what they mean in retirement. Financial satisfaction goes beyond having secure finances—it's about lifestyle. This chapter covers all the basics of saving and investing for retirement as well as other financial matters, including insurance and estate planning. The next chapter describes in detail how to create financial satisfaction. Then, Chapter Six shows you how to put it all together and make a financial plan.

One of the most crucial steps anyone can take is to start planning for retirement early. If you haven't begun yet, it's not too late—start now. This chapter will guide you through self-analysis, checklists, and charts to help you achieve a fulfilling and financially secure retirement.

FINANCIAL SATISFACTION IN RETIREMENT

The terms "financial satisfaction" and "financial security" both hold significance when discussing retirement; however, they emphasize different aspects. "Financial security" focuses on building a stable income for the retirement years sufficient to cover necessary expenses without the risk of running out of funds. It encompasses having one or more sources of reliable income, being debt-free, having adequate health care, keeping an emergency fund, and having a clear estate plan. Essentially, it underscores the protective measures and financial stability needed to safeguard one's retirement years.

On the other hand, "financial satisfaction" is more than mere security because it is about the personal fulfillment and enjoyment one derives from one's financial situation. It includes the ability to support a comfortable lifestyle, care for loved ones, and pursue individual interests and hobbies. Financial satisfaction is the sense of well-being and contentment that comes from having a secure financial status, one that allows retirees to live life to the fullest.

Financial satisfaction and financial security may be used interchangeably to a point. Both focus on achieving a secure economic foundation, but financial satisfaction also highlights the importance of personal fulfillment in retirement. Balancing them is part of a holistic approach to retirement planning that addresses both security and quality of life factors.

WHAT DOES FINANCIAL SATISFACTION LOOK LIKE

A general guideline for achieving financial security in retirement is to save enough money to enable you to live on 70% to 80% of your current income. This means you need to assess how your lifestyle would be affected when you are living on 70% of your present income.

Think about what financial satisfaction looks like for you. Consider the activities you want to pursue, such as hobbies and interests. If buying a vacation property or fulfilling a lifelong dream is important to you, then plan accordingly. Maybe you want to travel more, visit new places, or spend more time with your family. Your vision for retirement should guide your planning and help you navigate the challenges and opportunities that come your way.

Financial satisfaction in retirement involves having enough income to cover essential expenses, being debt-free, and enjoying a comfortable lifestyle. Here are some fundamentals:

- **Adequate Income.** Establishing a reliable source of income sufficient to cover all essential expenses, including housing, health care, food, and other daily living costs, without the concern of depleting funds. This income may derive from pensions, Social Security, retirement savings, investments, or other sources.

- **Debt-Free Living.** Ideally, entering retirement with minimal to no debt, including mortgages, car loans, and credit card debt. Being debt-free status allows for greater financial flexibility and reduces stress.

- **Health Care Security.** Having a comprehensive health care plan that covers medical expenses, including potential long-term care needs. Financial satisfaction includes not worrying about whether you can afford unexpected health issues or the hit to your savings.

- **Well-Funded Emergency Fund.** Maintaining an emergency fund to address unexpected expenses, such as home repairs, medical emergencies, or other unforeseen events, thus avoiding the need to withdraw funds from retirement savings for unexpected costs.

- **Ability to Care for Loved Ones.** For many, financial satisfaction in retirement includes the capability to help children, grandchildren, or other loved ones, whether through gifts, education funding, or other forms of support.

- **Inflation Protection.** Having investments or income streams designed to keep pace with inflation, thus ensuring that purchasing power is still robust throughout retirement.

- **Estate Planning.** Having a clear and well-structured estate plan that ensures asset distribution according to your wishes. This involves having a will, trust, or other legal instruments in place to minimize taxes and avoid legal complications for heirs.

- **Minimal Financial Stress.** Experiencing low levels of anxiety about money, secure in the knowledge that you have adequate funds to live comfortably for the rest of your life. This means having a solid financial plan in which you have confidence.

- **Comfortable Lifestyle.** Being able to uphold a lifestyle that aligns with personal values and desires with sufficient funds for hobbies, interests, travel, dining out, and other activities that bring joy and fulfillment.

- **Flexibility and Freedom.** Having the financial flexibility to adapt to changes in lifestyle, health, or family situation without significant financial strain. This might involve being able to relocate, take up new hobbies, or respond to unexpected life changes.

- **Philanthropy and Giving Back.** For some, financial satisfaction in retirement includes the capacity to donate to charities, support causes they care about, or leave a legacy through charitable giving.

- **Contentment with Financial Decisions.** Feeling at peace with the results of planning and management of retirement finances, without significant regrets about past decisions. This also entails confidence in your ongoing financial strategy.

To reach financial satisfaction in retirement, you need to take proactive measures. Set your retirement goals, create and adhere to a comprehensive retirement plan, manage the plan, adjust as necessary, and continuously enhance your financial literacy.

RETIREMENT AND FINANCIAL LITERACY

Strategic retirement planning requires financial literacy. Understanding how to manage your finances effectively is crucial for a successful retirement. By learning about budgeting, investing, and finance principles, you can create a personalized plan that ensures your financial security. Start learning early to better handle the financial challenges of retirement. Here are some steps to enhance your financial literacy.

Steps To Financial Literacy:

1. Develop financial skills, including personal fiscal management—budgeting, saving, investing, debt management, understanding credit, tax

literacy, insurance, inflation and interest rates, estate planning, consumer awareness, and retirement planning.
2. Educate yourself on the financial fundamentals of a retirement plan.
3. Take courses, attend seminars, read books on personal finance, and follow reputable financial news sources.
4. Keep up with changes in tax laws, interest rates, and market conditions that can affect your finances.
5. Apply what you learn by managing your own budget, savings, and investments.
6. Work with a financial planner, especially as you approach retirement, to ensure your plan is on track.

Improving your financial literacy is essential for making informed decisions, building wealth, and achieving financial satisfaction. Start early, as education is the foundation of financial success. By grasping the fundamentals of an effective financial plan, particularly for retirement, you can ensure a future that aligns with your goals and values.

FUNDAMENTALS OF YOUR RETIREMENT FINANCIAL PLAN

Understanding the financial fundamentals of your retirement plan is crucial for securing your future. There are many ways to allocate your savings and investments to ensure a steady income during retirement. From Social Security, 401(k)s, pensions, IRAs, and real estate to personal savings and part-time employment, familiarizing yourself with these options will help you make informed decisions.

SOCIAL SECURITY BENEFITS

If you have worked in the United States, you are entitled to register for Social Security. This program, managed by the Social Security Administration (SSA), offers a federal contribution-based system that provides benefits such as health, old age pension, unemployment, retirement, and disability income. It also extends these benefits to the spouses of qualified individuals.

Social Security provides a guaranteed source of income based on your earnings history. It is a key part of retirement planning for most Americans. The key aspects of it are:

Benefits. The amount of income individuals receive from Social Security is calculated based on how much they have earned in their lifetime. Their average indexed monthly earnings are then calculated for the 35 years in which they earned the most. Generally, Social Security payments replace about 56% of someone's preretirement income.

Spousal and Survivor Benefits. Social Security also offers spousal and survivor benefits, which provide additional income for those individuals.

Claiming Strategy. The age at which someone claims Social Security significantly affects their benefits. People can start receiving Social Security retirement benefits as early as age 62, but they aren't entitled to full benefits until they reach their Full Retirement Age (FRA). This depends on what year they were born. If someone starts taking Social Security benefits before their Full Retirement Age (FRA), their monthly benefit is reduced. The reduction is permanent and can be up to 30% less than what they would receive at their FRA. At FRA (66 to 67, depending on birth year), individuals receive 100% of their Social Security benefits as calculated based on their earnings history. See the table below.

Social Security Full Benefits Eligibility

YEAR	FULL RETIREMENT AGE (FRA)*
Born 1943–1954	66
Born 1955	66 and 2 months
Born 1956	66 and 4 months
Born 1957	66 and 6 months
Born 1958	66 and 8 months
Born 1959	66 and 10 months
Born 1960 *	67

The full retirement age for Social Security benefits does not go beyond 67 for individuals born in 1960 and later.

If someone delays claiming Social Security benefits beyond your FRA, your benefits increase by approximately 8% per year up until age 70. This increase adds up in the three or four years from FRA, so if an individual is earning income in those years, it pays to delay claiming Social Security.

The SSA provides statements with detailed information about how much you've paid into the program and estimates of how much you'll receive in benefits depending on the age at which you retire. You can get this information by creating an online "My Social Security" account with the agency by going to https://www.ssa.gov/. This account provides a personalized estimate of your Social Security Benefits based on your actual earnings record. You can request one by mail (at https://www.ssa.gov/forms/).

Regardless of how much you have earned or when you retire, you should never rely on Social Security as your sole source of income in retirement. It certainly will not be enough. Be sure to plan to have other sources of income. You can elect to receive your Social Security while you are still working, but if this is before your FRA, your lifetime benefit amount will be reduced. Starting with the month you reach full retirement age, there will not be a reduction in your benefits, no matter how much you earn.

EMPLOYER-SPONSORED RETIREMENT PLANS

The main two ways employers provide retirement benefits to their employees are through 1) a defined-contribution Pension Plan and 2) a defined-benefit Plan. If you work for a company as opposed to for yourself, familiarize yourself with the basics of these plans, which are covered in this section.

TRADITIONAL DEFINED-BENEFIT PENSION PLANS

A defined-benefit pension plan is a type of employer-sponsored retirement plan where an employee's retirement benefits are calculated based on a specific formula. There are two types: a traditional defined-benefit pension plan and a cash balance pension plan. In both, the employer is responsible for managing the plan's investments, bearing the investment risk, and ensuring there are sufficient funds to pay the promised benefits. There are also vesting schedules, which determine when employees have a right to the benefits. Someone typically must stay with the employer for a certain number of years to gain full rights to the benefits under the plan.

A defined-benefit pension plan guarantees a specific monthly benefit in retirement. The benefit is typically based on factors like a person's salary, years of service, and age at retirement. The employer typically funds these plans, although some may also need employee contributions. Other points about defined-benefit pension plans are:

Payment Options. Pensions often offer several payout options, such as a single life annuity (which pays benefits for your lifetime) or a joint-and-survivor annuity (which also continues payments to your spouse after your death).

Lack of Portability. If someone leaves their job before being fully vested, they might lose some or all their benefits. Because of this, defined-benefit plans are less portable than defined-contribution plans like 401(k)s.

Security. Pensions are generally seen as secure because they provide a predictable, guaranteed income for life. However, they depend on the financial health of the employer, and some pensions may be subject to underfunding risks, meaning the company did not set aside enough funds and/or manage the fund properly to cover their pension obligations.

Inflation Protection. Some pensions include cost-of-living adjustments (COLAs) to protect against inflation, although this is not always the case.

CASH BALANCE PENSION PLANS

A cash balance pension plan is a retirement plan that combines features of both traditional defined-benefit pension plans and defined-contribution plans like 401(k)s. It's considered a *hybrid plan* because it provides the security of a defined-benefit plan with the flexibility and portability of a defined-contribution plan. Employers contribute a percentage of an individual's salary to an account (a "pay credit") along with interest credits. Employees receive a statement showing their hypothetical account balance, which grows annually based on the set interest rate.

Guaranteed Benefit. The plan guarantees a benefit based on the balance in the employee's account.

Portability. Unlike traditional pensions, cash balance plans are often more portable, allowing employees to roll over the balance into an IRA or another retirement account if they change jobs.

Security. The plan offers more security than a defined-contribution plan because the employer guarantees the benefits, even if the underlying investments in the pension plan don't perform well.

Payout Options. At retirement or when leaving the company, employees can choose to receive their benefits as a lump sum or as an annuity (a series of payments over time).

DEFINED-CONTRIBUTION RETIREMENT PLANS

Another type of plan offered by employers is a defined-contribution plan. These include the 401(k), 403(b), 457(b), and Thrift Savings Plan (TSP) and are crucial for individuals working to build a secure retirement. Here's a breakdown of each plan, how it works, and other key considerations about each one:

401(k) Plan

A 401(k) is a retirement savings plan sponsored by private-sector employers. It allows employees to contribute a portion of their pre-tax income to a retirement investment account. The key points about 401(k) plans are:

Tax Benefits. Because contributions to the plan are pre-tax, the employee's taxable income is reduced, and they pay less taxes than they otherwise would. In addition, any investment earnings on amounts in the plan are also not taxed as income until withdrawal.

Contribution Limits. The federal government limits the amount that can be contributed to the plan tax-free. For 2025, the contribution limit is $23,500, with an added $7,500 in catch-up contributions allowed for those aged 50 or older. Plans have the option to allow additional catch-up amounts for employees aged 60 to 63 with a limit of $10,000 or 150% of the allowed regular catch-up limit. Check with a financial advisor or planner for contribution limit updates.

Employer Match. Many employers offer matching contributions, where they contribute a certain amount to your 401(k) based on your own contributions. This is essentially "free money" and a significant benefit.

Vesting. Employer-matched contributions may be subject to a vesting schedule, meaning an employee may need to stay with the company for a certain period to own the matched funds fully.

Investment Options. Most 401(k) plans typically offer a range of employee-selected investment options, including mutual funds, stocks, bonds, and target-date funds, each with a different level of risk. Carefully consider the options based on risk/return and consider diversifying to spread out risk. Seek the advice of a financial advisor if necessary. It is possible to experience losses in these plans.

Withdrawals. Withdrawals are subject to income tax; however, the idea is that usually, once retired, someone's income tax is lower than when they were working. If someone makes a withdrawal before age 59½, it is subject to a 10% early withdrawal penalty in addition to regular income tax. There are some penalty exceptions under certain circumstances, such as hardship withdrawals and separation from service at age 55 or older. Required minimum distributions (RMDs) must begin at age 73.

403(b) Plan

A 403(b) is like a 401(k) but is available to employees of public schools, universities, nonprofit organizations, and certain ministers. It functions similarly to a 401(k). It has the same tax benefits and contribution limits, but there are also differences. Key points about 401(k) plans are:

Tax Benefits. Like a 401(k), contributions are made with pre-tax dollars, and earnings grow tax deferred. Roth 403(b) options are also available for after-tax contributions and tax-free withdrawals.

Contribution Limits. The contribution limits for 2025 are the same as for 401(k) plans—$23,500, with an added $7,500 in catch-up contributions for those aged 50 or older.

Employer Contributions. Some employers offer matching contributions, though this is less common in 403(b) plans than in 401(k) plans.

Investment Options. Often, 403(b) plans include annuities and mutual funds as investment options, though they may offer fewer investment options compared to 401(k) plans.

Special Catch-Up Contributions: Employees with 15 or more years of service with the same employer may be eligible for an added catch-up contribution, though this is subject to specific conditions.

Withdrawals. The same rules apply as those for 401(k)s: withdrawals are subject to income tax; early withdrawals before age 59½ are also subject to the 10% penalty (the same basic penalty exceptions apply); and required minimum distributions (RMDs) must begin at age 73.

GOVERNMENT EMPLOYER PLANS

Federal, state, and local governments have plans that are similar to the ones in the private sector, but also different. The two covered here are the 457(b) plan and Thrift Savings Plans. This section does not cover government defined-benefit plans.

457(b) Plan

A 457(b) plan is a type of deferred-compensation plan modeled on 401(k)s but is primarily available to employees of state and local governments and certain nonprofit organizations. Private-sector businesses do not typically offer it. The basics of these plans are summarized here:

Public-Sector Availability. The standard 457(b) plan is not commonly offered by private employers. (It shouldn't be confused with a similar plan called a 457(f) plan that may be available to certain highly compensated employees in private companies or non-profit organizations.)

Tax Benefits. Like a 401(k), the contributions to a 457(b) plan are made with pre-tax dollars, and withdrawals during retirement are taxed as ordinary income.

Contribution Limits and Matching. The contribution limits are the same as 401(k)s, although employers may not match employee contributions to the plan.

Special Catch-Up Provision. Not only do 457 plans benefit from the same catch-up amount after age 50 as 401(k)s ($7,500 in 2025), but they also have special catch-up provisions. Plans have the option to allow additional catch-up amounts for employees aged 60 to 63 with a limit of $10,000 or 150% of the allowed regular catch-up limit. Additionally, a 457 has a "double limit" provision that applies to individuals in the three years leading up to "normal retirement age," which is usually considered to be 65 and means they can double their contributions, subject to the specific plan's rules and limits. Section 109 of the 2022 SECURE 2.0 Act permits 457 plans to optionally offer higher catch-up contributions in 2025 for participants ages 60 to 63 before the end of the tax year. The maximum catch-up limit is the greater of $10,000 or 150% of the regular catch-up limit.[4]

Investment Options. The investment options available in a 457(b) plan can vary widely depending on the plan provider and the specific plan offered by the employer. Both 457(b) and 401(k) plans generally offer similar types of investment options. Some 457(b) plans may have a broader range of low-risk options compared to 401(k) plans.

Withdrawal. Unlike 401(k) plans, there is no early withdrawal penalty for distributions taken before age 59½. However, withdrawals are still subject to ordinary income tax. Hardship withdrawals are more flexible since there are fewer restrictions on them.

Thrift Savings Plan (TSP)

The TSP functions similar to a 401(k), but is specifically designed for federal employees and members of the uniformed services, including the military. The main points on TSPs are:

Tax Benefits. Contributions can be made with pre-tax (Traditional TSP) or after-tax (Roth TSP; see more on Roth plans in the next section) dollars. Earnings grow tax-deferred in the Traditional TSP, while Roth TSP earnings can be withdrawn tax-free in retirement.

Contribution Limits. The contribution limits for 2025 are also $23,500, with an added $7,500 in catch-up contributions for those aged 50 or older.

Government Match. Employees under the Federal Employees Retirement System (FERS) and the Blended Retirement System (BRS) receive an automatic 1% of salary contribution, regardless of their own contributions. Additionally, employee contributions are matched dollar-for-dollar up to 3% of salary and 50 cents on the dollar for the next 2%. This means that a total possible match of 5% of salary.

Investment Options. The TSP offers a limited number of investment funds, including the G Fund (government securities), F Fund (fixed income index), C Fund (common stock index), S Fund (small-cap stock index), I Fund (international stock index), and Lifecycle Funds (L), a diversified mix of the five individual TSP funds.

Withdrawals. Early withdrawals before age 59½ are subject to a 10% penalty and regular income tax, with some exceptions. Required minimum distributions (RMDs) must begin at age 73.

Low Fees. The TSP is known for its extremely low administrative fees, which can significantly help long-term savings.

INDIVIDUAL RETIREMENT ACCOUNTS (IRAS)

Individual Retirement Accounts (IRAs) are tax-advantaged savings accounts that help individuals save for retirement. They offer various tax benefits to encourage people to save for their future financial needs. Here are the main types of IRAs and their features.

Traditional IRA:

A Traditional IRA is an individual retirement account that allows you to save pre-tax income, with earnings growing tax-deferred until withdrawal. In addition:

Contribution Limits. For 2025, the contribution limit is $7,000, with an added $1,000 catch-up contribution allowed for those aged 50 or older.

Tax Treatment. Contributions may be tax-deductible (fully if you are not covered by a retirement plan at work and possibly partially if you are), and withdrawals in retirement are taxed as ordinary income. Early withdrawals before age 59½ are typically subject to a 10% penalty plus regular income taxes unless you qualify for an exception.

Required Minimum Distributions. (RMDs) must begin at age 73.

Roth IRA:

A Roth IRA is like a Traditional IRA, but contributions are made with after-tax dollars. Because of this, earnings on savings and withdrawals are tax-free in retirement. Other things to know about Roth IRAs are:

- **Income Limits.** Roth IRAs have income limits for contributions. For 2025, the ability to contribute phases out for single filers with modified adjusted gross income (MAGI) above $150,000 and for married couples filing jointly above $236,000.

- **Contribution Limits.** Contributions amounts are the same as a Traditional IRA—$7,000 (under 50) or $8,000 (for those 50 and older).

- **Withdrawals.** You can withdraw your contributions (but not earnings) at any time, regardless of age. To withdraw earnings tax-free, the account must have been open for at least five years, and you must be age 59½ or older. Withdrawals can also be tax-free for specific situations, such as buying a first home (up to $10,000) or due to disability. There are no Required Minimum Distributions.

SIMPLE IRA (SAVINGS INCENTIVE MATCH PLAN FOR EMPLOYEES)

SIMPLE IRAs are for small businesses with 100 or fewer employees, and no other retirement plan is allowed. Employees are always fully vested. Note the following:

- **Contributions.** Employers are required to contribute either up to 3% of compensation or 2% mandatory.

Tax Treatment. Employer contributions to employees' SIMPLE IRAs are tax-deductible for the employer. Employee contributions are made on a pre-tax basis, reducing their taxable income. The SIMPLE IRA is a tax-advantaged retirement plan, benefiting both employer and employee. Earnings grow tax-deferred until withdrawal, at which point they are taxed as ordinary income.

Roth 401(k)

A Roth 401(k) combines features of both traditional 401(k) plans and Roth IRAs. It allows employees to contribute after-tax income, meaning that contributions are taxed in the year they are made. This plan is offered by employers, providing a way for employees to save for retirement with tax benefits upon withdrawal. Other points include:

Contributions. Employees can contribute to a Roth 401(k) up to annual contribution limits set by the IRS. These limits can change each year. For the 2025 tax year, the contribution limit is typically $23,500, with additional catch-up contribution amounts allowed for those aged 50 and older (7,500) and 60 to 63 ($11,250).

Portability. Roth 401(k) plans are portable, meaning that if an employee changes jobs, they can roll over their balance into another Roth 401(k) or a Roth IRA, maintaining the tax-advantaged status of their contributions. However, rolling over to a traditional 401(k) will result in the tax advantages being altered.

Employer Match. Many employers match employee contributions in a Roth 401(k). However, these matching contributions are made on a pre-tax basis and will be placed into a traditional 401(k) account, which means they will be taxed upon withdrawal.

Vesting. Employee contributions to a Roth 401(k) are always 100% vested, meaning the employee owns their contributions outright. However, employer matching contributions may be subject to a vesting schedule, which determines how much of the employer's contributions the employee can keep based on their length of service.

Tax Benefits. The main tax benefit of a Roth 401(k) is that investments in the account grow tax-free, while qualified withdrawals during retirement are tax-free. To be qualified, withdrawals must occur after age 59 ½ and at least five years after the first contribution was made.

Investing Options. Roth 401(k) plans offer various investment options, typically including mutual funds, stocks, bonds, and other investment vehicles. Employees can choose how to allocate their contributions among these options based on their risk tolerance and investment goals.

Annuities

An annuity is a financial product offered by insurance companies or financial institutions to provide steady income, often for retirement. Annuities help manage the risk of outliving savings by converting money into regular payments.

Tax-deferred Annuity. This annuity defers taxes on investment earnings until withdrawal. Other features include a growth phase—when contributions accumulate until you decide to withdraw, typically in retirement—and flexibility—withdrawals can be delayed for maximum tax-deferred growth, or different payout options can be chosen. Withdrawn earnings are taxed as ordinary income, with possible penalties for early withdrawal. The main benefit is that it is useful for supplementing retirement income with tax-deferred growth.

Fixed annuity. Provides guaranteed income with a fixed interest rate. It offers predictable, low-risk income but comes with fees. Income is taxed as ordinary income.

Variable annuity. Allows investment in subaccounts like mutual funds. It has the potential for higher returns and tax-deferred growth. Variable annuities typically have higher fees and investment risk; income is not guaranteed.

Immediate Annuity. Begins payments shortly after a lump sum payment. Like all annuities, it provides a reliable income stream.

When considering investing in an annuity, carefully review the annuity type, fees, and terms. Scheduled payments may provide security, but it also means annuities have limited liquidity, and they may be complex and costly.

ADDITIONAL RETIREMENT SAVINGS OPTIONS

Personal savings and investment strategies are crucial components in ensuring financial stability for your retirement, beyond retirement funding via conventional plans such as Social Security, 401(k), 403(b), 457(b), Thrift Savings Plans (TSP), and defined-benefit pensions. Below is a detailed overview of alternative or supplemental sources of retirement funding.

TAXABLE INVESTMENT ACCOUNT OR BROKERAGE ACCOUNT

Through a taxable investment or brokerage account, you have the flexibility to trade a diverse array of securities, including stocks, bonds, and mutual funds. Unlike IRAs, these accounts are not tax-advantaged, so you'll pay taxes on income and gains in the year they are earned. You can contribute unlimited amounts to a taxable brokerage account and withdraw anytime without penalties, with no required minimum distributions (RMDs). If you've maxed out your contributions to tax-advantaged retirement accounts, a taxable brokerage account is a good next step to save.

Funding retirement by saving and investing using stocks, bonds, and mutual funds involves balancing risk, return, and income generation. Each asset class has its own characteristics, making it important to understand these for a successful retirement strategy. This section presents the key considerations for each.

Stocks

Stocks represent ownership in a company and can offer significant long-term growth. Historically, they have provided higher returns than bonds or cash, making them useful for retirement savings. Considerations when investing in stocks include:

Volatility. Stock prices can be volatile and can fluctuate significantly in the short term, which is important to consider near retirement.

Dividend Income. Some stocks pay dividends, which can serve as regular income, though these are not guaranteed and can be cut when the company is experiencing financial difficulties.

Diversification. Diversify your stock holdings across sectors, industries, and regions to manage risk and mitigate the impact of poor performance in any one area.

Withdrawal Strategy. When withdrawing funds by selling stocks, especially in retirement, balance income needs with capital preservation.

Sequence of Returns Risk. Poor early investment returns can shorten your portfolio's lifespan. Minimize this risk by reducing withdrawals during down markets or using a bucket strategy for short-term and long-term needs.

Bonds

Bonds are debt securities issued by governments or corporations. They pay interest regularly and return the principal at maturity. Generally considered to be safer and less volatile than stocks, they are a common component of retirement portfolios. When considering investing in bonds, keep the following in mind:

Interest Rate Risk. Rising interest rates can reduce bond prices, affecting their value if they are sold before maturity.

Inflation Risk. Fixed-rate bonds may not keep pace with inflation, eroding the income's purchasing power. Consider Treasury Inflation-Protected Securities (TIPS).

Credit Risk. Corporate bonds risk default. Government bonds are safer but offer lower returns.

Duration. Longer-duration bonds are sensitive to interest rate changes. Reduce duration as you near retirement to minimize this risk.

Role in Retirement. Bonds provide steady income generation for covering living expenses and serve as a portfolio stabilizer since they offset stock volatility, thereby reducing overall risk.

Mutual Funds

Mutual funds pool investor money to purchase a variety of stocks, bonds, or other securities, which are managed by professional fund managers (search for "Mutual Funds versus ETFs Comparison—NURP"). Other aspects of mutual funds to keep in mind include:

Types of Funds include **Equity Funds** that invest in stocks, suitable for growth-oriented investors with higher risk but potential for higher returns; **Bond Funds** that are designed for income-oriented investors offering regular income with lower growth potential; and **Balanced or Target-Date Funds**, which hold a mix of stocks and bonds, adjusting to become more conservative as retirement approaches. They are popular for retirement planning due to automatic adjustments.

Fees and Expenses charged by mutual funds can vary widely. High fees can affect returns, so look for low expense ratios, especially in passively managed funds like index funds.

Performance. Actively managed funds aim to outperform the market with varying success, while passively managed funds track specific indexes and typically have lower costs and consistent performance over time.

Liquidity. Mutual funds can be bought and sold on any business day, so they are considered liquid. However, redemption fees or penalties may apply to transactions, depending on the specific terms of the investment.

Role in Retirement. Investing in mutual funds is ideal for retirees who prefer a hands-off approach and allows for diversification since a single mutual fund investment spreads exposure across a broad range of securities, reducing individual investment risk.

A taxable investment account offers flexible options for growing wealth with fewer restrictions than retirement accounts. If retirement account contributions are maxed out, continue saving by investing via a taxable brokerage account.

Savings Accounts

High-yield Savings Accounts are a safe, liquid option for storing cash, offering higher interest rates than traditional savings accounts. They can be useful in retirement for keeping emergency funds or short-term savings geared toward specific goals. Next are some saving account options.

Certificates of Deposit (CDs). These are time deposits with fixed interest rates over set periods and are low-risk and FDIC-insured, offering secure retirement savings. CDs have higher interest rates than regular savings accounts, but lock in your money for the term of the CD. Early withdrawal usually incurs a penalty.

Dividend-Paying Stocks. Dividend stocks provide regular income in retirement and potential capital appreciation. They offer higher returns than fixed-income investments, with dividends that may increase over time. However, dividends are subject to market risk since companies may reduce or cut dividends during times of poor performance or economic downturns.

Health Savings Accounts (HSA)

This account helps those with high-deductible health plans (HDHPs) save for medical expenses. They are ideal for maximizing savings toward retirement health care costs. To contribute, you must have an HDHP, defined in 2025 as having a minimum deductible of $1,650 for individuals or $3,300 for families. Other points about HSAs:

Contributions. Contributions are tax-deductible, and withdrawals for qualified medical expenses are tax-free. The IRS sets annual contribution limits. You can't contribute if enrolled in Medicare, but existing funds can be used for medical expenses, including Medicare premiums.

Withdrawals. After age 65, nonmedical withdrawals are subject to income tax but no penalty.

Benefits. HSAs serve as long-term savings for health care costs in retirement and complement other retirement savings plans.

REAL ESTATE AS A TANGIBLE ASSET AND FOR INCOME GENERATION

When planning for retirement, investing in real estate should be a crucial part of someone's investment strategy. Not only can it generate income, but it also appreciates in value. Additionally, in retirement, once someone has paid off the mortgage on their home, their living expenses are greatly reduced. If an individual or couple has invested in rental property, this property could become an affordable place to live in their older years.

Home Ownership

When owning a home (house, condominium, townhouse), an individual has a significant asset that contributes to their financial stability. A home serves as a long-term investment with the potential to increase one's net worth over time. Homeownership has distinct benefits including as an income stream, a way to diversify investments and appreciation.

Income Streams. Mortgage payments over the years build equity in a home, which can serve as a financial resource in retirement—whether at the time of selling the home or through accessing home equity loans. Owning your home means you won't incur monthly rent payments, which can be more than the mortgage and other monthly payments, but instead build equity in a valuable asset.

Diversification. At retirement, if someone's current home is larger than their current requirements, they can always downsize—for example, from a family home to a townhouse—which can free up cash for their other retirement needs while still providing the comfort of owning their own home. A home serves as a gathering place for family and friends, enabling vital social connections that enhance emotional well-being.

Benefits. Real estate typically appreciates over time, giving homeowners a potential financial cushion as they age. Homeowners may also receive help from tax advantages related to home ownership, such as deductions for mortgage interest or property taxes. Take the time to assess your home's value and think strategically about using this important asset to support your retirement lifestyle. One important consideration is the effect of taxes on the sale of a home. Consult with a professional to fully understand what happens when you sell and for strategies to avoid a big tax bill.

While homeownership does come with responsibilities, such as maintenance, repairs, and property taxes, the benefits can far outweigh the challenges when planning for a secure and fulfilling retirement. It's essential to consider how owning a home fits into your overall financial plan and personal goals for this next phase of life.

Rental Property

Rental real estate can generate stable income and appreciate over time, offering benefits like inflation hedging and tax advantages. Like other real estate, rental property can increase in value over time. It can be a lucrative but illiquid investment. It requires active management and is subject to market risks and financing concerns. However, after the purchase process, rental real estate can provide passive income, freeing up your time. The tax benefits are complex, so seek professional advice. Rental property can provide the following benefits:

Income Stream. Rental income provides consistent cash flow, which is valuable in retirement.

Diversification. Adding rental properties into your portfolio of assets provides diversification and balances risk with assets other than stocks and bonds. Property values and rental income often rise with inflation.

Tax Advantages. Deductions include mortgage interest, depreciation, and property management costs.

Including rental properties in your retirement strategy can enhance financial security and offer the benefits of real estate investment.

Reverse Mortgage Income

A Reverse Mortgage lets you turn home equity into cash, which can be used to add to your retirement income to help with expenses or lifestyle improvements without monthly payments or having to sell and leave your home. In this way, it diversifies the homeowner's retirement income sources.

Designed for those 62 and older, a Reverse Mortgage allows you to access your home equity while living in it. The loan must be repaid when you sell, move, or pass away. Because of this, the loan reduces the value of your estate. The benefits include:

- **No Monthly Payments.** Eases financial pressures.
- **Flexibility.** The money can be received as a lump sum, monthly payments, or in the form of a line of credit.
- **Stay in Your Home.** Reverse Mortgages allow homeowners who are less concerned about leaving a large estate to access their home's equity while continuing to live in it.

Consider the long-term effects on home equity and consult a financial advisor or planner to ensure it fits your retirement and estate-planning goals. This option offers financial flexibility and security for an enjoyable retirement.

Real Estate Investment Trusts

Real Estate Investment Trusts (REITs) offer a way to invest in real estate without managing properties directly. A Real Estate Investment Trust owns, operates, or finances income-producing real estate across various sectors. (search for "Are REITs good Investments in 2025?—Prudent Savings"). Investing in REITs provides exposure to different property types—commercial, residential, and industrial—without hands-on management since the properties are managed by professionals. Some points about REITs:

Liquidity. REITs are traded on major stock exchanges, offering liquidity.

Income Potential. REITs often offer attractive dividend yields.

Income Stream. REITs must distribute at least 90% of their taxable income as dividends, providing a reliable income stream.

Diversification. REITs diversify your portfolio by spreading risk across multiple property types and locations, protecting against sector volatility.

Research different REIT types and evaluate their performance, costs, and risks to align with your financial goals. REITs can enhance financial security and offer real estate benefits.

RETIREMENT INCOME STREAMS FOR FINANCIAL SECURITY

Some in retirement find that their income or funds fall short of their needs or that they want to wait as long as possible before accessing their retirement funds. So, many retirees choose to work part- or full-time after their mandatory or Social Security age to cover "income gaps" or preserve their assets. Another reason may be to stay active and to support having purpose.

As someone enters retirement, maintaining financial stability without a regular paycheck becomes crucial. Consider different income sources, such as part-time work or starting a small business. Each option comes with its own benefits and challenges, allowing you to tailor your approach to fit your unique needs.

Working After Retirement

Part-time work can boost financial stability by supplementing Social Security, pensions, or savings to help cover health care costs and unexpected expenses and reducing the need to withdraw funds from savings and investment accounts. It can also provide for "extras," such as travel, spa days, or hobbies.

Income while receiving Social Security benefits and pension income may affect those benefits. For example, if someone has elected to receive their Social Security before their "Required Retirement Age," income earned working may reduce the benefit. Retirees should plan for tax and other impacts and consider strategies to minimize liabilities.

Popular part-time jobs for retirees include consulting, freelancing, teaching, tutoring, retail, remote work, pet sitting, dog walking, house sitting, and tour guiding. AARP and similar organizations provide resources for finding part-time jobs.

Small Business in Retirement

Starting a small business in retirement keeps you active, generates income, and lets you pursue your passions. Approach it thoughtfully and strategically. Consider consulting, selling your crafts, teaching, writing, or other hobbies.

A small business can supplement your retirement income and provide flexible hours. Popular ideas include consulting, freelancing, tutoring, crafts, e-commerce, pet services, and home-based ventures. A small business can also become a family legacy or support the community. Some key points about starting a home business in retirement are:

Financial Risk. Assess the finances of the business, such as startup costs, income expectations, and potential risks. Avoid risking your retirement savings.

Health Considerations. Be realistic about whether you have the physical and mental capacity to operate a business, particularly if it involves manual labor or long hours.

Tax Implications. Consult a tax professional to follow tax laws and maximize business deductions and retirement contributions.

Time Commitment. The initial setup of a business may be time-consuming. In addition, think about how much time it will take to run the business. Assess if you're truly prepared for this versus preferring more leisure in your retirement lifestyle.

INSURANCE CONSIDERATIONS FOR RETIREMENT

A well-structured insurance strategy ensures that you and your loved ones are protected against life's uncertainties. Adequate insurance coverage can significantly mitigate risks and unforeseen expenses, thereby safeguarding your financial stability and providing peace of mind. Consider various insurance types, including life insurance, homeowners' insurance, auto insurance, umbrella insurance, and supplemental health care insurance. As your needs change, review and adjust your coverage accordingly.

Life Insurance

Life insurance is a financial product designed to provide financial protection to beneficiaries after the death of the insured individual. The key basics of life insurance, its types, and its benefits are the following:

Term Life Insurance. Provides coverage for a specific period, paying a death benefit if you die during the term. It is more affordable than permanent life insurance but does not accumulate cash value. (Search for "Life Insurance Policies. Key Provisions and Legal Implications").

Whole Life Insurance. Offers lifetime coverage with a savings component that grows over time. (Search for "Everything You Need To Know About Basic Life Insurance"). It can be used for estate planning, providing for heirs, or covering outstanding debts or estate taxes.

Final Expense Insurance. A small whole life policy designed to cover funeral and burial costs, typically offering coverage amounts from $5,000 to $25,000.

Universal Life Insurance. A flexible permanent life insurance policy that allows policyholders to adjust premiums and death benefits. It accumulates cash value based on current interest rates, which can vary.

Homeowners and Renters Insurance

These cover losses due to unforeseen events and include Homeowners and Renter's Insurance.

Homeowners Insurance. Provides basic structural damage, fire, and theft protection as well as liability protection. Review your coverage limits, especially if your mortgage is paid off or home value has increased. Consider adding riders for valuable items. Be aware of what generally isn't covered, like floods, earthquakes, and damage caused by pests.

Renters Insurance. Covers against theft and fire loss of personal belongings and provides liability protection for retirees who rent.

Auto Insurance

Covers liability for injuries and property damage from auto accidents as well as damage to your vehicle. Adjust coverage based on driving habits, consider usage-based plans, and increase liability coverage if you have significant assets. Drop comprehensive and collision coverage if your vehicle is older.

Umbrella Insurance

Provides added liability coverage beyond your existing policies, covering legal fees and settlements if you're sued for damages exceeding your coverage limits. Regularly review your policies to ensure they meet your evolving needs. Bundling multiple policies, such as homeowners and auto insurance, can help reduce costs (search for "State Farm vs. Alfa Homeowners Insurance Review").

Health Insurance

Chapter Seven, "Cultivating Good Health in Retirement," discusses health insurance considerations. It also addresses Long-Term Care Insurance for potential large expenses like nursing home care or in-home assistance.

WEALTH TRANSFER: *NAVIGATING YOUR FINANCIAL LEGACY*

Wealth Transfer involves the systematic transfer of assets and resources to others. Intergenerational transfer consists of the passing of financial expertise and assets, such as money, property, and other valuables, from one generation to the next. This process includes inheritances, gifts, or trusts from parents or grandparents to their offspring and highlights the necessity for strategic planning to maintain family wealth and ensure its enduring impact. Understanding intergenerational transfers is essential for enhancing financial security in retirement.

DO NOT RELY ON THE PROSPECT OF A WEALTH TRANSFER

Being the recipient of an inheritance or wealth transfer can enhance someone's retirement security, yet its timing and amount are unpredictable. Until received, do not depend on it as your primary source of retirement funds, even if a promised inheritance gives a psychological sense of security. It is prudent to remember that inheritances are not guaranteed; therefore, maintaining a personal savings strategy remains advisable.

On the other hand, when a wealth transfer is structured well so that its likelihood is secure, it can alleviate the necessity of saving aggressively for retirement. An inheritance or gift can significantly augment retirement savings, facilitating the attainment of financial objectives. Cash inheritances offer immediate funds for retirement savings, clearing up debts, or living expenses. Inheriting a home can reduce housing costs or be sold to support retirement. Rental property inheritances provide income but require time and management of tenants and maintenance.

Beneficiaries of wealth transfers should educate themselves on how to protect the gift or inheritance for their future by investing it wisely, such as in retirement accounts or other vehicles. Consult a financial advisor or estate planner to make effective use of your inheritance and align it with your retirement goals. See a financial planner or tax specialist to educate yourself and help you navigate any inheritance or gift taxes.

The certainty of such a transfer depends on effective estate planning by the person who has made out a will or established a trust and on how likely it may be that they change their mind. The next section provides some information for those preparing their estate plans.

CONSULT AN ESTATE PLANNING ATTORNEY

An estate planning attorney can help you create or update your will, set up trusts, and ensure your assets are distributed according to your wishes. Proper estate planning can reduce taxes, avoid probate, and provide for your heirs. Do not consider your estate plan to be "one and done." Review it regularly and periodically consult with your professional advisor(s) as life events, personal challenges, or economic shifts occur.

ESTATE PLANNING AND FINANCIAL SECURITY DOCUMENTS

When considering an estate plan, an individual or couple needs to have a legal strategy in place for managing and distributing their assets both during their lifetime and after they pass away. This approach protects their assets, provides for their loved ones, and ensures that their wishes are followed. Additionally, the right plan will aim to minimize estate taxes and maximize the value of inherited assets for beneficiaries through techniques such as gifting, charitable giving, and other tax-efficient methods.

Take the time to talk to your heirs about your plans and educate them about the financial management of any gift or inheritance. This not only prepares them for their future but also supports their financial security, which can create a positive ripple effect.

An estate plan includes tailored documents to protect your legacy and ensure your wishes are followed during your life and after. Planning for intergenerational transfers preserves your legacy, respects your wishes, and involves transferring property, investments, and continuing family traditions. Proper planning minimizes taxes and costs, ensuring more assets for your heirs through strategies like gifting and trusts. Clear plans prevent family conflicts, ensuring a smooth transition of assets.

Taking control of your financial future empowers you to make informed decisions that benefit you and your family.

Wills

A will is a legal document specifying how someone's assets should be distributed after their death. In it, a person names their beneficiaries, an executor for their estate, and appoints guardians for their minor children. Without a will, state intestacy laws dictate asset distribution, which might not match their intentions. The key components of a will are:

Executor. The person responsible for administering your estate, paying debts, and distributing assets according to a will (search for "What is a Last Will and Testament? Everything You Need to Know").

Beneficiaries. Individuals or organizations who will receive someone's assets, including in what percentage or amounts and specific bequests—stated items or gifts designated for named individuals (search for "A Guide to Naming Beneficiaries in Your Will or Trust").

- **Guardianship.** If you have minor children, you can name who will serve as a guardian to care for them (search for "Generate Last Will & Testament—Documentify").
- **Residuary Estate.** The remainder of someone's estate after specific bequests, debts, and expenses have been paid, if any, and what happens to it.

Updating Your Will. Regularly update your will to reflect life changes, such as marriage, divorce, the birth of children, or significant changes in your assets.

Trusts

Trusts are legal arrangements that allow someone to transfer their assets to it, to be managed by a trustee who will distribute them according to their instructions when they pass away. (Search for "How Does Inheritance Work? (Legal Transfer of Assets)—Tag Vault") Trusts can serve various purposes, including avoiding probate, providing for minor children or individuals with special needs, minimizing estate taxes, and protecting assets from creditors or beneficiaries' poor financial decisions. The main types of trusts are:

Revocable Living Trust. This type of trust can be changed or revoked during the lifetime of the grantor. The benefit is that a Revocable Living Trust allows your assets to pass to beneficiaries without going through probate. However, the grantor can change the terms or the assets in the trust at any time and even revoke the trust.

Irrevocable Trust. Once set up, this trust cannot be changed or revoked. It can provide tax benefits and asset protection, for example, from debtors or in a divorce.

Testamentary Trust. Set up is pursuant to the instructions in someone's will and only takes effect after their death. It names a trustee to manage the trust assets on behalf of beneficiaries such as minor children or others.

Special Needs Trust. Provides for a disabled beneficiary without affecting their eligibility for government benefits.

Some of the key points about trusts include:

Trustee. A trustee is appointed to manage the trust's assets and carry out its terms. This can be an individual or a corporate trustee.

Funding the Trust. Assets must be transferred into the trust during the grantor's lifetime or at death through their will or other estate planning tools.

Distribution Terms. These specify how and when the trust's assets will be distributed to beneficiaries.

Non-Will-Related Beneficiaries

Life insurance policies, retirement accounts, and payable-on-death (POD) bank accounts will ask the holder to name the beneficiary(s) that the policy or account pays upon the holder's death. This is because such payouts override the person's will.

Both primary and contingent beneficiaries should be named. Primary beneficiaries receive the asset upon the holder's death, while contingent beneficiaries are named in case the primary beneficiary predeceases the holder. Beneficiary designations should be regularly reviewed and updated to ensure they reflect someone's current wishes and align with the provisions of their will and other estate planning documents.

Power of Attorney (DPOA)

Both Durable Power of Attorney (DPOA) and Financial Power of Attorney (FPOA) are legal documents that allow one person to act on behalf of another as their agent. These documents are crucial for effective estate planning because they name an agent to act in the event someone is temporarily or permanently incapacitated. Consult a legal professional to create these documents properly and according to state laws. However, they serve different purposes and have distinct features.

Durable Power of Attorney. The key characteristic of a DPOA is its durability. It is designed to still be effective despite the principal's incapacitation, ensuring that their affairs can be managed without interruption. (Search for "Understanding Statutory Power of Attorney—Boxed Out Law"). This means that the agent can continue to act on behalf of the principal when they are unable to make decisions for themselves. A DPOA must be created while the principal is competent. It may need specific language for its durable feature, proper notarization, and witnesses as per state laws.

DPOAs can be used for a wide range of situations, including health care decision-making, managing personal affairs, and handling financial matters, but their scope can be general or limited. It allows the agent to handle various designated aspects of the principal's affairs, which can include both financial and nonfinancial matters, such as health care decisions or legal matters.

Financial Power of Attorney. This legal document grants an agent authority to make financial decisions and handle financial matters on behalf of the principal, such as managing bank accounts, investments, real estate transactions, and other financial decisions. Financial Powers of Attorney may be general or specific to certain transactions but is primarily used to manage financial affairs, making them particularly useful when the principal is away, hospitalized, or otherwise unable to manage their finances directly (search for "Top 10 Things to Know About POA | Forbes & Forbes Law").

A Financial Power of Attorney (FPOA) can either be durable or nondurable. A nondurable FPOA becomes invalid if the principal becomes incapacitated, while a durable FPOA continues to be effective even if the principal is unable to make their own financial decisions.

TAKEAWAYS FROM SAVING FOR RETIREMENT

Financial satisfaction in retirement depends on planning. The main points of this chapter were:

Financial security in retirement depends on financial literacy.

Planning for retirement is more than relying on Social Security or a pension.

Today, most people need to save for retirement. Explore the many options for doing so, from employer plans such as 401(k)s, 403(b)s, 457(bs), and TSPs to self-saving plans such as IRAs and Annuities.

Understand the value of investing in real estate for the retirement benefits.

Consider working or operating a small business while retired for additional income and to preserve retirement assets.

Protect yourself with adequate insurance coverage, appropriate estate planning, and Power of Attorney documents.

CHAPTER FIVE

FINANCIAL SATISFACTION: CHALLENGES AND STRATEGIES

---

*Retirement is wonderful if you have two essentials—
much to live on and much to live for.*
—UNKNOWN

Different roads sometimes lead to the same castle.
—GEORGE R. R. MARTIN

*Strategy is a fancy word for coming up with
a long-term plan and putting it into action.*
—ELLIE PIDOT

Those individuals who are part of a racial or ethnic community, women, LGBTQ+ individuals, someone with disabilities, or a low- to moderate-income worker face unique challenges to saving and financial planning. Systemic barriers, wage disparities, limited savings opportunities, and, for women, longer life expectancies are some of the hurdles they might encounter. When multiple overlapping identities—such as race, gender, socioeconomic status, sexual orientation, and disability—intersect, the impact on someone's finances may be catastrophic.

When such individuals understand their unique challenges, targeted strategies can be developed to improve their retirement outcomes and ensure their financial security and well-being in retirement. This review aims to examine diversity-related issues in retirement planning and offers insights to help those affected by these issues navigate such complexities effectively. It's crucial to recognize and address these factors.

THE SAVINGS ISSUES OF DIVERSE DEMOGRAPHICS

Many members of racial and ethnic communities encounter specific challenges in retirement planning. For example, lower lifetime earnings and wage disparities can significantly affect the ability to save. Additionally, many have limited access to employer-sponsored retirement plans, further impacting savings potential. These individuals must overcome these challenges in order to build a secure and prosperous future. The first step is to find culturally competent advisory services or education resources to improve financial literacy as someone navigates the complexities of retirement planning as a member of a diverse community. The second step is to develop targeted financial strategies to achieve better retirement outcomes.

No matter your age or employment status, start to think about and plan for retirement by taking the following actions:

> Tap into local community organizations, non-profits, and faith-based groups that offer financial advice, resources, and support tailored to their specific needs.

> Participate in programs and resources provided by local community centers, libraries, faith-based organizations, and community colleges to support retirement planning. Create community networks for sharing financial planning resources and strategies.

Look for culturally aware financial advisors and inclusive retirement planning resources. Cultural differences influence attitudes toward retirement, family duties, and financial decisions. It is essential to find advisors familiar with your community's nuances or multilingual financial planning resources.

Make a detailed budget that focuses on saving for retirement, cutting spending, and managing health care. Set clear, reachable goals to guide your financial planning. Start today and, if possible, start when you are as young as possible.

Factor in potential caregiving expenses in retirement planning and consider long-term care insurance to mitigate financial strain.

Encourage employers to sponsor and set up retirement savings plans and financial education resources for workers, highlighting the importance of fair workplace benefits.

Advocate for government policies that improve retirement savings—such as increasing the minimum wage and requiring automatic enrollment in 401(k) programs—can help address income disparities and enhance retirement security within your community.

By acknowledging and addressing the unique challenges faced by your community, you can work towards improving financial security and overall well-being for yourself and others.

WOMEN AND CAREGIVERS

Women also face specific challenges to financial satisfaction and living well during their retirement years. The most significant challenge remains the gender pay gap, which results in lower lifetime earnings—and therefore Social Security benefits and lower lifetime savings—compared to men. As discussed, statistics show that women live longer than men, which means they will need to be able to fund a longer retirement period. So, on top of earnings challenges, they need more savings than men do.

Most women have the strength and resilience to navigate the unique issues they face in order to secure their financial future and retirement years. Though the gender pay gap has often resulted in lower lifetime earnings, know that the determination to budget and save can overcome this hurdle. Their longevity and enduring spirits mean that it is likely they will require a substantial savings amount, but this is achievable with strategic planning. In addition, their tendency to cultivate friendships and form lasting ones will help them to ward off possible social isolation in retirement.

Caregivers who take time out of the workplace to look after others—children, aging parents, or other family members—can experience the negative impact of many years of lost income at retirement. Some caregivers take lower-level or part-time positions to allow them to devote themselves to their loved ones. This also affects their career progressions because they've lost the time when others are moving into higher-level and better-paying positions. In this way, caregiving reduces lifetime earnings, whether the caregiver is a man or a woman. The result is that caregivers risk having insufficient funds to support themselves later in life.

Those who give of themselves in service to others discover that the time dedicated to caregiving is invaluable and enables them to cultivate valuable skills, such as resourcefulness, budgeting, and experience in negotiating with various organizations and support systems that will prove helpful in the future. In addition, they are likely to develop strong social networks that may offer essential emotional support and shared resources during their retirement years.

Despite the challenges you may face as a woman and/or a caregiver, it is still possible for you to shape your financial future with confidence and foresight. Some points for you follow:

Despite reduced or limited income, still make savings a priority by belt-tightening and living on a detailed budget, one that keeps current expenses to a minimum and provides a cushion for unexpected future expenses to ensure that savings can be maximized. Remember that any dollar not spent today is a dollar for the future.

Establish retirement accounts early, such as IRAs, and regularly make contributions to them, no matter how small the amounts, although as much as possible is best. If you are still employed and you have employer retirement accounts available to you, take full advantage of the "free money" of employer matching contributions.

Educate yourself about investment options and strategies, and consider working with a financial planner knowledgeable about the unique financial challenges of women and caregivers.

Join groups, participate in programs, and network with others for support and financial insights. Join women- or caregiver-focused financial literacy organizations, programs, or workshops. Engaging with these types of communities builds financial literacy and provides access to the knowledge and experience of others with similar challenges.

Explore alternative income sources, such as gig or part-time work, and seek to develop passive income streams, such as renting to a roommate, if possible, to supplement your income.

Consider health care needs in retirement planning, as medical expenses can be a significant burden. Purchasing long-term care insurance when you are younger when it is cheaper and engaging in regular health assessments can help manage these potential costs.

Despite the economic challenges faced by them, women and caregivers can still work towards achieving a secure and fulfilling retirement.

SAME-SEX COUPLES

Members of the LGBTQ+ communities face many of the same challenges that women and diverse communities do: lower wage and savings levels, and the advice for them is the same. The members of these communities should avail themselves of community-oriented financial resources for financial literacy to help them set up budgets and savings plans. For some members, adequate access to health care and insurance is even more critical, so this must be made a priority.

As for same-sex couples, navigating retirement planning can be complex, but with the right strategies and resources, they can ensure a secure and fulfilling future together. Understanding your rights and benefits, especially regarding Social Security and health care, is crucial for you. Prepare your legal documents thoroughly and engage with financial advisors who are knowledgeable about LGBTQ+ issues to safeguard your assets and wishes. Stay informed, proactive, and connected with supportive communities to overcome challenges and build the retirement you deserve.

To address these challenges, consider taking the steps listed below:

Review and understand your legal rights and benefits as a same-sex couple, including the differences in those rights when you are or are not legally married. This includes understanding the implications of each with respect to Social Security, pensions, and inheritance rights. Familiarize yourself with Social Security rules about spousal and survivor benefits.

Seek financial planning resources tailored to diverse family structures. Engaging with financial advisors and institutions knowledgeable about the LGBTQ+ community can enhance planning outcomes.

Create an estate plan that protects partners and establishes them as the beneficiary. Set up clear directives for the transfer of assets. Properly prepare and update legal documents like wills, trusts, powers of attorney, and health care directives to protect assets and fulfill both partners' wishes. A plan must address legal, tax, and health care challenges in retirement. Realize that with no estate plan, the probate court will administer a person's assets. Probate courts do not recognize long-time partners if they are not married.

Ensure that you both have adequate life insurance coverage.

Keep yourself updated on any changes in laws and policies that may affect your rights and benefits as a same-sex couple, particularly those related to retirement, taxation, and health care.

TRANSGENDER INDIVIDUALS

A transgender individual planning for retirement may face unique legal, financial, and societal considerations in addition to those encountered by their broader LBTQ+ community. Legal recognition of gender identity can affect access to benefits and health care. Income disparities, employment discrimination, and career interruptions due to transitioning can have negative impacts on retirement savings. The cost of transitioning and gender-affirming care may use up existing savings and leave little funds available for ongoing retirement saving.

If society is to address the unique financial issues faced by transgender individuals, a comprehensive approach is necessary, one that includes legal and insurance protections, inclusive workplace policies, and targeted resources to promote financial literacy and security.

To address these challenges, consider the points that follow:

Stay informed about legal rights related to employment, health care, and retirement benefits for transgender individuals. Knowing your rights can help you advocate for fair treatment and protection.

Anticipate potential health care expenses in retirement, including ongoing medical care related to gender transition. Explore health insurance options and long-term care plans that provide necessary coverage.

Seek out financial advisors and planners experienced in working with transgender individuals and the LGBTQ+ community. They can give tailored advice that accounts for unique challenges and considerations.

Connect with LGBTQ+ community organizations that offer resources, support, and networking opportunities. Engaging with peers can provide valuable insights and encouragement.

INDIVIDUALS LIVING WITH DISABILITIES

As a person living with a disability and planning for retirement, you may often face unique challenges. These include potential barriers to full-time employment, lower lifetime earnings, and higher health care costs due to specialized care needs. Additionally, accessibility, housing modifications, and long-term care services can pose significant expenses. Remember, you are not alone on this journey. There are resources and support networks available to help you navigate these challenges effectively.

Some actions you can take are listed below. Explore supplemental insurance options and long-term care insurance can help prepare for future care needs. Understand how to maximize Social Security Disability Insurance (SSDI) and Supplemental Security Income (SSI). Eligible individuals should carefully consider the timing of when to start receiving retirement benefits to ensure maximum monthly payouts.

These include potential barriers to full-time employment, lower lifetime earnings, and higher health care costs due to specialized care needs. Additionally, accessibility, housing modifications, and long-term care services can pose significant expenses. Remember, you are not alone on this journey. There are resources and support networks available to help you navigate these challenges effectively.

Some actions you can take are listed below:

Explore supplemental insurance options and long-term care insurance can help prepare for future care needs.

Understand how to maximize Social Security Disability Insurance (SSDI) and Supplemental Security Income (SSI). Eligible individuals should carefully consider the timing of when to start receiving retirement benefits to ensure maximum monthly payouts.

Establish an Achieving a Better Life Experience (ABLE) Account allows individuals with disabilities to save for qualified expenses without affecting their SSI, Medicaid, or other benefits. Money withdrawn from these accounts can be used for various expenses such as housing, transportation, health care, and education.

Consider a Supplemental or Special Needs Trusts (SNTs), another option that enables individuals with disabilities to receive financial support from family members or other sources without risking their government benefits. Funds in these trusts can be used for many needs, including health care, education, recreation, and transportation.

Work with financial advisors who have experience helping clients with disabilities and understand their unique challenges.

Connect with local and national organizations that provide resources, advocacy, and support can help individuals navigate benefits, find accessible housing, and access community services.

LOW- AND MODERATE-INCOME INDIVIDUALS

Workers who earn 50% or below the median income where they live (low) or 50 to 80% of the median income (moderate) face many of the same challenges discussed earlier. They have less ability to save and often have a lack of financial literacy resources. Many individuals in sectors such as retail, food service, and hospitality may be earning the minimum wage or below the average hourly income in their areas. Just covering living expenses may be a challenge for these workers, let alone setting aside money for the future.

In addition, many such workers may not have access to employer-sponsored retirement plans, such as 401(k)s or pension plans, either because they are not available or due to their part-time status or employer policies. Even when such plans are available, participation rates can be low because workers just can't afford it.

Low- and moderate-income workers might find themselves living paycheck to paycheck. Rising housing costs often consume a significant portion of their income, leaving little for retirement savings. Essential expenses like food and transportation can further strain financial resources, while health care costs—including premiums and out-of-pocket expenses—add to the burden. All of which can lead to high levels of debt and credit card payments, so they live in a negative savings situation. Finally, they cannot afford professional financial advice. All of this can make retirement planning feel daunting, if not impossible.

Despite these obstacles, if you are a low- to moderate-income earner, you can still benefit from accessible financial education, advice from others, and community resources if you seek it out. Furthermore, the experience in resilience and agility gained from being a gig worker (short term or temporary work assignments) can help you to secure work in retirement as well. You *can* chart a path toward a secure retirement. You can take proactive steps to build your financial future and remember that even small actions can lead to significant changes.

Here are some action steps to get you started:

Create a budget detailing your income and expenses to uncover any area where you can save on expenses. Regularly pay close attention to your spending. Allocate some portion of income toward saving for retirement, no matter how small. Also, build a small emergency fund to cover unexpected costs, aiming for three to six months of living expenses.

Educate yourself on the amount and cost of the debt you are carrying. Set alerts to pay all credit card debt on time to avoid costly late fees. That $25-35 late fee could be set aside for your retirement.

Explore retirement saving options. Certain states have introduced retirement savings programs for workers without access to employer-sponsored plans, such as "Secure Choice" plans. These programs typically offer low-cost, automatically enrolled IRAs that enable workers to save through payroll deductions. (More information about Secure Choice can be found at Georgetown Center for Retirement Initiatives or Guideline).

Consider that even without having an employer-sponsored retirement plan, you can still prioritize saving for retirement and get the tax advantages of doing so by opening an Individual Retirement Account

(IRA). Even small contributions can add up over time, and investment earnings on them help your savings grow. A Roth IRA is particularly beneficial for low-income individuals as contributions are made with after-tax dollars, allowing for tax-free withdrawals in retirement.

If you are eligible to enroll in an employer-sponsored retirement plan, such as a 401(k) or Roth 401(k), take full advantage of any employer matching contributions, as this is essentially free money that can boost your retirement savings.

Delay claiming Social Security benefits as long as possible—ideally up to age 70—to maximize future monthly payments. This strategy is particularly important for those who will rely heavily on Social Security in retirement. For those who are or were married, understanding how spousal and survivor benefits can improve Social Security income for the household.

Look for opportunities to generate added income through part-time jobs or gig work that can be directed toward retirement savings.

Seek out local workshops, community programs, or online resources that offer financial education and retirement planning advice. Increasing your financial literacy can enhance your ability to make informed decisions.

Join local community organizations or groups focused on financial literacy. Networking with others in similar financial situations can provide valuable insights and support for retirement planning.

Keep your vision and long-term retirement goals in mind to stay motivated. Having a clear picture of your future can help you prioritize saving over short-term spending.

Chapter 5: Financial Satisfaction: Challenges and Strategies

While saving for retirement on a low-to-moderate income can be challenging, strategic planning and taking advantage of available resources can make a significant difference. Starting early, utilizing employer plans, and seeking education are key steps in building a secure financial future.

GENERATIONAL COHORTS AND RETIREMENT FINANCIAL PLANNING

Understanding the influence of generational cohorts is crucial for shaping effective retirement financial planning strategies. Each generation—from Baby Boomer to Gen X and Millennial—brings unique experiences that shape their approach to retirement, influenced by cultural, economic, and technological changes. By exploring these cohorts, we can identify the distinct challenges and opportunities each group faces.

For Baby Boomers, the focus may be on maximizing Social Security benefits and health care planning, while Gen Xers might be more concerned with balancing retirement savings with current financial responsibilities. Millennials, on the other hand, may prioritize long-term investment strategies and use technology in their financial planning. Recognizing these nuances is essential for developing tailored strategies that align with their values and aspirations. This section discusses how factors like income levels, access to retirement savings plans, and social attitudes affect different financial planning approaches for each generational cohort.

BABY BOOMER

The Baby Boomer generation (roughly born between 1946 and 1964) forms a sizable part of today's retiree population, and its members have diverse financial situations, savings habits, and retirement plans. Many of them have already retired or are approaching retirement. Some say they will never retire. With a life expectancy much longer than past generations, they may need to plan for longer retirement periods, considering the potential need for income and health care over an extended period.

Overall, Baby Boomers should take a proactive approach to financial planning for retirement. If they have not yet retired, their next decision is whether they can afford to retire now or if they should wait until they are better positioned financially. Baby Boomers can start by answering these questions:

When will you be eligible to receive full Social Security, pension, or other retirement plan benefits?

What would your monthly retirement income be?

What would your monthly expenses be?

Would your monthly income be enough to cover your monthly expenses if you didn't work?

Do you have enough money to retire now?

If not, how could you increase your income and lower your expenses to save more (for example, with catch-up 401(k) savings, or earn more on your existing assets to help close the gap?

Baby boomers, you must carefully assess your financial situation and your retirement plan. Determine where you are in terms of savings and investments, what your retirement income looks like or will be, and your expected expenses is a good start to deciding when to retire. So, go deeper and do the following next steps:

Identify your various sources of retirement income, including Social Security benefits, pensions, and earnings on retirement savings accounts such as 401(k)s, 403(b)s, 457(b)s, Thrift Savings Plans, and IRAs, other investment income, rental income, and part-time work.

Prioritize maximizing your contributions to retirement savings accounts.

Maximize savings and keep an emergency fund to handle unexpected expenses.

Manage debt and prioritize paying off high-interest debt.

Consider funding annuities to give you a guaranteed income stream for life and ensure you don't outlive your savings.

Consider downsizing your housing, if your current home is larger than you need, to reduce expenses such as property taxes, maintenance, and utilities,

Understand your Medicare coverage and supplemental health care options and choose the right plan that balances cost with coverage.

Estimate health care expenses and health insurance premiums expenses that you will pay after you leave full-time employment.

Consider long-term care insurance to protect against potentially high health care costs in retirement.

Contribute to a Health Savings Account (HSA) if you are still working, not covered by Medicare yet, and eligible.

Seek advice from a qualified professional to better prepare for a financially secure and comfortable retirement.

For Baby Boomers who are already retired, the main concern is to take steps to make sure savings last throughout retirement. This requires some careful planning and employing smart fiscal management. Here are a few tips:

If you haven't done so, formulate a budget to ensure you don't outspend your income and dip into savings. Plan for inflation, which can erode buying power over time. Make sure your budget reflects the potential for rising costs beyond inflation, especially in health care. Regularly review and adjust your budget to align with changes in your financial situation or unexpected expenses.

Adopt a strategic withdrawal plan and manage how and when to withdraw money from retirement accounts like 401(k)s and IRAs to ensure savings last.

Minimize income taxes by considering the tax effects of withdrawals from taxable, tax-deferred (like traditional IRAs), and tax-free accounts (like Roth IRAs).

Understand your Required Minimum Distributions (RMDs) and plan your RMDs alongside other income sources to manage your tax bracket effectively.

Maximize Social Security benefits if possible. If you haven't yet claimed Social Security, consider delaying benefits until age 70. Coordinate the timing of your and your spouse's claims to optimize the combined payout.

Refine your investment strategy for a diversified portfolio that includes a mix of stocks, bonds, and other assets like real estate or dividend-paying investments. Diversification helps manage risk and offers growth opportunities.

Explore some income-generating alternative investments to have less dependence on low interest rate bonds and saving accounts or adjust spending to cope with reduced income.

Investigate the advantages of downsizing to a more affordable home versus staying in your existing one. Look into whether selling or renting works better for you financially, from an estate planning perspective, and with respect to taxes. Explore the options of keeping a large home that may be impractical or too expensive versus downsizing to a more affordable home.

Consider moving to a different city, state, or country with a lower cost of living or better amenities for retirees, weighing the benefits of a new location against the potential downside of moving away from family and friends.

Manage health care costs and understand your Medicare and health insurance options. Choose the right supplementary plan that balances cost with coverage. Evaluate the best prescription drug plan to buy.

Ensure that wills, trusts, and other estate planning documents are up to date, especially as family dynamics change or as the financial situation evolves.

Discover how best to pass on wealth to heirs by navigating tax implications, setting up trusts, and ensuring that beneficiaries are clearly designated.

Set up a Financial Power of Attorney, Health Care Proxy, and Advance Medical Directive in the event you become temporarily or permanently incapacitated.

Plan for a retirement that could last 20 to 30 years or more due to increased life expectancy.

Seek advice from a qualified professional to ensure that you are on track to keeping a financially secure and comfortable retirement.

GEN X

Born between 1965 and 1980, Generation X started their careers during a major shift in retirement saving. Companies moved from pensions to 401(k)s, and Gen Xers had to take on more responsibility for their retirement planning. While all generations undergo recessions and economic downturns, Gen X experienced the 2008 financial crisis. Their concerns have been the level of their student debt, caring for both children and aging parents, and doubts about the future of Social Security.

Here are some important steps for Gen Xers to plan for a financially secure retirement:

Maximize contributions to retirement accounts like 401(k), 403(b), IRAs, and other tax-advantaged options to take full advantage of any free money employer matching and tax benefits. Maximize allowable "catch-up" contributions.

Despite the temptation to take early Social Security, plan to hold out as long as possible by waiting until age 70.

Build a diversified investment portfolio that balances risk and return based on your goals and periodically review it.

Create and stick to a budget to help track expenses, find areas for saving, and prioritize financial goals, including retirement.

Prioritize paying off high-interest debt while saving for retirement.

Create an emergency fund with three to six months' worth of living expenses.

Plan for current health care costs, including premiums, deductibles, and co-pays, by taking advantage of Health Savings Accounts and retirement costs by looking into long-term care insurance while it's affordable.

Work to secure a variety of retirement income sources in addition to Social Security, such as pensions, retirement savings accounts, regular savings, rental income, and part-time work.

Continually clarify retirement goals by estimating future income and expenses and adjust savings and investments accordingly.

Enhance financial literacy by attending workshops, working with financial advisors, and staying informed about changes in laws and investment trends.

Regularly review and adjust your retirement plan as circumstances change.

By taking these steps, Gen Xers, you can better manage competing financial priorities and ensure a stable retirement.

MILLENNIAL (GEN Y)

The Millennial generation, born roughly between 1981 and 1996, also has its own challenges and opportunities when it comes to retirement planning. Due to their facility with technology, Millennials may have experienced career success early, enabling them to focus on building wealth and financial stability. While retirement may seem distant for them, if they develop financial discipline and start saving for retirement early, they can build long-term financial security.

One of the factors affecting saving for retirement by Millennials is pressure on income levels. Even those with higher education have seen slower wage growth, partly due to entering the workforce during the 2008 financial crisis. Those Millennials getting by through the gig economy and frequent job changes may not have begun to save for retirement since many gig workers lack employer-sponsored plans.

While many Millennials may be involved in saving for retirement despite earnings pressures, they also face a number of demands on their income. Repaying high levels of student loan debt can hinder their ability to save, so trying to repay debt while also saving for the future is a balancing act. They are faced with high living costs, especially for housing, and higher home prices, making homeownership difficult. The continued rise in living costs further strains budgets, complicating saving efforts.

Despite financial pressures from student loans and high living costs, Millennials have a significant advantage in retirement planning—time. Focus on the suggestions for Gen Xers and also work on these actions:

> Save and invest for retirement early to allow for the power of compound interest to work in your favor because even small contributions made early on can grow substantially over time.

> Leverage technology and automation to make saving for retirement easier. Automatic contributions to retirement and savings accounts ensure consistent saving without needing to manage finances actively.

> Utilize budgeting apps or tools to watch spending habits and adjust as needed.

Refinance or prioritize the repayment of high-interest rate debt.

Take advantage of other employer benefits, such as Health Savings Accounts (HSAs), Flexible Spending Accounts (FSAs), employee stock purchase plans (ESPPs), and employer-sponsored financial education programs.

Plan for longevity and develop a plan that allows you to save more money than you think you will need. Given advances in health care, you may live longer than earlier generations, so it's important to save more to ensure you don't outlive your retirement funds.

Remain adaptable and open to adjusting retirement plans as your circumstances change or unexpected policy, laws, or financial challenges may cause revisions to the retirement plan.

Millennials, you can set yourself on a path toward a comfortable retirement. Develop sound financial habits and stay fully informed about retirement planning strategies, and you have every chance of achieving long-term financial security and satisfaction.

GEN Z

Born between 1997 and 2012, the members of Generation Z are either still in school, in college, or at the beginning of their work life. The COVID-19 pandemic affected this generation the most since they had to go online to continue their schooling, lost valuable social opportunities, or had to seek remote employment. Many Gen Z graduates have high student loan debt levels combined with high post-Covid inflation-driven food and other costs of living, which have outpaced wage growth. Many have delayed saving for retirement due to this financial squeeze and because the Gen Zers relying on the gig economy involvement rarely have access to traditional retirement savings plans.

What's critical for Gen Zers is concerns about the future of Social Security. This combined with longer life expectancies, means starting early and being serious about saving for retirement must be their two most critical goals.

Although retirement may seem distant, it's important for Gen Z to start financial planning early, especially in their 20s. Some suggestions are listed below:

Enhance financial literacy in budgeting, saving, investing, and debt management. Use budgeting apps or tools to check and adjust spending.

Establish good financial habits such as tracking spending, living within your means, avoiding credit card debt, and setting and tracking short-term and long-term savings goals.

Manage student loan debt effectively.

Start a retirement plan early and seek employers offering retirement benefits.

Balance earning money with enjoying life for long-term well-being.

MICROGENERATION OR CUSP COHORTS

Those who are members of Microgenerations should follow the advice given to the larger generation they are a part of. Cuspers, born between two generations, have some experience of the cultural, historical, and technological shifts from both. They benefit from the financial prudence of the older generation and the innovation of the younger. By using these strengths, Cuspers, you can create a resilient and adaptable retirement plan, aligning with their values and goals, and confidently navigate retirement complexities.

YOUR FINANCIAL PLAN AND MAKING YOUR MONEY LAST

Creating a financial plan for retirement is essential for ensuring that your money lasts throughout your retirement years—after all, you don't want to be the retiree who must live off instant noodles and nostalgia. With increasing life expectancies and evolving economic conditions, strategic retirement planning is more important than ever before for managing risks and making informed decisions about finances. The guidance that follows can help you to effectively navigate this process and provide for a retirement that you can enjoy.

ASSESS YOUR FINANCIAL SITUATION AND FINANCIAL FUTURE

The first step in financial planning is to perform some analysis to assess your current finances and project what your retirement income, expenses, assets, and liabilities will be and then to set realistic savings goals. Evaluating your future finances allows you to adjust strategies for inflation, health care costs, and lifestyle changes. Then, following up with regular assessments will help you cut costs, save more, and invest wisely, boosting your confidence and sense of control over your financial future. Developing a financial plan fosters peace of mind and reduces stress—both now and in the future because it allows you to enjoy retirement without financial worries. Here are steps for reviewing your financial situation.

Evaluate your current financial situation:

Calculate Net Worth. List all your assets, such as savings, investments, property, vehicles, personal valuables, and retirement accounts. Next, list your liabilities, which include debts and obligations like mortgages, student loans, credit card debt, personal loans, and unpaid taxes. Subtract the total liabilities from the total assets, and the result is your net worth.

Review income sources. Find all sources of income, including salaries, pensions, Social Security benefits, and rental and investment income.

Track Monthly Expenses. Create a detailed budget for housing, utilities, groceries, insurance, debt repayment, subscriptions, discretionary spending, and short-term savings goal categories. Stick to the budget by tracking what you spend. Eliminate as many unnecessary expenses as possible and allocate as large an amount for retirement savings as possible.

Improve your understanding and skills in personal finance, budgeting, and investing.

State your retirement objectives:

Retirement Date. Decide on an expected date you'll retire.

Consider Preferences. Take into account several scenarios for retirement location, housing arrangements, social engagement, and overall lifestyle.

Estimate Retirement Expenses. Project future expenses based on your desired lifestyles, including health care and travel costs. With different scenarios, you'll have different expense totals.

Estimate your future income needs:

Use the 80% Rule. Aim for having a retirement income that is 70 to 80% of your pre-retirement income to keep your lifestyle.

Assemble All Future Income Sources. What income streams will you have in retirement from Social Security benefits and pensions and investment, rental, and work earnings? Include any income that may result from an inheritance (how certain is it?).

Factor in Inflation. Consider how inflation will affect your expenses over time.

Compare your income to the different expense levels of your hoped-for lifestyle scenarios. Are any of the lifestyle preferences unaffordable? Which one means that expenses are covered comfortably? Can you save more to attain your preferred lifestyle?

TAKEAWAYS FROM FINANCIAL SATISFACTION

Today has everything to do with how satisfying and secure your retirement will be as the takeaway from this chapter show:

Face any financial challenges that you experience as a member of a diverse demographic or generational cohort. It is still possible to have savings goals and work toward them.

Embrace financial literacy.

Create a budget with your current income, expenses, and debt, and set up a savings plan.

Track sticking to your budget and savings plan.

Start to think about what lifestyle you'd like in retirement, what it would cost, and how much income you'd need for it.

CHAPTER SIX

ARTFUL PLANNING: DEVELOPING YOUR FINANCIAL PLAN

A goal without a plan is just a wish.
—ANTOINE DE SAINT EXUPERY

Great things are not done by impulse, but by a series of small things brought together.
—VINCENT VAN GOGH

Planning is bringing the future into the present so that you can do something about it now.
—ALAN LAKEIN

Artful financial planning for retirement is akin to an artist who is crafting a masterpiece just for you. It involves creating a personalized strategy that balances your immediate needs with long-term goals, using various financial tools and investment options. This approach allows for proactive monitoring of how the strategy is working and allows for making adjustments to ensure that your plan stays on track as circumstances change.

In the last chapter, you developed an understanding of your current financial condition as well as what level of income you may need for your retirement lifestyle choices. Your artful financial retirement plan is how to get you from one to the other.

Planning Your Retirement Steps

A plan is just a series of steps and actions that keep you fully informed so you can make the choices that are right for you—and adjust them as necessary. The guide that follows outlines a straightforward structure for creating a financial plan for retirement. It includes essential aspects of planning while allowing for flexibility and personalization.

Set up a retirement savings plan:
  a) **Set Financial Goals.** Name specific objectives, such as:
     Consult a financial planner or advisor.
     Contribute a percentage of your salary for saving (e.g., 6% to a 401(k)).
     Save a total target amount (e.g., $500,000 in a 401(k)).
     Contribute to a Roth IRA.
     Purchase long-term care insurance.
  b) **Develop a Savings Strategy.** Decide how much you will save monthly based on your income, expenses, and financial goals (a).

Plan for health care expenses:
  a) **Evaluate Health Insurance Options and Costs.** Learn how Medicare and supplemental and prescription drug insurance work.
  b) **Consider Long-Term Care Needs.** Evaluate medication requirements and buy long-term care insurance.

Review retirement accounts and investments:
  a) **Analyze Savings.** Assess your retirement accounts and investment strategies.
  b) **Ensure Diversification.** Verify that your portfolio is diversified to

balance risk and returns. Consider switching to a lower-risk diversification strategy as retirement grows closer. If possible, consult a financial advisor on this.

c) **Monitor Financial Goals.** Regularly evaluate the effectiveness of your savings and investment strategies in terms of asset values and returns.

Understand Social Security benefits:

a) **Review Your Statement.** Obtain and analyze your Social Security statement, if you haven't been receiving it, to understand your estimated benefits.

b) **Decide on Your "Claiming Age".** Evaluate the implications of claiming Social Security early versus waiting until full retirement age or later.

Make a table of retirement income sources:

Social Security. Choose when to start benefits.

Pensions. Understand the details of your pension plans, including payout options.

Retirement Accounts. List balances and develop a plan for rollovers and withdrawals from 401(k)s, IRAs, and other retirement-saving vehicles.

Annuities and Investments. Understand the terms of annuities and other investments, including the tax consequences related to income earned from them.

Part-Time Work. Estimate potential income from part-time work. Develop a plan for how to freelance or consult while retired.

Real Estate. Evaluate the current market value of your property and whether there are any tax consequences from selling.

Other Income Sources. Add any other income sources (e.g., rental income, side businesses, or expected income from inherited assets).

Create a detailed expected retirement budget. Regularly review and adjust the budget to reflect actual spending habits and changing circumstances.

Include:
- **Essential Expenses.** These include housing, utilities, insurance, groceries, and, possibly, car expenses.
- **Discretionary Expenses.** These are those you could cut out if necessary but perhaps make life more enjoyable (e.g., travel, entertainment, shopping, hobbies.
- **Saving.** Do you plan to save in retirement, for example, for short-term goals, such as gifts to family or health costs? Add this to the budget.

Think about how you want to approach wealth transfer. It's never too early to start. Consider:
- **Beneficiaries.** At a minimum, you must designate the beneficiaries of your retirement accounts. Who should these individuals be? Children, a spouse or partner, a relative, or a friend?
- **Wills, Trusts, Gifts, Other Wealth Transfers, and Power of Attorney.** Carefully consider your wishes and work with an estate planner or attorney to put them in place.

MAKING YOUR MONEY LAST

Artful planning is not just about having sufficient resources for your desired retirement lifestyle. It is also about ensuring that your money will last throughout retirement, even when someone's life span is quite long. For most people, it is a top concern as they transition into their new phase of life. It's common to worry about outliving your savings, especially with the rising costs of living and health care.

Such fears can be alleviated by learning and understanding the financial strategies and best practices for effectively managing your assets and income so you can relieve anxiety and build a secure financial future.

A COMPREHENSIVE GUIDE TO HAVING ENOUGH FOR RETIREMENT

Here are some key money management strategies to get you started.

1. Consider delaying Social Security benefits. If possible, claim Social Security benefits at full retirement age or even age 70 to increase the monthly benefit, which increases your monthly income.

2. Explore part-time work opportunities. Consider working, consulting, or gig opportunities to supplement your income. This can help reduce the amount you need to withdraw from your retirement accounts.

3. Control Spending:
   - **Stick to Your Budget**. Track your spending against your budget to ensure you're living within your means ("5 Ways To Reduce Your Retirement Stress—Forbes").
   - **Be prepared to Belt-Tighten**. Adjust your budget if your income changes or you experience unexpected expenses by cutting back on discretionary and other nonessentials like dining out, travel, and luxury purchases. Do not use credit card debt to get you over the crunch.
   - **Manage Health Care Costs**. Medical and dental costs can be some of the largest expenses in retirement. Consider options like Medicare Advantage plans and supplemental insurance. You can also save for these costs with a health savings account (HSA) before you are eligible for Medicare to have a source of funds to pay for these costs. Prioritize preventive care and healthy living to reduce the likelihood of costly medical issues.

4. Manage your investments well:
   - **Diversify for Lower Risk**. Ensure your investment portfolio is diversified across asset classes (stocks, bonds, real estate) to manage risk while providing additional potential growth. A balanced portfolio might include a mix of stocks, bonds, and cash, with the specific allocation depending on your risk tolerance, time horizon, and income needs.
   - **Dividend-Paying Stocks.** Invest in high-quality, dividend-paying stocks that provide a steady income stream along with potential capital appreciation. Dividend income can supplement other sources of retirement income and help preserve your principal.
   - **Bond Laddering**. Invest in a series of bonds with staggered maturities, ensuring that bonds mature at separate times, providing regular income and reducing interest rate risk. Bond laddering provides predictable income and reduces the impact of interest rate fluctuations on your portfolio.
   - **Consider Annuities.**
     - **Immediate Annuities.** Purchasing an Immediate Annuity with a lump-sum payment secures regular, guaranteed income with immediate payments for life or for a specified duration. This provides financial security by ensuring you won't outlive your money. However, it limits your access to the annuity value and may reduce your financial flexibility.
     - **Deferred Annuities.** It's possible to buy an annuity that begins payouts later, often when you're older, to provide income later in life. This can be a hedge against longevity risk, ensuring you have income if you live longer than expected.
     - **Variable and Fixed Annuities.** Variable Annuities offer the potential for investment growth, while fixed annuities provide a guaranteed return. Annuities can be complex and come with fees, so it's important to understand the terms and costs before purchasing.

- **Rebalance.** As you near retirement, rebalance your portfolio periodically to align with your risk tolerance and retirement goals. Adjust your investment portfolio to be more conservative while keeping some growth investments. Rebalance annually or when there's a significant market shift that alters your asset allocation (for more information search the web for "Retirement Planning: Best Investment Options to Secure Your Future").

5. Create a withdrawal plan:
    - **The 4% Rule.** A common guideline is to withdraw 4% of your retirement savings in the first year and adjust that withdrawal amount for inflation each subsequent year. This strategy aims to provide a steady income while preserving your savings and purchasing power over a 30-year retirement period ("How to Create a Retirement Income Plan: A Guide"). Realize that the 4% rule is a general guideline, not a one-size-fits-all solution. Factors such as market conditions, life expectancy, and your specific financial situation may require adjustments.
    - **Bucket Strategy.** Divide your retirement savings into three "buckets" based on when you will need the money: short-term (0-5 years), medium-term (6-10 years), and long-term (10+ years). This strategy helps manage risk by keeping short-term funds in safer, more liquid investments while allowing longer-term funds to continue to grow in higher-risk, higher-return investments.
    - **Dynamic Withdrawal Strategies.** Adjust your withdrawals based on market performance and changes in your spending needs. For example, reduce withdrawals during market downturns to preserve capital. A dynamic approach can help extend the life of your portfolio by adapting to changing circumstances.

- **Plan for Taxes.** Carefully address the tax consequences of withdrawals from retirement accounts.
    - **Taxable vs. Tax-Deferred Accounts.** The best strategy is to withdraw funds from taxable accounts first to allow your tax-deferred accounts to continue to grow tax-free for longer. However, be mindful of capital gains taxes incurred when investments in taxable accounts are sold. Coordinate withdrawals with a financial advisor to improve tax efficiency.
    - **Required Minimum Distributions (RMDs).** Starting at age 73, you must take RMDs from your traditional IRA, 401(k), and other tax-deferred accounts. Failing to do so results in a hefty tax penalty. Plan your withdrawals to minimize taxes, such as taking distributions in years when you're in a lower tax bracket.
    - **Roth Conversions.** Convert some of your traditional IRA or 401(k) funds to a Roth IRA, especially when your taxable income is lower. Roth IRAs offer tax-free withdrawals in retirement. This strategy can reduce your required minimum distributions (RMDs) and lower your taxable income in the future.

6. Addressing Longevity Risk
    - **Longevity Insurance.** Purchase longevity insurance (a type of deferred annuity) that starts paying out at a later age, such as 85, providing income if you live longer than expected. This strategy can give you peace of mind and ensure you have income in your later years.
    - **Staggered Retirement Withdrawals.** In order to preserve funds for your later years, withdraw funds conservatively in the early years and gradually increase them as you age and your life expectancy decreases. This approach can help prevent the money from running out in later years.

7. Regularly review and adjust your plan and stay flexible:
   - **Annual Check-Ups.** Review your retirement financial plan annually to ensure it's still on track. Assess your spending, investment performance, and any changes in your financial situation. Be prepared to adjust your withdrawal rate, investment strategy, or spending habits as needed.
   - **Monitor Market Conditions.** Stay informed about market conditions and economic trends that could affect your retirement savings. In times of market volatility, consider adjusting your portfolio, reducing withdrawals, or cutting expenses temporarily to preserve your savings.

8. Seek out professional advice. This is discussed in detail in the next section.

GET GUIDANCE: FINDING A RETIREMENT PLANNING ADVISOR

If you can afford it, work with a financial advisor or planner to develop a personalized retirement savings and investment plan. Assess Your Needs. Identify the aspects of retirement planning you need help with, such as estimating future expenses, maximizing Social Security benefits, or deciding on a withdrawal strategy. Knowing your financial goals and comfort level regarding risk will guide you as you evaluate suitable advisors.

Get Referrals. Seek recommendations from friends, family members, or colleagues who have experience with financial advisors. Personal referrals can offer valuable insights. Ask other professionals, like accountants or attorneys, for recommendations. Consult online platforms, such as:

Financial Planning Association (FPA). Provides a directory of financial planners.

National Association of Personal Financial Advisors (NAPFA). Lists fee-only financial advisors.

XY Planning Network. Focuses on financial planning for younger generations and offers a directory of advisors

Seek Out Fiduciary Advice. Prioritize *fiduciary* financial advisors who are legally required to act in your best interest. Ask for referrals from friends or use online resources like SmartAsset's free tool to find qualified fiduciary advisors.

Focus on Services and Expertise. Determine if a retirement advisor offers the services you need, such as retirement income planning, tax-efficient withdrawal strategies, Social Security optimization, pension planning, annuity purchases, investment portfolio management, estate planning guidance, and health care cost planning.

Look for Specialized Credentials. Note whether a prospective financial planner has any specialized credentials, like Certified Financial Planner™ (CFP®), Chartered Retirement Planning Counselor (CRPC), Retirement Income Certified Professional (RICP), Chartered Financial Consultant (ChFC), Accredited Financial Counselor (AFC) and Chartered Financial Analyst (CFA). Certifications are issued by a sponsoring organization and indicate that a professional has met rigorous education, examination, experience, and ethical standards.

Find an Advisor Who Works with Clients Like You. Choose an advisor experienced with retirees or those approaching retirement, as they will better understand your needs and concerns.

Investigate Their Investment Philosophy and Tools. Ask about the advisor's investment philosophy, risk management approach, diversification techniques, and asset allocation strategies. Inquire about their methods for generating reliable income streams and the use of financial planning software.

If working with a financial planner isn't in your budget, self-educate by taking advantage of community resources, online organizations, books (such as this one), and articles. If you make planning for retirement a priority, you will learn what you need to provide for yourself effectively.

STORIES OF GEN XERS' SUCCESSFUL RETIREMENT PLANNING

Generation Xers Elizabeth and Travis have each put in place successful plans for retirement. Here's what they did in their own words.

AS A SINGLE WOMAN, IT'S ALL ON ME

My retirement planning journey embodies my theme, "As a Single Woman, It's All on Me." This is because I've been divorced for over 20 years. As an African American woman, I take immense pride in having rebuilt my life and achieving significant financial and other milestones. After my separation and divorce, I made the bold decision to relocate to a new city. This move opened up new opportunities, and I eventually became the CEO of a nonprofit organization.

My determination to be self-reliant has been a driving force in my life. I purchased my own home and focused diligently on saving for retirement by maximizing my 401(k) contributions and making sure I took full advantage of my employer's matching contributions. My commitment to retirement planning has meant that I save 15% of my pre-tax income for my retirement savings plan. Now, with approximately ten years to go before retirement, I'm excited to prepare for the next chapter of my life. I plan to establish a consulting firm that will sustain me beyond retirement. Now in my late 50s, I feel proud of what I've accomplished so far and look forward to what I can achieve once I'm retired.

ELIZABETH'S ADVICE

Throughout my work life, I've made it a priority to mentor younger men and women in their 30s, 40s, and 50s. Here's some key advice I love to share: Don't delay setting up a retirement savings plan; taking charge of your finances early can lead to positive results and a more secure future. Always communicate openly about finances, especially if you're in a relationship. It's crucial to discuss financial matters with your significant other before marriage. By comparing attitudes and reaching agreement on goals for spending, saving, and retirement plans, you'll help to build a strong foundation for your future together. Remember, it's all on you to take charge of your life and finances. You have the power to achieve great things.

TRAVIS'S RETIREMENT JOURNEY: A FOCUS ON FINANCIAL LITERACY AND PLANNING

As a Gen Xer in my mid-50s living in the Southeast, I've dedicated over 30 years to working at a financial services company, where I currently serve as a systems engineer. I landed this job right out of college, and from the very beginning, I hoped to retire early, which has guided my planning. One significant advantage of the company where I work has been the opportunity to work closely with wealth and investment managers—experts in managing money and trusts. I've learned a great deal by asking questions and seeking their valuable advice. Over the years, I have also actively enhanced my financial literacy by listening to radio programs during my commute and engaging in activities that educate me on saving, investing, and securing financial independence.

I started saving for retirement early. Both my wife and I take full advantage of our 401(k) plans and employer matching. Currently, I also contribute to a Roth 401(k), so I am saving approximately 12% in total of my income in combined contributions. While I feel good about my proactive approach, my biggest fear is running out of money in retirement. I also worry about developing costly habits or interests once I stop working that may require additional support.

My job satisfaction has faded; it now feels more like a means to an end. Therefore, my current focus is on supporting my family and ensuring my children complete their education and launch their careers before I retire. With two children still in school, I plan to wait until they finish their studies before officially retiring. In about five years, I hope to embrace this next chapter.

Looking ahead, my wife and I have purchased land with the dream of starting a small farm in retirement. We are genuinely excited about our future and the adventures that await us in this new chapter of life.

TRAVIS'S ADVICE

To everyone reading this, I encourage you to start saving and investing early for retirement. Think about your plans at least 25 years before you intend to retire so your money can benefit from compound interest—you'll begin to see your savings grow over time.

If you're working in the gig economy or as a contract worker, consider opening an IRA and setting up automatic contributions. When purchasing a home or a car, avoid borrowing too much money if possible; if you must, opt for the shortest repayment period. Focus on building your assets and equity through ownership and paying off your bills. Remember, retirement investment is a long-term plan, and as you approach your retirement date—perhaps 10 years out—consider becoming more conservative with your investments. Don't shy away from expanding your financial literacy and learning about investing; it's a crucial step toward a secure and fulfilling retirement.

ACTION PLAN

Consider Elizabeth and Travis, both resilient individuals who effectively manage their respective retirement savings and consistently adhere to the principles outlined in this chapter. Develop a financial retirement plan that is inspired by their successful approaches. This book is dedicated to supporting you as you work to attain financial stability and satisfaction during retirement the way Elizabeth and Travis have.

Complete the worksheet below using the information you have gathered and the ideas provided in this chapter and align it with your vision and goals for retirement. It is also recommended to consult with a financial advisor or planner to review and create a personalized and effective plan.

Chapter 6: Artful Planning: Developing Your Financial Plan

Financial Planning Worksheet
Fundamentals of My Retirement Financial Plan

Estimated – Retirement Age_____   **Retirement Date** _____

Timely Enrollment for Social Security Benefits

Today - *My Current Status*

_____

Change - *What I Need to Do*

_____

Retirement Plan - *What Will Be in Place When I Retire (Your Goal)*

_____

Eligibility for Defined-Benefit Pensions

Today - *My Current Status*

_____

Change - *What I Need to Do*

_____

Retirement Plan - *What Will Be in Place When I Retire*

_____

Contributions to a 401(K)

Today - *My Current Status*

_____

Change - *What I Need to Do*

Retirement Plan - *What Will Be in Place When I Retire*

Contributions to a 403(b)

Today - *My Current Status*

Change - *What I Need to Do*

Retirement Plan - *What Will Be in Place When I Retire*

Contributions to a 457(b)

Today - *My Current Status*

Change - *What I Need to Do*

Retirement Plan - *What Will Be in Place When I Retire*

Participation in a Thrift Savings Plan

Today - *My Current Status*

Chapter 6: Artful Planning: Developing Your Financial Plan

Change - *What I Need to Do*

_____

Retirement Plan - *What Will Be in Place When I Retire*

_____

Types and Contributions to Individual Retirement Accounts (IRAs)

Today - *My Current Status*

_____

Change - *What I Need to Do*

_____

Retirement Plan - *What Will Be in Place When I Retire*

_____

Type and Contributions to Annuities

Today - *My Current Status*

_____

Change - *What I Need to Do*

_____

Retirement Plan - *What Will Be in Place When I Retire*

_____

Additional Retirement Savings Options

Type and Contributions to Taxable Investment Account or Brokerage Account
Today - *My Current Status*

___

Change - *What I Need to Do*

___

Retirement Plan - *What Will Be in Place When I Retire*

___

Type and Contributions to Savings Accounts
Today - *My Current Status*

___

Change - *What I Need to Do*

___

Retirement Plan - *What Will Be in Place When I Retire*

___

Retirement Income Streams for Financial Security

Type of Real Estate Assets, Approximate Expenditure, and Income
Today - *My Current Status*

___

Change - *What I Need to Do*

_____

Retirement Plan - *What Will Be in Place When I Retire*

_____

Plan to Work After Retirement and Potential Income

Today - *My Current Status/Plan*

_____

Change - *What I Need to Do*

_____

Retirement Plan - *What Will Be in Place When I Retire*

_____

Establish a Small Business—Business Plan, Approximate Expenditure and Income

Today - *My Current Status/Plan*

_____

Change - *What I Need to Do*

_____

Retirement Plan - *What Will Be in Place When I Retire*

_____

Managing an Inheritance

Today - *My Current Status*

Change - *What I Need to Do*

Retirement Plan - *What Will Be in Place When I Retire*

Key Insurance Considerations for Retirement

Life Insurance

Today - *My Current Status*

Change - *What I Need to Do*

Retirement Plan - *What Will Be in Place When I Retire*

Homeowners and Renters Insurance

Today - *My Current Status*

Change - *What I Need to Do*

Chapter 6: Artful Planning: Developing Your Financial Plan

Retirement Plan - *What Will Be in Place When I Retire*

_____

Auto Insurance

Today - *My Current Status*

_____

Change - *What I Need to Do*

_____

Retirement Plan - *What Will Be in Place When I Retire*

_____

Umbrella Insurance

Today - *My Current Status*

_____

Change - *What I Need to Do*

_____

Retirement Plan - *What Will Be in Place When I Retire*

_____

Health Insurance

Today - *My Current Status*

_____

Change - *What I Need to Do*

_____

Retirement Plan - *What Will Be in Place When I Retire*

Estate Planning and Financial Security Documents

Establish a Will

Today - *My Current Status*

Change - *What I Need to Do*

Retirement Plan - *What Will Be in Place When I Retire*

Establish a Trust

Today - *My Current Status*

Change - *What I Need to Do*

Retirement Plan - *What Will Be in Place When I Retire*

All Named Beneficiaries *(i.e., insurance policies, 401(k), savings accounts)*

Today - *My Current Status*

Chapter 6: Artful Planning: Developing Your Financial Plan

Change - *What I Need to Do*

_____

Retirement Plan - *What Will Be in Place When I Retire*

_____

Established a Durable Power of Attorney

Today - *My Current Status*

_____

Change - *What I Need to Do*

_____

Retirement Plan - *What Will Be in Place When I Retire*

_____

Established a Financial Power of Attorney

Today - *My Current Status*

_____

Change - *What I Need to Do*

_____

Retirement Plan - *What Will Be in Place When I Retire*

_____

Challenges to Achieving Financial Security

Diversity Influences to Consider

Today - *My Current Status/Influences*
_____

Change - *What I Need to Do*
_____

Retirement Plan - *What Will Be in Place When I Retire*
_____

Generational Cohort Issues to Consider *(Baby Boom, Gen X, Millennial, Gen Z)*

Today - *My Current Status*
_____

Change - *What I Need to Do*
_____

Retirement Plan - *What Will Be in Place When I Retire*
_____

Expected Money or Assets from Intergenerational Transfer

Today - *My Current Expectation*
_____

Change - *What I Need to Do*
_____

Retirement Plan - *What Will Be in Place When I Retire*

_____

Financial Plan and Making Your Money Last

Thorough Evaluation of My Financial Status and Future Prospects

Today - *My Current Status*

_____

Change - *What I Need to Do*

_____

Retirement Plan - *What Will Be in Place When I Retire*

_____

Complete My "Artful Financial Retirement Plan"

Today - *My Current Status*

_____

Change - *What I Need to Do*

_____

Retirement Plan - *What Will Be in Place When I Retire*

_____

Establish a Plan to Make Your Money Last

Today - *My Current Status*

_____

Change - *What I Need to Do*

_____

Retirement Plan - *What Will Be in Place When I Retire*

_____

This worksheet is a summary of where you stand in terms of your retirement planning. It should show you in what areas there is room for improvement. Hang onto it and update it often to track your retirement goals.

TAKEAWAYS FROM ARTFUL PLANNING

As you reflect on the insights presented up to this point, the following takeaways serve as essential reminders of the key retirement planning principles for achieving financial security and satisfaction in retirement. These points highlight the importance of proactive planning, informed decision-making, and the strategies necessary to create a stable financial future. By internalizing these takeaways, you will empower yourself to navigate your retirement with confidence, ensuring that you can not only meet your financial needs but also enjoy a fulfilling and enriched lifestyle. Let's review these vital takeaways to solidify your understanding and prepare you for a rewarding retirement journey:

A well-rounded retirement financial plan is essential for ensuring your needs are met throughout retirement. Take the time to assess your financial situation and create a detailed strategy.

Carefully manage your investments to balance earnings growth and risk, keeping in mind your retirement timeline and financial goals.

Engage with financial advisors and estate attorneys for expert guidance. Their insights can help you make informed decisions and navigate complex financial landscapes.

Regularly Review Your Plan. Consistently assess and update your retirement plan as circumstances change, such as fluctuations in income, expenses, or personal goals.

Formulate a solid withdrawal strategy that outlines how and when you will access your retirement savings. This helps ensure that your funds last as long as you need them.

Understand how taxes will affect your retirement income and plan accordingly. Be mindful of longevity risks, so take steps to ensure your savings can support you throughout your lifetime.

Once retired, adopt a mindful approach to spending. Create a budget that reflects your priorities and helps you keep financial stability.

Stay flexible and willing to adjust your financial strategy as needed to respond to unexpected expenses or shifts in your retirement lifestyle.

Focus on Financial Satisfaction. Remember that achieving financial security in retirement is not just about money—it's about creating a fulfilling life. Align your financial goals with your personal values and desires for a satisfying retirement.

By following these takeaways, you can enhance your financial security and satisfaction in retirement, ensuring a stable and enjoyable future as you embark on this new chapter of your life.

PART

III

THRIVING IN
RETIREMENT

CHAPTER SEVEN

ANCHORING RETIREMENT IN PURPOSE AND MEANING

Retirement is not a life without purpose; it is the ongoing purpose that provides meaningfulness.
—ROBERT RIVERS

What you get by achieving your goals is not as important as what you become by achieving your goals.
—HENRY DAVID THOREAU

Life is not measured by the number of breaths we take, but by the moments that take our breath away."
—MAYA ANGELOU

Retirement is more than financial security; it opens the door to new adventures and is about finding new purpose and meaning in your life. Transitioning from a career to a post-work life can be both challenging and rewarding. Work may have defined your self-perception, sense of success, and social identity, but ending full-time employment presents an opportunity to redefine these aspects. In retirement, you have the chance to pursue personal interests and align your passions, values, and goals. Approach this stage with curiosity and an open mind, and you'll build new connections and find contentment. Discovering a new purpose is key to thriving in your retirement years.

LOSING MEANING AND FINDING IT AGAIN

How does someone find fulfillment when retirement takes away work's structure? Transitioning from having a work identity requires that those in retirement rethink their sense of self and purpose outside the workplace. Retiring can be so much more than engaging in personal interests and activities. For someone to truly enjoy their "longevity bonus"—the many healthy years after retirement—they must explore what gives them meaning and align that with what they do to feel a sense of purpose.

As you embark on your retirement journey, consider the insights of Dr. Viktor Frankl, the author of *Man's Search for Meaning*. He believed that true happiness comes from having a purpose, rooted in meaningful experiences. While achieving personal desires often can contribute to happiness, seeking meaning encourages you to focus outward on caring for others, contributing to your community, and making a positive impact. Purpose transforms that meaning into actionable goals, guiding you toward the difference you want to make. Without this foundation, it's easy to feel anxious, lose confidence, or struggle with direction in retirement.

Take inspiration from the story of Joan, a retired elementary school teacher. After leaving her career, she initially felt aimless because her identity had been tied to her job. Recognizing her need for purpose, Joan started volunteering at a local literacy program for underprivileged children. This opportunity allowed her to share her teaching skills while fostering a love of reading among the kids. Through her volunteer work, Joan found fulfillment in making a positive impact and built meaningful connections with the children and their families.

By shifting her focus from personal wishes and goals to a desire to contribute to her community, Joan transformed her retirement into a meaningful, vibrant, and rewarding chapter of her life. Taking action to mentor students gave her a newfound sense of purpose, which not only brought her happiness but also alleviated the feelings of anxiety and uncertainty that many retirees face without it. Like Joan, you can discover that seeking meaningful experiences and caring for others can lead to a fulfilling and purpose-driven retirement, illustrating the powerful link between meaning and happiness.

OPENING UP

Brené Brown, professor, author, and motivational speaker, believes that purpose is deeply connected to vulnerability, connection, values, resilience, and authenticity. Living intentionally and with courage will significantly enrich your life. By recognizing your imperfections and aligning your actions with your core values, you can cultivate meaningful connections and uncover your true purpose in retirement.

Take the story of Michael, a retired corporate executive who faced the transition to retirement with both excitement and apprehension. Initially, he struggled without the structured environment of work and felt isolated. Instead of retreating, Michael decided to embrace his vulnerability and seek ways to connect with others. He enrolled in a local community center program focused on personal development and social engagement. Through this program, Michael explored his core values—family, mentorship, and social responsibility. He found purpose by volunteering with a youth mentoring program, where he could share his professional experiences and listen to the challenges faced by younger generations. This engagement not only fostered enriching relationships but also helped him to recognize the importance of resilience—accepting that successes and setbacks were integral parts of his journey.

By aligning his actions with his values, Michael discovered a renewed sense of purpose: to empower others and create a lasting impact in his community. His experience shows that embracing vulnerability, focusing on what truly matters, and nurturing connections can lead to a fulfilling and meaningful retirement. As you explore your own path, remember that while your journey to new purpose and meaning is just beginning, focusing on purpose ensures that your retirement years can become some of the most fulfilling and meaningful of your life.

A RETIREMENT MINDSET

Despite any fears or anxieties about retirement (Chapter 2), those who keep a positive mindset as they transition into retirement are most likely to thrive. Cultivating an optimistic outlook about retirement allows someone to view it as a fresh beginning and an opportunity to explore new interests and passions. By engaging in meaningful activities and reflecting on the legacy they wish to leave, anyone can navigate this stage with confidence and renewed direction.

To fully realize the potential of your retirement, examine and discard any limiting beliefs leftover from your work life and embrace empowering ones that allow you to open to new opportunities. Establishing purpose and connection during retirement may require effort, but the benefits are substantial. An outlook of being willing to be vulnerable, positive, curious, and courageous will engender a newfound sense of freedom, which will, in turn, open you to new possibilities and experiences. By maintaining a positive mindset, you can ensure that your retirement years become some of the most fulfilling and meaningful periods of your life.

DISCOVERING NEW MEANING AND PURPOSE IN RETIREMENT

Embarking on the journey to discovering a new meaning and purpose in life is a deeply personal endeavor that requires thoughtful introspection, reflection, and a willingness to embrace new experiences. It may be that some have already undergone this process once or twice in their lives before retirement.

The pursuit of meaning and purpose is strongly associated with long-term happiness and joy. It involves an exploration of one's inner self, gaining deeper insights into one's identity, and remaining open to various aspects of life. It is typical for this journey to require time and entail some trial and error. Adhering to a series of steps or following a structured method can help this process, making it more straightforward and gratifying.

STEPS TO BUILDING A LIFE OF PURPOSE AND MEANING IN RETIREMENT

Crafting a retirement filled with fulfillment, connection, and significance requires some reflection and inner exploration. Here are the key steps to guide you in building a meaningful life during this transformative phase:

1. **Reflect on Past Fulfillment**. Take time to think about experiences in your life that have brought you joy and satisfaction. What activities or roles made you feel truly alive? Consider how the fulfilling experiences in your past can inform the present and your future endeavors. Reflecting on your history helps reveal the patterns and themes that resonate most deeply with you, providing a solid foundation for your retirement purpose.

2. **Explore Current Values and Passions**. Identify your core values and current passions at this stage of your life. What values do you want to live by now (e.g., honesty, integrity, being of service, kindness)? What do you care about most? What do you feel passionate about? Is it family, creativity, advocacy, community service, or lifelong learning? Understanding your values and passions will guide you in selecting

activities and pursuits that align with who you are now rather than who you were in your career. Make a list of your 1) top five values and 2) top five passions and brainstorm how to incorporate them into your daily life.

3. **Identify New Opportunities**. Look for new activities, hobbies, or volunteer roles that excite you. This is an ideal opportunity to explore interests you have always wished to pursue but have not had the time for. Consider joining clubs, taking classes, or participating in community organizations, which can spark creativity and open doors to connections and friendships. Activities such as mentoring, lifelong learning, exploration, and self-development can provide deep personal satisfaction and fulfillment.

4. **Envision the Future**. Formulate a specific idea of your desired retirement lifestyle. Imagine your ideal day, week, or year. What activities would fill your time? Who do you spend it with? Write down your vision and think about the steps needed to achieve it. This can serve as a motivating roadmap for your retirement journey, keeping you focused on your purpose.

5. **Overcome Barriers**. Recognize the inner and outer barriers that may hinder you from pursuing your purpose, such as self-doubt, fear, financial constraints, or health limitations. Develop strategies to overcome these challenges. Whether it means fostering a positive mindset, seeking advice on financial planning, finding ways to stay healthy, addressing these barriers head-on in other ways can enhance your ability to engage fully in retirement.

The following worksheet summarizes the "Steps to Building a Life of Purpose and Meaning." As you answer the questions, some ideas and themes will emerge.

Steps to Building Purpose and Meaning Worksheet
Reflect on Past Fulfillment

1. What activities or roles have brought you the most joy and satisfaction in the past?
   _____
   _____

2. What have been your proudest achievements, and what made them meaningful?
   _____
   _____

3. When have you felt most alive and engaged?
   _____
   _____

Explore Current Values and Passions

1. What excites or inspires you right now?
   _____
   _____

2. What values or principles feel most important to you at this stage in life?
   _____
   _____

3. What hobbies, causes, or interests are you curious to explore further?
   _____
   _____

4. How can your unique skills and experiences help others?
   _____
   _____

Look For New Opportunities

1. How can your unique skills and experiences help others?
   _____
   _____

2. What contributions would you like to make to your family, community, or the world? _____
   _____

3. If given the opportunity, what new skill or experience would you choose to pursue? _____
   _____

Envision the Future

1. What kind of legacy do you want to create in this next chapter?
   _____
   _____

2. What would give you a sense of accomplishment and fulfillment moving forward?
   _____
   _____

3. How do you want your days to feel—energized, relaxed, meaningful, or adventurous?
   _____
   _____

Overcome Barriers

1. What fears or uncertainties are holding you back from pursuing a renewed purpose?
   _____
   _____

2. What small steps can you take today to move closer to a purposeful life?
   _____
   _____

Set Life Goals

What are three life goals you hope to pursue during your retirement that will bring you fulfillment and meaning?

1. _____
2. _____
3. _____

By following these steps—reflecting on your past, aligning with your current values, seeking new opportunities, envisioning your future, and overcoming barriers—you can build a life in retirement that is rich in purpose and meaning. By embracing your unique experiences and planning with intention, you can cultivate a sense of purpose that not only enhances your well-being but also fosters meaningful connections with others. Ultimately, you have the power to transform this stage of life into a truly extraordinary and enriching experience.

DIVERSITY AND INFLUENCES ON FINDING MEANING AND PURPOSE

Many factors affect individuals—various backgrounds, generational cohorts, and demographic diversity, such as race and ethnicity, gender identities, sexual orientations, socioeconomic statuses, and disabilities—can all influence how individuals view themselves, their families, and their communities, and significantly impact their approach to retirement. In many cultures, self-worth may be tied to professional accomplishments, while others may prioritize familial roles and responsibilities. Cultural perspectives can shape retirees' decisions to focus on caregiving or mentorship, as well as their level of engagement in community service and volunteer work.

Additionally, the cultural and ethnic environment someone grew up in can influence their attitude toward aging and inform whether they view retirement as a time for celebration or as a daunting transition. Financial practices naturally vary across cultures also, reflecting different values related to saving and investment. Recognizing how these cultural influences help or hinder someone as they seek new meaning and purpose in retirement is a useful part of the process.

Your background offers a unique lens through which to explore what will be meaningful to you in retirement as you reflect on your cultural values and the connections you maintain with family. By recognizing and valuing these elements, you can craft a retirement plan that genuinely reflects who you are and what matters to you. Engaging in caregiving, leveraging community support, and pursuing interests aligned with your passions can lead to a fulfilling retirement experience.

MEANING AND PURPOSE ACROSS GENERATIONS

As individuals transition into retirement, their search for meaning and purpose will be uniquely theirs. Yet, each generation brings its own values, life experiences, historical context, and aspirations to the retirement experience, which can ultimately influence the retirement path of those in the generation and how they approach their exciting new chapter in life.

Retirement is a time to embrace your individuality. Yet, much like owning cultural, ethnic, and other demographic impacts on you, it also helps to appreciate the broader journey of your generation. Seeing how the individuals in your generation as a whole cope and thrive can point the way to purpose and meaning for you as well.

BABY BOOMERS BUILDING A SOCIAL SUPPORT NETWORK

As traditionally socially engaged individuals, Boomers see retirement as a unique opportunity to continue pursuing purpose and meaningful connections beyond their working years. They can leverage their wealth of skills and experience to volunteer, start new ventures, or immerse themselves in personal growth, something that has always been important to them. By reflecting on their core values—perhaps even going back to the ones of their youth—and seeking ways to engage in mentorship, charitable work, or activism, they will quickly align with what truly matters to them.

If you are a Boomer, explore hobbies or skills you've always wanted to pursue, such as music or art, or consider starting a community advocacy project that aligns with your values and purpose. By embracing these pursuits, you can enhance your sense of fulfillment, engage with others in meaningful ways, and make a positive impact in your community, creating a rewarding and enriching chapter in your life.

GEN XERS

Those who are part of Generation X value authenticity and independence, and retirement is a chance to channel that into meaningful contributions. Retirement can be a time when they consider how they can champion causes that resonate with them and seek opportunities to engage in community efforts, teach, volunteer, or mentor others. In other words, Gen Xers should dive deeper into their interests—whether it's traveling to give talks, writing, or exploring creative outlets—that enrich their lives and those around them.

By applying your adaptability and commitment to making a difference, Gen X, you can create deep connections and contribute to the social initiatives that matter most to you. Embracing this purpose will lead to a retirement filled with intention and significance.

MILLENNIALS

Millennials often prioritize social responsibility and collective impact, which can hugely shape their retirement experience. By combining the skills gained in their professions with a passion for serving others, members of the Millennial generation can find ongoing purpose and fulfillment during their retirement years, transforming their commitment to social responsibility into a powerful avenue for personal growth.

Use retirement as a time not only to deepen your commitment to what you are passionate about, such as environmental sustainability and community collaboration, but also to engage in personal development. Seek opportunities to participate in meaningful projects that empower others—volunteer work, mentorship, or activism—that align with your values. Create spaces for dialogue and collaboration in your communities, allowing you to pool resources with like-minded individuals. Yet, also consider learning new skills or taking up new interests.

Chapter 7: Anchoring Retirement in Purpose and Meaning

GEN ZERS

Many Gen Zers are driven by values such as social justice and environmental advocacy, positioning these individuals as a generation of change-makers. As the members of Generation Z look ahead at retirement, they will likely focus on how they can pursue opportunities that reflect their ideals and seek ways to bridge cultural divides through creative and educational initiatives.

Your retirement plans, Gen Zer, might include engaging in community service, mentorship, or activism to allow you to contribute to a better world. Explore ways to share your vision. Stay true to your passions and embrace your role as a global citizen, finding purpose and fulfillment as you work to create positive change in the world around you.

MICROGENERATION MEMBERS AND CUSPERS

When someone identifies with two generational narratives or feels a disconnect from both, retirement can be a chance for them to carve out a unique space for themselves. Reflect on the dual generational experiences that shape your identity and explore new avenues for fulfillment. Consider engaging in intergenerational activities that bridge gaps or seek mentorship opportunities where you can both learn and teach. Use this phase of your life to build connections in your community, engage in personal reflection, and remain open to learning. By navigating your path authentically, you can set up a profound sense of purpose, honor both your histories and aspirations, and find meaning in contributing to a supportive and inclusive society.

Each generation will face a unique retirement reality—one informed by the broader historical, cultural, and economic environments they grew up in, together with the environment that will shape their retirement years. The members of every generation will have opportunities to achieve life goals and fulfill their purpose in their retirement phase.

Identifying what resonates most with you and aligning your activities accordingly is essential for creating a meaningful and fulfilling retirement. Consider how you can actively look for meaning and purpose. Engage with your community, express your creativity, and set up new connections. By doing so, you will not only enhance your own life but also positively affect those around you.

A PURPOSEFUL RETIREMENT MAY NOT BE WHAT YOU EXPECT

Jack and Enrique are examples of those who decide to thrive in retirement no matter the obstacles.

JACK'S STORY OF RESILIENCE AND PURPOSE

My story is one shaped by love, resilience, and a commitment to truly "Live This Life." My late wife and I had big dreams of traveling the world together. We poured our resources into those dreams, even paying off our house twice, all while looking forward to a joyful and secure retirement. But life doesn't always follow the script we lay out. When my wife fell ill, everything changed. I spent the next 20 years as her caregiver, ultimately leaving my corporate job in telecommunications to support her full-time. This journey, while challenging, became a path of discovery for me—an unexpected early retirement that allowed me to embrace life's uncertainties with a positive mindset. I learned that life is both fleeting and precious, and every moment is worth cherishing.

After my wife's passing, I made a promise to honor her memory by fully embracing the next chapter. I am committed to living life to the fullest by pursuing what was once our shared dream—embracing different cultures, exploring new places, seeking fresh experiences, and building meaningful relationships. And that's exactly what I'm doing!

JACK'S ADVICE

To those younger generations out there, let me share some advice: take the time to envision what retirement could look like for you. Think about the legacy you want to leave behind for your children and family. Listen to the wisdom of those who came before you—it could help shape your own journey. Life is too short not to live it fully!

Jack's story shows that life has many twists and turns, but having goals and purpose helps you navigate it. Let's look at another example of planning with purpose.

A NEW CHAPTER: *ENRIQUE'S JOURNEY*

It wasn't a single moment; rather, it was decades of planning that led me here. I often asked myself, "If not now, when?" I was ready to embrace something new. As I contemplated my finances, I wondered, "When is enough money truly enough?" Fortunately, I realized that my hard work and diligence since the age of 19 had created the opportunity for a life beyond work. I wanted to focus on my health, deepen my relationships with my spouse and kids, and explore new hobbies that would allow me to grow, give back, and approach the next chapter with purpose and energy.

Honestly, one of my biggest fears was losing my sense of purpose. Since my teenage years, I had dreamed of becoming a pilot, and I achieved it. To me, being a pilot was not just a job—it was my identity, providing structure and motivation each day. I worried that without it, my life might feel empty instead of fulfilling, and I feared losing my relevance.

Change itself was another source of anxiety. I knew who I was in the military, but I questioned who I would be without the title, the missions, and the constant demands.

Yet, I came to realize that these fears could serve as invitations—opportunities to redefine myself and my purpose. My focus shifted from mere achievement to finding significance and prioritizing a life that reflects what truly matters—independent of a paycheck but rich in meaning. I stopped trying to replicate the structured pace of my past and instead leaned into learning more about myself. I created meaningful relationships and began giving back to others. I started making time for leisurely walks and reading purely for enjoyment.

Eventually, new goals emerged. I began volunteering in ways that allowed me to contribute without the risk of burnout. I picked up hobbies that I had admired from afar—activities that challenged me and reminded me that I was still learning and evolving. What am I doing with my time post-retirement? Some days are intentionally slow—enjoying meals without the pressure of a clock, taking time for longer workouts at the gym, or simply sleeping in. Other days are filled with activities but on my terms. I've embraced creative and active hobbies, exploring ones that aren't just "quick and easy." I cherish the quality time spent with my spouse and kids, being truly present rather than just nearby.

Travel is also on my agenda—not just for vacations but for meaningful visits to places I've always wanted to see. I've discovered ways to give back through mentoring and local volunteering, sharing my knowledge in rewarding, fulfilling ways. I no longer measure my days by productivity; instead, I focus on my presence. This newfound perspective has been a gift I didn't fully appreciate until now.

Chapter 7: Anchoring Retirement in Purpose and Meaning

ENRIQUE'S ADVICE

My advice to younger generations and those from diverse communities is to start early with the intention of retiring on your own terms. Even if you don't, whether you're in your 30s, 40s, or 50s, it's never too late to begin thinking about the life you want to lead. Retirement isn't just about money; it's about freedom, identity, health, and purpose. The sooner you align your life with what truly matters to you, the more choices you will create for yourself down the road.

For individuals from historically marginalized or underserved communities—women, people of color, LGBTQ+ individuals, low-income workers, and people with disabilities—I see you because I am you. I understand that the path may be steeper, resources can be limited, and the system isn't always designed for your success. Your perspective, resilience, and lived experiences are powerful tools and assets. Own your story. Ask questions, demand clarity, and seek out mentors and allies who understand your journey.

Don't wait for retirement to start living. Build a community wherever you can—learn, share, and uplift one another. Your future is worth fighting for, worth planning for, and absolutely worth dreaming about. Retirement should be a continuation of a meaningful life, not the beginning of one.

PURPOSE STATEMENT EXAMPLES

Retiring with a purpose provides an opportunity to thrive and experience fulfillment, connection, and enjoyment daily. You can shape this stage of life into one with purpose and passion; approach it with confidence.

As you plan your transition into this stage of your life, it is useful to reconsider what retirement means for you and how you can incorporate purpose and meaning into it. Remember Jack and Enrique's stories and advice as you develop your ideas for how to have meaning and purpose in retirement.

Crafting a retirement purpose statement can clarify your thoughts and goals and can serve as a light during your retirement journey. Naturally, your ideas of purpose can change, and then you just have to rethink it and restate it.

Most life purpose statements include one or more of the following:

Embracing Growth and Discovery. This means staying curious and open to new experiences. Whether it's traveling to unfamiliar places, exploring creative hobbies, or learning a new skill, continuous growth keeps someone's mind sharp and their spirit fulfilled.

- **Nurturing Meaningful Connections.** Many people want to focus more on their relationships with family, friends, and community in retirement. Building deeper connections not only brings joy but also provides support and companionship.

- **Contributing and Give Back.** This is about using one's time, talents, and wisdom to make a positive impact. Whether through volunteering, mentoring, or supporting a cause, contributing to something greater than oneself can bring profound satisfaction.

- **Prioritizing Your Well-being.** Sometimes, between work and raising a family, people stop taking care of themselves as they should. Many want to make retirement a time to rectify this. Having a purpose that is about caring for one's physical and mental health is valid and important. This includes staying active, eating well, and seeking out activities that bring you peace and joy. Preventive health care and regular self-care practices are key to thriving.

- **Align with Your Values.** This is about acting on what matters to someone. Whether it's spirituality, environmental stewardship, lifelong learning, or creative expression, a purpose that is about pursuing activities that reflect someone's core values will bring deeper fulfillment.

- **Embrace Financial Confidence.** Some want to focus their purpose on taking care of themselves and others financially, so it is about thoughtfully managing their finances and maintaining a clear view of their resources for peace of mind. This also includes wanting the ability to gift wealth to loved ones and leaving a legacy.

This chapter of life is yours to design. By leading with purpose, staying engaged, and nurturing both your own growth and the well-being of those around you, you can create a retirement that is not only fulfilling but truly inspiring.

We have discussed the process of creating a life purpose statement for retirement to help keep you focused as you pursue your aspirations and despite challenges. The following examples of life purpose statements are illustrations and can guide you in developing your own. These examples are organized by a main theme, as shown:

Health and Wellness
"To ensure my physical and mental well-being, I will engage in regular exercise, support a balanced diet, and prioritize preventive health care. Additionally, I will advocate for health initiatives that inspire others to embrace and sustain a healthy lifestyle."

Faith and Spiritual Growth
"To deepen my spiritual journey and share my faith with others, creating a supportive community where individuals can explore their beliefs and find solace and strength together."

Promote Lifelong Learning
"To inspire adults to engage in lifelong learning, empowering them to enhance their skills, adapt to change, and cultivate a sense of purpose in their lives."

Cultivate Lifelong Growth
"To continuously seek new experiences and insights that expand my understanding of the world and myself. Through curiosity and personal development, I will remain open to growth, learning from others, and evolving in this new chapter of life."

Travel the World
"To explore diverse cultures around the globe, fostering connections and understanding through travel, while seeking adventure and personal growth."

Cultural Exploration
"To travel and become immersed in diverse cultures, gaining deeper perspectives and fostering a greater appreciation for the world's richness."

Social Connections
"To strengthen my existing relationships and build new friendships through community engagement and social activities."

Foster Meaningful Connections
"To build and nurture relationships that celebrate diversity and shared experiences. By engaging in thoughtful conversations and celebrating the traditions and stories of others, I will create moments of joy, connection, and mutual learning."

Creative Expression

"To pursue my artistic passions like painting, writing, photography, or music, using creativity as a form of self-expression and joy."

Recreation and Adventure

"To savor new adventures, hobbies, and leisure activities that bring joy, relaxation, and fulfillment."

Giving Back to My Community

"To uplift my local community by volunteering my time and skills, fostering positive change, and working toward a more equitable and supportive environment for everyone."

Mentor Young People

"To mentor and work with our youth, inspiring them to believe in their potential and nurturing their natural talents so they can confidently pursue their dreams and make positive contributions to the world."

Leadership Consultant

"To serve as a consultant dedicated to empowering the next generation of leaders, providing them with the tools, knowledge, and confidence needed to drive meaningful change and inspire others in their communities."

Advocacy and Philanthropy

"To use my life experience to support and advocate for social causes, contributing time, energy, or resources to make a positive impact."

Environmental Stewardship

"To care for the environment through sustainable practices, advocating for conservation, and taking part in eco-friendly initiatives."

Environmental Advocate

"To champion environmental stewardship by promoting sustainable practices and raising awareness, ensuring that future generations can thrive in a healthy, vibrant planet."

Financial Wisdom and Legacy

"To ensure my financial well-being, manage my resources responsibly, and leave a meaningful legacy for loved ones and future generations."

CREATE A RETIREMENT LIFE PURPOSE STATEMENT

Now, put it all together. With your answers to the "Steps to Building Purpose and Meaning Worksheet" fresh in your mind, combine these with the ideas and examples provided earlier to write your life purpose statement for a fulfilling retirement below.

_____
_____
_____
_____
_____

TAKEAWAYS FROM ANCHORING RETIREMENT IN PURPOSE AND MEANING

Entering retirement offers a vital opportunity to cultivate a renewed sense of purpose. This next chapter is not an end but a chance to explore new interests, build meaningful relationships, and engage in activities that resonate with you. Having a strong sense of meaning and purpose will enhance your mental and emotional health, helping you navigate the changes that come with this transition.

The key takeaways from Chapter Seven include:

- Approach the retirement phase in a state of openness and willingness to be vulnerable.

- Understand the importance of having meaning and purpose in retirement.

- Reflecting on your past experiences, what has been important to you, and aligning with your values can lead to meaning and fulfillment.

Understanding how others have crafted meaning and purpose can help you to see what might work for you.

- Formulate a statement of purpose and refer to it when considering a new step.

Retirement is a chapter of life that is yours to design. By leading with purpose, staying engaged, and nurturing both your own growth and the well-being of those around you, you can create a retirement that is not only fulfilling but truly inspiring.

CHAPTER EIGHT

CULTIVATING GOOD HEALTH FOR A VIBRANT RETIREMENT

The road to a healthy life is not a sprint, it's a marathon.
—UNKNOWN

A healthy lifestyle is the foundation of a happy life.
—UNKNOWN

Take care of your body, it's the only place you have to live.
—JIM ROHN

Healthy aging involves staying active and independent by practicing self-care and maintaining well-being throughout life. It consists of adopting behaviors and making lifestyle choices that support longevity, vitality, and quality of life in later years. It also includes enhancing health literacy and developing a plan to maintain wellness as one ages and ensure access to quality health care.

As you age, your body undergoes various changes, increasing the risk of chronic illnesses such as heart disease, diabetes, arthritis, cancer, and dementia. However, it is possible to promote a longer and healthier life. It's never too early or too late to start living healthfully—your retirement can be your best chapter if you prioritize your well-being.

EMPOWERING YOURSELF THROUGH HEALTH LITERACY

As you navigate your retirement journey, developing health literacy is essential for making informed health decisions. Health literacy is the ability to obtain, understand, and use health information effectively. It empowers you to understand health details, navigate health care systems, and communicate confidently with your providers. Improving your health literacy can significantly enhance your access to health care services and positively affect your overall health.

Retirement is great for becoming more health literate—simply because people have more time to do so. To become knowledgeable about your health, educate yourself about the human body, healthy habits, and common ailments. Find out what community resources are available to educate yourself on these topics further. With knowledge from health literacy, people are more likely to adopt a healthy lifestyle, which can lead to better health outcomes, reduced health care costs, and an improved quality of life during retirement.

Part of health literacy is to learn how the health care system and Medicare work. Learn how to familiarize yourself with your health insurance options and find and use all available resources. In addition, focus on how best to communicate with health care professionals by asking as many questions as needed and requesting as much information and data as possible.

Your health is your greatest asset—investing in your health literacy will pay off in countless ways.

Chapter 8: Cultivating Good Health for a Vibrant Retirement

HEALTHY LIFESTYLE CHOICES AND BEHAVIORS

In retirement, embracing healthy aging through your lifestyle choices is crucial. Here are some key habits that promote a healthy lifestyle both now and in your retirement years.

Nutritious Diet

The first step toward health is to focus on what you put in your body, so stick to a balanced diet rich in fruits, vegetables, whole grains, lean proteins, and healthy fats. Aim to minimize processed foods, sugary drinks, and excessive salt. Consider adopting a Mediterranean or plant-based diet, both of which are linked to healthy aging and longevity. The Mediterranean diet emphasizes whole foods, healthy fats, and a variety of fruits and vegetables. It includes olive oil as a primary fat source, along with fish, poultry, beans, and whole grains, while limiting red meat and dairy. A plant-based diet primarily focuses on foods derived from plants, including vegetables, fruits, whole grains, nuts, seeds, and legumes, while minimizing or eliminating animal products.

Resources and websites:

- Mediterranean Diet Foundation— https://dietamediterranea.com/en/nutrition/
- Mediterranean Diet— https://my.clevelandclinic.org/health/articles/16037-mediterranean-diet
- Oldways—(resources, recipes, meal plans) https://oldwayspt.org/
- Plant-Based Dietitian—https://healthspandietitian.com/
- Forks Over Knives— (recipes, meal plans) https://www.forksoverknives.com/
- Minimalist Baker—(simple plant-based recipes) https://minimalistbaker.com/

Regular Exercise

Stay active with a mix of aerobic activities like walking, jogging, swimming, or cycling, paired with strength training. Aim for at least 150 minutes of moderate-intensity exercise or 75 minutes of vigorous activity each week, along with muscle-strengthening exercises on two or more days. There are some excellent websites that provide resources for incorporating regular exercise into your routine like 9 Simple Ways to Be Healthy Again—Peak Wellness. https://www.peakwellness.in/post/9-simple-ways-to-be-healthy-again

> Resources and websites:
>
> Mayo Clinic—comprehensive exercise guidelines and tips for beginners. https://www.mayoclinic.org/
>
> American Heart Association—recommended exercises for heart health, including aerobic activities and strength training. https://www.heart.org/
>
> ACE Fitness—information on fitness programs, videos, and certifications. Includes workout plans for aerobic and strength exercises. https://www.acefitness.org/

Adequate Sleep

Aim for 7 to 9 hours of sleep each night. Stick to a regular schedule, create a relaxing bedtime routine, and optimize your sleep environment.

> Resources and websites:
>
> National Sleep Foundation—offers information on sleep health, tips for better sleep, and guidelines for healthy sleep patterns. https://www.thensf.org/
>
> American Academy of Sleep Medicine—provides resources on sleep disorders, sleep hygiene tips, and educational materials on restorative sleep. https://sleepeducation.org/

Avoid Harmful Habits

Retirement can give you the space you need to finally let go of unhealthy habits. Stay clear of smoking and limit alcohol intake to boost your cardiovascular and overall health.

Resource and websites:

National Institute on Alcohol Abuse and Alcoholism (NIAAA)— offers resources on alcohol use, drinking guidelines, and support for quitting or reducing alcohol. https://www.niaaa.nih.gov/

National Institute on Drug Abuse (NIDA)— offers resources on drug, tobacco, nicotine, and e- cigarettes use and addiction https://www.drugabuse.gov

Maintain a Healthy Weight

Achieve and sustain a healthy weight with nutritious food and regular exercise to lower the risk of chronic diseases.

Resources and Websites:

CDC Healthy Weight—information on balanced nutrition, physical activity, and lifestyle changes for a healthy weight. www.cdc.gov/healthyweight

ChooseMyPlate.gov—tips on portion sizes, food groups, and dietary choices for weight management. www.choosemyplate.gov

Regular Medical and Dental Health Checkups

Schedule regular check-ups for medical screenings and vaccinations. Early detection of diseases can significantly enhance life quality. Also make sure you get to the dentist. Good oral health is vital to overall well-being and can prevent conditions like heart disease and diabetes. Regular dental care ensures you can eat, speak, and smile comfortably as you age. And dental expense is often out of pocket. which makes preventative care even more important.

Resources and websites:
- Healthfinder—information on preventive health care services, screenings, and vaccinations from the U.S. Department of Health and Human Services. https://odphp.health.gov/myhealthfinder
- American Academy of Family Physicians (AAFP)—guidelines on routine health check-ups, preventive services, and health tips for all ages. https://www.aafp.org/home.html
- American Dental Association (ADA)—information on dental check-ups, oral hygiene, and overall well-being. https://www.ada.org/
- Centers for Disease Control and Prevention (CDC) Oral Health resources on oral health, preventive care, and impact on heart disease and diabetes. https://www.cdc.gov/oral-health/index.html

Cognitive Stimulation for Brain Health

Engage in brain-challenging activities like learning new skills, using technology, playing an instrument, or joining a book club to maintain mental sharpness and potentially delay cognitive decline.

Resources and websites:
- Alzheimer's Association—provides cognitive health resources, including mental activities, brain health tips, and materials for preventing cognitive decline. https://www.alz.org/
- AARP Brain Health—offers strategies to maintain cognitive function, including brain games and mental engagement activities. https://www.aarp.org/health/brain-health/

Manage Stress

As is well known, chronic stress negatively impacts health. Learn and use stress-reduction techniques, such as mindfulness, deep breathing, and yoga. Go on walks in nature and engage in activities you enjoy. Time spent with loved ones can also reduce stress. If you still need help coping with stress, seek out friends to talk to or community resources that might offer short-term therapy.

Resources and websites:

> Mindful—resources on mindfulness, meditation, and stress reduction. www.mindful.org
>
> Headspace—meditation app with guided stress management exercises. www.headspace.com

Social Connections

A supportive social network helps combat loneliness, contributes to overall happiness, and promotes healthy aging in your retirement years. As much as possible, retain and nurture existing relationships with family, friends, and community members, and seek ways to develop new ones. Attend or participate in community events to engage in shared experiences with others.

Resource and Website:

> **AARP Connect**—AARP offers resources for social connections, including online communities, events, and activities for older adults to foster engagement and prevent loneliness. aarp.org/connect

Positive Outlook

As discussed in Chapter Seven, a positive mindset can help you engage in new experiences and create purpose and meaning in your life. More than that, research has shown that a positive attitude can significantly affect your health and longevity. If optimism doesn't come naturally to you, look into courses, workshops, or spiritual resources that can show you the way.

Resources and Websites:

> Greater Good Science Center—offers insights on positive mindset, gratitude, resilience, and well-being. www.greatergood.berkeley.edu.
>
> Positive Psychology Center—provides resources by Dr. Martin Seligman on optimism, mental health, and life satisfaction. www.ppc.sas.upenn.edu

By incorporating these and other healthy choices into your retirement lifestyle, you can age gracefully and potentially reduce the risk of chronic diseases in your later years. When it comes to health care, every individual's needs may vary. Consult with health care professionals such as physicians, physical therapists, and nutritionists to obtain personalized advice to support a healthy lifestyle. Take self-care seriously and embrace your health care journey.

GET THE MOST OUT OF INSURANCE

There is a lot that can be done in order to stay healthy, yet aging does entail physical decline. Perhaps more than any other time in a person's life, having adequate insurance coverage is a necessity in retirement. For one thing, it means someone has access to health care, and for another, without coverage, medical expenses can have a catastrophic effect on retirement savings and, as a result, the quality of life in retirement.

Medicare Health Insurance Benefits

Medicare is a federal health insurance program that provides essential coverage for individuals aged 65 and older, as well as certain younger people with disabilities and those facing specific health conditions. This program is designed to help you access the health care services you need as you age.

As you approach your retirement, understanding Medicare is essential for securing your health and well-being. Your journey with Medicare begins by enrolling in Medicare Part A during your initial enrollment period, which starts three months before you turn 65 and lasts for seven months. This proactive step is vital to ensuring timely access to benefits and establishing a foundation for your health care needs.

Medicare has four components that you should familiarize yourself with:

- **Part A (Hospitalization):** This covers inpatient care in hospitals and skilled nursing facilities, hospice care, and some home health services. Most people don't pay a premium for Part A if they or a qualifying spouse have worked and paid Medicare taxes for a certain period. Part A in-patient hospital services have a deductible.

- **Part B (Medical Insurance).** Part B covers essential medical services like doctor visits, outpatient care, and durable medical equipment ("Understanding Parts of Medicare Explained. A Guide"). Most people become eligible when they turn 65 and may automatically enroll if they are already receiving Social Security benefits. You will have to pay a monthly premium for Part B, so be prepared for that expense and factor it into your financial plan. Part B also has a deductible and coinsurance fees.

- **Part C (Medicare Advantage).** This plan combines coverage from both Part A and Part B and often includes added benefits like vision and dental services. Offered by private companies approved by Medicare, these plans provide flexibility in your health care choices.

- **Part D (Prescription Drug Coverage).** If you need prescription medications, Part D helps cover those costs. Make sure to enroll during the right period to avoid penalties later.

To supplement Medicare, consider **Medigap (Medicare Supplement Insurance)**, which covers any gaps in your coverage, such as deductibles and coinsurance. In addition to the premium you pay for Part B, you will have to pay an additional monthly premium for Medicare Supplement

Insurance. Still, financially, it provides peace of mind that your medical expenses will be covered.

For detailed information on Medicare and to learn more about your eligibility, visit the Medicare official website. Understanding your options is an important step in making informed health decisions. It is beneficial to be knowledgeable about how to use the available benefits effectively.

Employer-Sponsored Health Insurance

Those that retire early may still have medical insurance coverage under their former employer's plan. Or you may be covered under a specific retiree health plan they offer. Let's explore the key aspects you should consider.

Retiree Health Plans

Some employers provide retiree health plans designed to offer health care coverage for retired employees and their dependents. These plans may mirror the benefits you enjoyed as an active employee, but keep in mind that they could have different premiums, copayments, and coverage options. It's important to review the specifics of your retiree health plan, as benefits can vary significantly, and employers may change or even drop them over time. Make sure you understand what is available to you.

Medicare as the Primary Payer

If you're age 65 or older, you may be eligible for Medicare, and you can often enroll in Medicare while keeping your employer-sponsored health insurance. In this case, Medicare generally becomes your primary payer for covered services, while your employer-sponsored plan functions as secondary or supplementary insurance. This combination can give you added flexibility and financial support as you navigate your health care needs in retirement.

Spousal Coverage

If your spouse is still working and has employer-sponsored health insurance, you might be eligible to be covered as a dependent on their plan. This option can be beneficial if you do not have access to retiree health benefits (such as Medicare yet) or find COBRA coverage to be prohibitively expensive. Always check to see what options are available to you and consider how they align with your health needs.

Consolidated Omnibus Budget Reconciliation Act (COBRA)

You may also have the choice to continue your current employment-based health insurance when you retire. Under the Consolidated Omnibus Budget Reconciliation Act (COBRA), you can keep your employer-sponsored health insurance for a limited time after leaving your job, including retirement. COBRA typically allows coverage to continue for up to 18 or 36 months, depending on your circumstances, providing you with the safety of insurance coverage during your transition.

Health Insurance Marketplaces

Health Insurance Marketplaces are essential for retirees who retire before becoming eligible for Medicare. These marketplaces offer valuable coverage options that can help you navigate this important transition.

Under the Affordable Care Act (ACA), Health Insurance Marketplaces offer a range of insurance plans, often with income-based subsidies, making them a vital resource if you need coverage before you are eligible for Medicare at age 65. If you do not have access to employer-sponsored coverage during this period, purchasing insurance through a Marketplace can provide you with the health insurance you need.

Early Retirees. If you retire before age 65, you might lose access to employer-sponsored health insurance. This is where the Health Insurance Marketplaces come in—insurance coverage bought there will fill the gap by offering plans that ensure you have continuous coverage until you qualify for Medicare.

Premium Tax Credits. If you have a moderate to low income, you may be eligible for premium tax credits that reduce the cost of insurance you buy through the Marketplace. This can make health insurance much more affordable during the years leading up to Medicare eligibility.

Coordination with Medicare. When you reach age 65, it is important to transition from a Marketplace plan to Medicare, as you cannot keep your Marketplace coverage while receiving Medicare. Plan this transition carefully to avoid any gaps in coverage and potential penalties for late enrollment in Medicare.

Coverage for Younger Spouses. If one marriage partner qualifies for Medicare, but their spouse doesn't yet, the spouse can purchase insurance on the Health Insurance Marketplace to secure coverage until their Medicare eligibility. This ensures that a spouse has access to health care once the older partner has retired.

By exploring the options available through Health Insurance Marketplaces, you can take proactive steps to ensure that you and your family have the health care coverage you need as you transition into retirement. Remember, you have the power to make informed decisions about your health insurance, helping to secure a healthier and more confident retirement for yourself and your loved ones.

Retiree Medical Savings Accounts (RMSAs)

Some employers offer Retiree Medical Savings Accounts as part of their retirement benefits. These accounts enable you to set aside funds in a tax-advantaged manner for health care expenses not covered by Medicare or other insurance. This can be a valuable resource for managing out-of-pocket costs as you age.

As you approach retirement, it is crucial to carefully review your health care coverage options, including available employer-sponsored plans. Ensuring you have adequate coverage for your health care needs during retirement can make a significant difference in your overall well-being.

Consulting with a benefits administrator or financial advisor can help you navigate your options and make informed decisions about health care coverage in retirement. Remember, you deserve a retirement filled with health and peace of mind.

MAXIMIZING YOUR HEALTH INSURANCE BENEFITS

Navigating health insurance can be challenging, but it is possible to know how to make the most of your benefits so that they fully support your health and well-being. There are some strategies and tips to help you maximize your health insurance benefits:

- **Understand Your Plan.** Take the time to review your health insurance plan in detail. Familiarize yourself with what's covered, including preventive services, specialist visits, prescriptions, and emergency care. Knowing the specifics will empower you to make informed decisions about your care.

- **Utilize Preventive Services.** Many health insurance plans cover preventive services at no cost to you, such as annual wellness checkups, vaccinations, and screenings. Make sure to schedule these services regularly—they're key to detecting potential health issues early and staying on top of your health.

- **Stay In-Network.** If your plan has a network of providers, try to use in-network doctors and facilities whenever possible. This typically leads to lower out-of-pocket costs and ensures that you are receiving care that aligns with your plan's benefits.

- **Communicate with Your Provider.** Don't hesitate to ask your health care provider about your coverage during appointments. They can help clarify what services are covered and guide you in using your benefits effectively.

- **Keep Track of Your Expenses.** It is essential to keep accurate records of all medical expenses, including bills, receipts, and insurance statements. This will help you budget, watch your spending, understand your out-of-pocket costs, and provide valuable information when filing claims or resolving billing issues.

- **Know Your Rights and Responsibilities.** Understand your rights as a policyholder. Familiarize yourself with the process for appealing denied claims and ask your insurance company about your options if you feel a service should be covered.

- **Take Advantage of Additional Resources.** Many health insurance plans offer added benefits, such as wellness programs, telehealth services, or discounts on gym memberships. Explore these options and incorporate them into your health routine to enhance your overall wellness.

Plan for Medications. If you take prescription medications, review your prescription drug plan's formulary to understand which drugs are covered and at what cost. Ask your doctor about potential alternatives that may be more affordable, and always inquire about generics.

Review Your Coverage Annually. Health insurance plans can change from year to year. Take time during open enrollment to review your options and adjust as necessary. This is your chance to ensure you have the best coverage for your current health needs.

- **Ask for Help When Needed.** If you're feeling overwhelmed, don't hesitate to seek help. Whether it's speaking with a benefits coordinator at your workplace, consulting a financial planner, or working with a health care advocate, there are resources available to help you understand and maximize your benefits.

By actively engaging with your health insurance and using these strategies, you can ensure that you're making the most of your benefits. Remember, empowered decision-making is key to supporting your health and enhancing your quality of life. Your health is a priority—take charge and advocate for yourself.

LONG-TERM CARE: PREPARING FOR THE FUTURE

As you think about your retirement, it is important to consider long-term care (LTC) and how it can support you in maintaining your quality of life.

CHARACTERISTICS OF LONG-TERM CARE

Long-term care includes a variety of services designed to assist individuals who may need help with daily activities due to aging, chronic illness, disabilities, or cognitive impairments. It encompasses settings such as in-home care, adult day care centers, assisted living facilities, and skilled nursing homes, all aimed at providing personal care, medical support, and rehabilitation.

Long-term care aims to support someone's overall well-being by promoting independence and ensuring they receive care for their physical, emotional, and social needs. This includes help with activities of daily living (ADLs) such as bathing, dressing, eating, and mobility (personal care) as well as ongoing health monitoring and medication management (medical care) and access to therapy options, such as physical, occupational, or speech therapy, especially after surgery or illness (rehabilitation services).

Long-Term Care Insurance

If someone is considering long-term care, it's wise to investigate LTC insurance policies that specifically cover these services. While premiums can be high and coverage varies, researching the options is essential to finding a policy that will meet long-term care needs. Resources such as the National Association of Insurance Commissioners (NAIC) website provide tools to compare insurance companies and policies. Consulting with a financial advisor or insurance broker who specializes in long-term care can also offer personalized guidance.

Deciding whether to obtain LTC insurance involves weighing several factors related to your medical situation:

- Evaluate the likelihood that you will require help with daily activities as you age by evaluating your current health and family medical history.
- Consider the risk of developing chronic conditions such as arthritis or diabetes.
- Think about the availability of family members to provide care.
- Assess whether you may need professional care for safety and daily activities.
- Reflect on the importance of limiting or reducing the burden on family caregivers.
- Understand the value of protecting your financial assets to ensure you can afford necessary care without depleting your savings.

By understanding your and your family's expected needs regarding long-term care, you can make informed decisions about long-term care insurance as you move toward retirement.

Other Long-Term Care Options

For those who choose not to invest in long-term care insurance, there are alternative funding options, including using funds from a Health Savings Account (HSA), personal savings, or withdrawals from retirement accounts. Additionally, if necessary, someone could tap into their home equity through a reverse mortgage or a home equity line of credit (HELOC) to pay the costs.

Consult a financial planner about funding future care costs, and ensure that your legal documents, such as wills, powers of attorney, and advance medical directives (see the next section), are in place to manage your finances and health care if necessary. This proactive approach will empower you to navigate your retirement with confidence and secure the care you deserve.

PREPARING LEGAL ADVANCE CARE DOCUMENTS

The day may come when a person is temporarily or permanently incapacitated and is unable to make their wishes known about their care. For this reason, certain legal documents can be put in place to ensure that someone's wishes are respected and followed. These legal documents typically include a Living Will, a Medical Power of Attorney (also known as Durable Power of Attorney for Health Care), and a Health Care Proxy. These documents empower individuals to take control of their health care decisions before they may be unable to do so, which provides peace of mind for both you and your loved ones. To guarantee that your wishes are followed, it is crucial to have these legal documents in place.

Living Will

A Living Will is a legal document that clearly outlines someone's preferences for medical treatment and end-of-life care in case they become unable to express their wishes. (Search for "Do I need a Living Will?—Senior

Centers"). It covers important decisions about life-sustaining measures, such as resuscitation (CPR), mechanical ventilation, tube feeding, dialysis, and palliative care. A Living Will typically takes effect when a person becomes incapacitated and cannot communicate their desires directly. Until then, they keep the right to make their own medical choices.

Although a Living Will provides instructions about medical preferences, it does not assign someone to make decisions on your behalf. It serves as a guide for health care providers and family members. This document is legally binding in most states, meaning that health care providers must adhere to the instructions outlined in it, provided it follows state laws. To designate an agent to make decisions on your behalf, you can pair a Living Will with a Medical Power of Attorney or Health Care Proxy.

Medical Power of Attorney

A Medical Power of Attorney or Durable Power of Attorney for Health Care is a legal document that appoints a trusted person (an agent or proxy) to make medical decisions on someone's behalf if they are unable to do so. Depending on their state, this document can grant broad powers to their appointed agent so they can make a wide range of health care decisions—not just those related to end-of-life care. It empowers someone to act as another's voice in health-related situations, allowing them to adapt to changing circumstances and make decisions that align with their preferences. This document takes effect when a physician decides that an individual is incapacitated. However, some Medical Power of Attorney documents can specify that an agent's authority begins immediately or under certain other conditions.

Health Care Proxy

A Health Care Proxy is a document that appoints a healthcare agent to make decisions on your behalf when you are unable to do so. This document focuses specifically on health care decisions, particularly treatment preferences, and is typically more limited in scope compared to a broader Durable Power of Attorney for Health Care. It is intended strictly for health care decisions, not financial or legal matters, and may cover decisions about treatments and care plans. A Health Care Proxy goes into effect when a doctor assesses that someone is unable to make their own health care decisions.

Distinguishing Advance Care Documents

Preparing Advance Care documents ensures your health care preferences are clear and respected. They allow you to specify choices and provide instructions to guide your loved ones during difficult times, ensuring your decisions are honored even if you cannot communicate.

The chart below explains the role of each type of Advance Care document to help you understand their unique purposes and scope.

Advance Care Documents

FEATURE	LIVING WILL	MEDICAL POWER OF ATTORNEY	HEALTH CARE PROXY
PURPOSE	Outlines specific medical treatment preferences.	Appoints someone to make health care decisions.	Appoints someone to make health care decisions.
SCOPE	Limited to predefined scenarios, often end-of-life care.	Broad, includes all health care decisions.	Limited to health care decisions, often narrower in scope.
ACTIVATION	Activated when incapacitated.	Activated when incapacitated or as specified.	Activated when incapacitated.
ROLE OF OTHERS	No person appointed—the document serves as a guide.	Appoints an agent to decide for you.	Appoints a proxy to decide for you.
FLEXIBILITY	Less flexible; only covers specific instructions.	More flexible; allows for real-time decisions.	Similar to a Medical Power of Attorney, but often simpler.

Together, a Living Will and a Medical Power of Attorney or Health Care Proxy are essential components of an individual's health care planning. They ensure that your medical preferences are respected and that someone trusted is available to make decisions if you are unable to do so.

CHALLENGES TO ACCESSING HEALTH RESOURCES

Addressing how to maintain health and address health issues is one of the primary goals of retirement planning. However, this can be more challenging for those who have directly experienced limited access to quality health care during their lives and the results of health disparities that arise from such problematic access. This issue is critical because it directly affects the well-being and overall quality of life of those affected as they age.

Additionally, a person's generational cohort may influence how they perceive and prioritize health, making it important to understand the unique challenges specific to your generation. Doing so will empower you to seek solutions actively. Addressing the concerns you share with your generation now will not only enhance your own experience but also contribute to building healthier communities for everyone.

ACCESS TO QUALITY HEALTH CARE AND HEALTH DISPARITIES

Because access to quality healthcare and resources is essential in retirement, it often requires more focused planning to ensure members of diverse and underserved communities obtain these benefits. These groups are more likely to face health disparities driven by social determinants of health (SDOH), which include factors or levels of economic stability, education, neighborhood and environment and social supports that influences healthcare access. Recognizing these health inequities and understanding how they may affect you can help you better navigate your transition into retirement and advocate for your health needs.

For example, if you live in a neighborhood with limited access to grocery stores that sell healthy food options (an SDOH related to your environment), you may struggle to eat a nutritious diet, which can affect your long-term health. This, in turn, can lead to higher health care costs and increased risk of chronic conditions, making it essential to find ways to mitigate these impacts on your retirement health. You may have to travel outside your neighborhood to obtain healthier food options, and this can take some planning.

We all deserve quality, affordable health care that is safe, effective, culturally competent, and accessible. To receive this care, explore resources such as government programs, community health centers, and the insurance available on your state's Health Insurance Marketplace (e.g., HealthCare.gov). Federally Qualified Health Centers (FQHCs) offer essential services like primary care, dental, and mental health care based on a sliding fee scale. Additionally, State Health Insurance Assistance Programs (SHIPs) provide free, unbiased help with Medicare, Medicaid, and other insurance options, helping you make informed decisions.

Take advantage of discount programs or prescription savings cards like GoodRx or Single Care to lower medication costs and consider using retail health clinics for affordable options on minor illnesses and preventive care. And it can't be said enough that engaging in education and awareness programs can also enhance your health literacy, empowering you to make informed health care decisions.

By staying informed and proactive, you can access the quality health care you need, mitigating disparities and improving your overall well-being. Remember, you have the strength and resources to advocate for your health and, in so doing, ensure a vibrant retirement ahead.

HEALTH CONSIDERATIONS ACROSS DIFFERENT GENERATIONS

Something else to consider relates to the health and wellness concerns of your generational cohorts. Each generation is influenced by medical progress, historical events, technological advancements, and societal changes that may affect its members' perspectives about and behaviors regarding health, wellness, and aging. There may also be unique social, economic, educational, lifestyle, and environmental factors that affect health risk and outcomes depending on the cohort.

Understating the health-related challenges of generational cohorts provides added context for promoting health and wellness in retirement. No matter what stage you are at in planning for retirement, understating your generational cohort can, in a general way, help you to focus on key health considerations. Next, you will find some health tips that each generational cohort might consider as its members plan for and approach retirement.

Baby Boomers

Boomers (1946–1964) are receiving or aging into Medicare. Some of them may still be working and may be receiving employer-sponsored health insurance as well as Medicare. According to the Centers for Disease Control and Prevention (CDC), Baby Boomers are now facing quite a few potential health challenges. Boomers must be aware of these ailments and make sure their doctor(s) are testing for them during wellness exams. They include:

Type 2 diabetes

Heart disease

Hypertension (high blood pressure)

Cancer, all forms, including breast and prostate in particular

Alzheimer's disease and other forms of dementia

Depression and anxiety

Substance abuse issues, including alcoholism and prescription drug abuse

Arthritis and joint replacement

Osteoporosis

Vision and hearing loss

Sexual health issues, including erectile dysfunction, menopause-related symptoms, and decreased libido

Respiratory illnesses such as influenza (flu), pneumonia, and respiratory syncytial virus (RSV)

While Baby Boomers tend to be avid consumers of health information, they must also do the following:

Find a primary care physician, specialist, dentist, and health care professional that they trust. Responsibly manage any chronic conditions. Be sure to follow your health care provider's advice on preventive measures, medications, other treatments, and adaptive strategies.

Continue to stay abreast of current preventive health practices, health information, treatments, interventions, and new medical breakthroughs and developments.

Proactively manage their health and wellness, emotional health, chronic illness, and health challenges.

Prioritize mental health. Boomers must learn how not to be afraid to talk to their doctor about anxiety and depression

Engage in cognitive exercises, maintain social connections, and adopt a brain-healthy diet to help manage age-related issues.

Adopt an open mind and broader view of wellness.

Generation Jonesers

As members of Generation Jones (1955–1965), the members of this Cusper cohort are nearing or are in retirement. Some may face chronic conditions like hypertension, high cholesterol, diabetes, and cardiovascular disease. Age-related issues such as arthritis, osteoporosis, vision and hearing loss, urinary incontinence, cognitive decline, dementia, and Alzheimer's are significant concerns for you.

Generation Jones is at the end of the Baby Boomers, so the same advice applies to them. One difference may be that this cohort needs to educate themselves on Medicare and Medicare Supplemental Insurance and work out how to fill the insurance gap if someone retires before age 65. Another important issue to address is that the members of this microgeneration may not have considered or planned for long-term health care or made out their Advance Medical directives yet, so they must make both of these a priority.

Gen Xers

The majority of Gen Xers (1965 to 1980) are still some years away from applying for Medicare, so they might currently be relying on employer-sponsored health insurance, COBRA, or coverage from the Health Insurance Marketplace. The members of Generation X were the first to grow up in an era where health information was readily available on the Internet. They also experienced direct-to-consumer advertising for prescription drugs and consumer activism within health care. Having witnessed the AIDS crisis and the rise of health advocacy, Gen Xers have more discriminating attitudes toward health than earlier generations. This includes a growing awareness and acceptance of mental health care.

Generation X is being called the current "sandwich generation," those individuals who are balancing the responsibility of caring for aging parents while at the same time raising and supporting their own children. Gen Xers tend to be hungry for information, tech-savvy, and comfortable using digital tools.

In terms of health care, Gen Xers should continue to make the most of a variety of information sources, including family members, coworkers, doctors, pharmaceutical company websites, medical journals, television programs, online news sites and other media, books, and technology gadgets such as wearable devices to monitor health metrics. Additionally, Gen Xers can pursue the following strategies:

Prioritize routine checkups with a primary care physician and other health care professionals to monitor overall health. Regular screenings, vaccinations, and preventive care are essential for early detection and management of potential health issues. Maintaining open communication with health care providers and being sure to be proactive about recommended tests—such as cholesterol, blood pressure, and cancer screenings—can significantly enhance long-term wellness. Active engagement in preventive care helps address emerging health risks before they become serious and supports healthier aging.

Manage any chronic health conditions that have developed, such as Type 2 diabetes, hypertension, heart disease, high cholesterol, arthritis, obesity, sleep apnea, back pain, specific cancer risks, and chronic respiratory conditions. Managing these conditions will be important as you age.

Monitor your health for signs of depression, anxiety, and stress-related conditions that may be due to the pressures of balancing careers, family responsibilities, and financial challenges. Share concerns with your physician and seek professional help as needed.

Consider incorporating holistic and integrative medicine into health management routines and to complement traditional medical care. These approaches include holistic therapies that address the mind-body connection (such as meditation and yoga), using herbs and traditional natural healing substances through nutritional counseling, and acupuncture, massage, and chiropractic therapy. Alternative therapies and holistic medicine can promote ongoing wellness and support the effectiveness of traditional medicine to help manage chronic conditions, reduce stress, and improve overall health.

Take full advantage of workplace wellness programs, which may offer benefits such as stress management workshops, counseling services, fitness incentives, and mindfulness training. Utilizing these resources can help manage stress, improve work-life balance, and support overall well-being. Engaging in workplace wellness initiatives also fosters a proactive approach to supporting health, both in your careers and as you prepare for retirement.

Seek affordable health insurance and health care options by using resources such as government programs, community health centers, and insurance marketplaces (see "Navigating Health Disparity and Inequity, Opportunities and Strategies"). Learning to navigate health care expenses and insurance benefits is crucial for managing costs effectively. Understanding coverage details, such as premiums, deductibles, copayments, and out-of-pocket limits, empowers them to make informed decisions, access necessary care, and plan for long-term health needs.

Reach out to caregiver support programs such as the National Alliance for Caregiving and local community resources for information and help in managing caregiving responsibilities. These programs can provide guidance, resources, and emotional support to help you effectively fulfill your caregiving role.

Improve your health literacy by continuously learning about managing chronic conditions, preventive care, mental health, and navigating the health care system. This knowledge empowers you to make informed decisions, effectively communicate with health care providers, and access necessary resources and services.

Xennials

Also, Cuspers, Xennials were born at the intersection of Gen X and Gen Y (Millennials) (1977–1985). Unlike Gen X, they aren't quite staring down the barrel of retirement yet; however, most are in midlife, though the later-born ones have just turned forty. The members of this cohort may have begun to face more significant health challenges now that they are past the vibrant physical condition of youth. They may already be experiencing early signs of musculoskeletal issues like back pain, arthritis, or joint problems or even find that members in their group have been diagnosed with more serious conditions such as cancer. Concerns about health care insurance and affordability might be weighing on their minds and affecting their financial and emotional well-being.

The members of this cohort, as busy as they are, must still make time to:

Get serious about regular wellness checkups and preventive care.

Engage in activities that promote work-life balance, reduce stress, and prevent burnout.

Embrace digital health tools like fitness trackers and health apps while also valuing traditional health care models.

Seek affordable health care and insurance options and consider whether buying long-term care insurance now, at more affordable rates, is even possible.

Carter Babies

Carter Babies, born during the presidency of Jimmy Carter from 1977 to 1981, often juggle their own health needs with those of their children and aging parents. They are Cuspers, so this group straddles Gen X and Millennials (Carter Babies and a smaller cohort within the Cusper generation of Xennials). Thus, they share the concerns of both cohorts and, like them, their family responsibilities combined with work life can lead to stress and burnout, which negatively affects overall well-being.

At midlife, keeping a healthy lifestyle becomes more challenging for this cohort since metabolism slows and the level many have attained at work means demanding schedules. Like Gen Xers, Carter Babies are susceptible to chronic conditions such as hypertension, high cholesterol, diabetes, and cardiovascular disease, along with age-related issues like arthritis, osteoporosis, and sensory loss. Additionally, you face concerns about health care costs and the need for long-term care as you approach retirement.

Here are some actions they can take to address these challenges:

Prioritize regular exercise, mindful eating, and self-care to support a healthy lifestyle.

Seek out family-friendly health options and preventive care.

Build a financial plan that includes savings for medical expenses and long-term care.

A WORRYING TREND FOR GEN XERS AND MILLENNIALS

Health reporting reveals a concerning trend for Generation X, Millennials, and Generation Z. Members of these cohorts are in poorer health compared to earlier generations at the same age. According to a study by Zheng and Ohio State researchers, these generations exhibit worse physical health, including higher instances of metabolic syndrome and chronic inflammation, compared to Baby Boomers at the same age. They also engage in more unhealthy behaviors such as alcohol use and smoking and experience higher levels of depression and anxiety l., 2021).

Millennials and Gen Zers

Despite research showing that Millennials and Generation Z often experience poorer health outcomes compared to previous generations, these groups tend to be more health-conscious. This heightened awareness is likely due to increased access to information, which has improved their understanding of healthy habits and shifted attitudes toward mental health. As a result, Millennials (born 1981–1996) and Generation Z (born 1997–2012) are more proactive in seeking health education before consulting healthcare providers and are more inclined to adopt healthier behaviors. However, many have encountered setbacks during adolescence and early adulthood, especially related to mental health issues like anxiety and depression, often worsened by social and academic pressures. These challenges can have long-lasting effects on their overall health, with unhealthy habits such as chronic stress and poor sleep increasing their risk of developing conditions like heart disease or diabetes later in life.

Early Millennials, now approaching middle age, are embracing a holistic approach to health, prioritizing overall well-being by addressing physical, mental, and emotional aspects of their health. Research suggests that Gen Zers (1997–2012) are likely to adopt a similar holistic approach to health as Millennials, even though some Gen Zers are still in their teens. Both generations may benefit from following these key practices:

Prioritizing preventive care.

Engaging in routine checkups.

Managing stress and mental and emotional wellness.

Committing to being insured by looking for and securing affordable health insurance.

Exploring solutions to health disparity and inequity may offer further opportunities for improvement.

Zillennials

Zillennials (1993–1998) are Cuspers who bridge the gap between Millennials and Generation Z, so they have experiences and outlooks similar to both those generations. Members of this cohort may just be settling into a career path, so they are working on financial discipline and goal-setting and evaluating their options for saving for retirement.

While retirement may seem far off, the individuals in this cohort must begin to think in terms of long-term health maintenance and be proactive about their health, prioritizing prevention over treatment by adopting healthy habits like regular exercise, balanced nutrition, and avoiding smoking and drinking in excess. However, they must also combat issues stemming from digital overload and a sedentary lifestyle, which can lead to poor posture, obesity, and digital eye strain.

To ensure that they approach their retirement years in good health, Zillennials can follow the guidance given to Millennials and Gen Zers. Such a microgeneration has distinct health behaviors and attitudes influenced by life experiences, cultural context, and technological exposure. Recognizing these differences can help in tailoring health interventions, products, and services to better address your needs. By taking these steps, you can set up a solid foundation for long-term health and wellness. These strategies can support both generations in keeping and improving their overall health and wellness.

VITAL HEALTH AND WELLNESS PLANNING FOR A FULFILLING RETIREMENT

As someone embarks on creating their comprehensive health plan for retirement, the aim is to build a retirement health plan that includes adequate insurance coverage and that connects you with a supportive health care team and system dedicated to promoting healthy aging.

The place to begin is to assess whether insurance coverage includes a broad range of services, including primary care physicians, specialists, hospitals, assisted living, rehabilitation facilities, and other health care professionals and resources.

The next step is to determine if health care is accessible and affordable where you live (or plan to live). It's essential to prioritize access to quality health care. Patrica's story showed how important that is. Check state and community rankings using resources like *U.S. News & World Report*. Their "Healthiest Communities" rankings offer valuable insights into health care access, healthy behaviors, health conditions, mental health, and outcomes, allowing you to evaluate the quality of care available in your current and future communities.

By staying informed and ensuring access to quality care, you can significantly enhance your overall health and well-being as you transition into retirement. This and the other proactive steps in the discussion that follows will empower you to support a vibrant, fulfilling lifestyle as you age.

STRATEGIES FOR MAINTAINING GOOD HEALTH IN RETIREMENT

Develop a detailed health plan early and update it regularly to ensure optimal effectiveness and positive results. The plan should help you to:

- **Assess Health Care Needs.** Evaluate your current and expected health care needs to figure out the level of coverage needed.

- **Analyze Health Insurance Options.** More than just coverage, look at which providers accept a type of insurance to be sure it provides access to quality services, including primary care and specialized health care professionals.

- **Do Research on Accessibility.** Utilize resources like *U.S. News & World Report* to compare health care access and affordability in your state and community. Explore the Healthiest Communities Rankings to understand health access, behaviors, and outcomes in your current and future neighborhoods. Some places may be attractive places to live, but you would have to travel out of state for advanced care.

- **Prioritize Routine Wellness Checkups.** Practice sound self-care techniques to support and manage health proactively.

- **Manage Chronic Health Conditions.** Develop a plan with your health care team to ensure ongoing care and support.

- **Organize and Manage Medications.** Set up a system to take medications at the right times and in the right amounts. If necessary, set up phone alerts or enlist a buddy to help you.

- **Take Advantage of Community Resources.** These could include wellness education and programs, fitness classes, and mental health services.

- **Update Your Detailed Health Plan Regularly.** Be sure it is optimally effective and delivers positive results.

COMPREHENSIVE HEALTH PLANNING

To assess where you stand in terms of being proactive about your health status and identify areas of improvement, complete this "How Proactive Am I About My Health" worksheet.

How Proactive Am I About My Health?

Health Literacy
Effectively communicate with health care providers, asking questions and expressing my concerns to ensure my clear understanding and active participation in my health care decisions.

Current Age _____ **Date** _____

Today - *My Current Skill*

_____

Change - *What I Need to Do*

___

Retirement Plan – *What Will Be in Place When I Retire (Your Goal)*

___

Easily read and understand health-related materials, such as medication labels, prescription directions, dosages, test results, health risks, and educational resources.

Today - *My Current Status*

___

Change - *What I Need to Do*

___

Retirement Plan – *What Will Be in Place When I Retire*

___

Evaluate the reliability, accuracy, and credibility of health information from various sources, including family, friends, websites, media, social media, and health care providers.

Today - *My Current Skill*

___

Change - *What I Need to Do*

___

Retirement Plan – *What Will Be in Place When I Retire*

___

Use health information to make informed decisions about preventive measures, treatment options, and lifestyle choices that promote health and well-being.

Today - *My Current Skill*

___

Change - *What I Need to Do*

___

Retirement Plan – *What Will Be in Place When I Retire*

___

Understand how to access health care services, including scheduling appointments, arranging transportation, filling out forms, navigating insurance coverage and co-pay requirements, and billing.

Today - *My Current Skill*

___

Change - *What I Need to Do*

___

Retirement Plan – *What Will Be in Place When I Retire*

___

Use Electronic Health Record (EHR) or Electronic Medical Record (EMR) that many health care providers use to keep track of health information and able to access my own health records through online portals. These portals are sometimes referred to as "MyChart" or similar names.

Chapter 8: Cultivating Good Health for a Vibrant Retirement

Today - *My Current Status*

___

Change - *What I Need to Do*

___

Retirement Plan - *What Will Be in Place When I Retire*

___

Utilize community resources such as local libraries, health columns in newspapers, reliable online resources, health podcasts, radio, and television programs, as well as programs offered by hospitals, community colleges, non-profits, faith-based organizations, and health events like fairs and free screenings to enhance health literacy.

Today - *My Current Status*

___

Change - *What I Need to Do*

___

Retirement Plan - *What Will Be in Place When I Retire*

___

Attend local health care events (e.g., health fairs, public workshops, or free screenings) that provide health information.

Today - *My Current Status*

___

Change - *What I Need to Do*

___

Retirement Plan – *What Will Be in Place When I Retire*

_____

Healthy Lifestyle

Assess my overall wellness and physical health and have a plan for my current wellness management strategies.

Today - *My Current Status*

_____

Change - *What I Need to Do*

_____

Retirement Plan – *What Will Be in Place When I Retire*

_____

Regularly check in on my emotional wellness, cognitive health, and mental health and engage in practices to support them.

Today - *My Current Status*

_____

Change - *What I Need to Do*

_____

Retirement Plan – *What Will Be in Place When I Retire*

_____

Consider how well I'm practicing a healthy lifestyle and whether there are resources that can support me in this.

Today - *My Current Status*
_____

Change - *What I Need to Do*
_____

Retirement Plan – *What Will Be in Place When I Retire*
_____

Health Insurance
Maintain good comprehensive health insurance coverage, even though I have retired early and am not yet eligible for Medicare.

Today - *My Current Status*
_____

Change - *What I Need to Do*
_____

Retirement Plan – *What Will Be in Place When I Retire*
_____

Educate myself about Medicare, including being informed about when I am eligible to/must enroll.

Today - *My Current Status*
_____

Change - *What I Need to Do*
_____

Retirement Plan – *What Will Be in Place When I Retire*

___

Understand Medicare Parts A and B and my Medicare Advantage options (Part C). Understand whether I will need a Medicare Supplemental Insurance Plan and a Prescription Plan (Part D) and what the best coverage for me is.

Today - *My Current Status*

___

Change - *What I Need to Do*

___

Retirement Plan – *What Will Be in Place When I Retire*

___

Long-term Care
Regularly consider my long-term care needs and review long-term care insurance and other options to address them as I age.

Today - *My Current Status*

___

Change - *What I Need to Do*

___

Retirement Plan – *What Will Be in Place When I Retire*

___

Plan to construct a long-term care plan with my health care professionals and family.

Today - *My Current Status*

_____

Change - *What I Need to Do*

_____

Retirement Plan – *What Will Be in Place When I Retire*

_____

Advance Care

Have my advance care preferences in writing through the necessary documents and have notified the relevant individuals as to where these documents are located.

Today - *My Current Status*

_____

Change - *What I Need to Do*

_____

Retirement Plan – *What Will Be in Place When I Retire*

_____

Challenges and Opportunities

Explore the health-related challenges I face in retirement and evaluate how well-prepared I am.

Today - *My Current Status*

_____

Change - *What I Need to Do*
_____

Retirement Plan – *What Will Be in Place When I Retire*
_____

Examine the possible health-related challenges I might encounter in retirement and outline my preparation strategies.

Today - *My Current Status*
_____

Change - *What I Need to Do*
_____

Retirement Plan – *What Will Be in Place When I Retire*
_____

Retirement Health and Wellness Action Plan

Using the results of the "How Proactive Am I About My Health?" worksheet, create a Retirement Health and Wellness Action Plan. Write six action steps that briefly outline how you will address any deficiencies in your retirement health planning that were identified when you completed the worksheet. Periodically review and revise these action steps as needed.

1. _____
2. _____
3. _____
4. _____
5. _____
6. _____

Patricia's story shows how to adjust health planning when a health challenge develops.

Chapter 8: Cultivating Good Health for a Vibrant Retirement

PATRICIA'S JOURNEY: *NAVIGATING HEALTH CHALLENGES, BUT HEADING IN THE RIGHT DIRECTION*

Now in my early 70s, I dedicated over 40 years to social work—spending more than two decades as a case manager and independent contractor. At this pivotal moment in my career, while many of my peers are transitioning into retirement, I find myself feeling uncertain about taking that step.

For roughly 30 years, I lacked access to employer-sponsored retirement savings plans. While I do have an IRA account, I didn't maximize my contributions. Poor financial advice and my own fear of being misled by financial advisors played a significant role in this, compounded by the daily demands of life that left me feeling overwhelmed and distracted. As a result, I'm now questioning whether my retirement savings and Social Security benefits will be enough to support my desired lifestyle. I own two houses as assets, but I'm unsure how to leverage them effectively for my retirement security.

Over the last three years, I have faced health-related issues. Fortunately, I had managed to buy health insurance through my state's Health Insurance Marketplace for eight years until I became eligible for Medicare at age 65. However, two years ago, a wake-up call prompted my current concerns: I underwent back surgery, which has resulted in ongoing mobility issues that require me to use a cane. This situation has forced me to reconsider my retirement plans and the feasibility of a comfortable transition in the near future.

Additionally, I am responsible for my 100-year-old mother, who lives with me. She retired 40 years ago with a pension, Social Security benefits, and health care coverage. Currently, she is unable to live independently. Access to quality health care has been essential for her, providing necessary medical attention and support from professionals. Since my surgery, having a home health aide assist my mother with daily activities (activities of daily living) has been important in ensuring she receives adequate care while also allowing me time for recovery. This situation demonstrates the importance of reliable health care access for both of us and its impact on our well-being and quality of life.

Recognizing the urgent need for a structured retirement plan, I have recently sought guidance from a financial planner to develop a comprehensive strategy. I'm also considering home modifications to accommodate my mobility constraints. Although I hope to explore new hobbies in retirement, I haven't yet pinpointed specific interests. My passion for helping others and working with children is key. While I feel I'm now on the right path, I acknowledge that I need ongoing support and encouragement as I navigate this journey.

Chapter 8: Cultivating Good Health for a Vibrant Retirement

PATRICIA'S ADVICE

I encourage you to consider planning for retirement early. Retirement may come sooner than expected, as when unforeseen health issues could necessitate leaving full-time employment. Preparing in advance is vital to ensure your financial stability and peace of mind.

TAKEAWAYS FROM CULTIVATING GOOD HEALTH FOR A VIBRANT RETIREMENT

You are your own best health advocate. Understand your health needs and be tireless in getting the care you deserve. Remember these takeaways:

Health literacy empowers and leads to critical healthy lifestyle choices

Get the most out of insurance by understanding the available options and how they work and ensure that you are covered up until you are eligible for Medicare.

Consider your long-term health needs and whether you should purchase long-term care insurance.

Realize the importance of Advance Care documents so that your wishes will be fulfilled if you are incapacitated.

It is critical to evaluate whether—for demographic or location reasons—you don't have adequate access to quality health care resources. Make it a priority to address this.

Assess where your retirement health planning is falling short and decide on some corrective action steps.

CHAPTER NINE

FOSTERING EMOTIONAL WELLNESS IN RETIREMENT

Feelings are something you have; not something you are.
—SHANNON L. ALDER

Emotional wellness is a key component of overall health and well-being; it's okay to ask for help.
—UNKNOWN AUTHOR

The most important decision you make is to be in a good mood.
—VOLTAIRE

When approaching retirement, many people can find that this significant life change leads them to question their identity and future. While it's crucial that retiring individuals focus on financial matters, it's equally important for them to prioritize their emotional wellness during this transition. Moving from a structured work routine to a new lifestyle can be challenging and may lead to feelings of uncertainty, stress, and anxiety.

Many retirees experience social isolation, which can lead to loneliness and even depression. As they distance themselves from the workplace connections they once had, they might feel less engaged with friends, family, and community networks. This disconnection can heighten feelings of loneliness and make it difficult to find meaning and support. It's natural to miss the interaction and camaraderie that work provided, but recognizing these feelings is an empowering first step toward crafting a fulfilling retirement.

Anyone planning for retirement must also proactively develop a plan for supporting their emotional wellness as well. Emotional wellness is about understanding, managing, and expressing one's emotions effectively. It involves building self-awareness and resilience and fostering healthy relationships, which can help someone navigate the challenges of aging while promoting personal growth and enriching experiences.

To enhance your emotional wellness, be attentive to your emotional well-being. If you notice signs of depression, anxiety, or stress, address them promptly. Sometimes, taking seemingly small actions can put you back into balance, and other times, more substantive support may be necessary; don't hesitate to seek it when you need it.

This section will cover strategies for monitoring your emotional health throughout retirement. Addressing emotional challenges is key to enjoying a fulfilling and vibrant retirement. By prioritizing your emotional wellness, you can approach this new phase of life with confidence and purpose. Remember, caring for your emotional well-being is essential for a satisfying and meaningful retirement.

MONITORING AND ASSESSING EMOTIONAL BALANCE

In retirement, emotional well-being encompasses your overall state of happiness and life satisfaction that results from achieving emotional wellness. Feeling content with your life, the presence of positive emotions, and a sense of fulfillment in your daily experiences are signs of emotional well-being. If these signs are lacking or you are experiencing high and low mood swings, then this means you are out of emotional balance.

High emotional well-being shows that you are not only coping well with the changes that come with retirement but are also enjoying a rich and meaningful life, which can lead to a deeper sense of purpose and connection with others. This chapter discusses emotional wellness and the specific tools and practices for effectively monitoring and addressing it.

ENGAGE IN SELF-REFLECTION

To support emotional well-being, regularly check in with yourself. Take a moment to pause, monitor, and assess your feelings. Regular self-checks are important because they allow you to address any emotional issues early, preventing them from escalating and negatively affecting overall wellness. This practice helps you stay aware of your emotional state and identify any areas that may need attention.

Daily Journaling and Check-ins

Take some time every day to write down your thoughts, feelings, and experiences. Reflecting on your emotions can help you spot patterns and name areas that need attention. Periodically perform an emotional assessment by regularly pausing and checking in with yourself. Pay attention to both positive and negative emotions and think about what might be influencing them.

Routinely Gauge Stress Levels

Consider how often you feel stressed and how you manage it. If stress feels overwhelming or constant, you might need to explore better coping strategies. Identify the source of the stress. Is it finances, family, or social isolation?

If you are still working, assess whether your work and personal life are in balance or not. Continuous work stress or lack of personal time can harm your emotional wellness.

Reflect on how you manage stress. Healthy options include exercising, talking to a friend, or practicing mindfulness. Unhealthy options might be overeating, substance abuse, or withdrawing from social activities. Think about your resilience and how you've bounced back from setbacks in the past. Resilience is a key part of emotional health.

Track Your Moods

Keep a journal to track your emotions throughout the day, noting any triggers or patterns. Use apps like Daylio or Moodfit to monitor your emotions and gain insights into your emotional well-being.

Consider Physical Symptoms

Pay attention to your mind-body connection by noting any physical symptoms that might be related to emotional distress, like headaches, stomach issues, changes in appetite, or unexplained aches and pains. Similarly, keep an eye on your sleep habits. If getting to sleep or staying asleep is difficult, there may be underlying reasons that need to be identified. Good sleep is crucial for emotional and physical well-being.

Reflect on Personal Fulfillment

Think about how fulfilled you feel in your personal and professional life. Are you lacking a sense of meaning or purpose? Or did what used to work as a life purpose stop working for you? A strong sense of purpose contributes significantly to emotional well-being. Reflect on your accomplishments and how well you are meeting your personal goals and set yourself a goal of finding a new purpose.

Reflect on the quality of your relationships and social interactions. Strong social connections are vital for emotional health. It may be that you need to engage with others more, either through your community or by reaching out to friends and family.

Seek Feedback and Help

Ask for feedback from people you trust to gain insights into your emotional well-being. You could also seek professional support for this. Consider talking to a therapist or counselor for an objective assessment and to help you come to a deeper understanding of your emotional state. Counseling can also help you to notice if patterns are emerging that are similar to past mental health challenges.

If you are coping with grief, whether over the loss of your work life or a loved one, practice more self-care and reaching out to others. Join a grief support group or seek therapy.

Utilize Assessment Tools

Employ online resources to gain insights into your emotional health. Some helpful tools include:

> The National Institutes of Health's (NIH) "Emotional Wellness Checklist"
>
> "Feeling Stressed? Ways to Improve Your Well-Being," NIH
>
> "Mindfulness for Your Health: The Benefits of Living Moment by Moment," NIH
>
> "Patient Health Questionnaire" (PHQ-9), American Psychological Association

By using these practices and self-assessment tools, you may gain a better understanding of your emotions and assess your emotional well-being. If you are experiencing feelings of depression, stress, or anxiety about retirement, do not ignore them. Seek help and take steps to manage these feelings to promote overall emotional health.

FACING MENTAL HEALTH CHALLENGES IN RETIREMENT

If you are experiencing feelings of depression, anxiety, or stress, manage your emotional wellness by seeking suitable interventions to address the underlying causes of what you are experiencing. Many of the mental health challenges faced during retirement—the loss of identity, social isolation, financial concerns, and adjusting to health changes—have already been discussed. Others have experienced struggling with these challenges, so you are not alone in this.

If the situation starts to feel overwhelming, face your emotions head-on and take proactive steps to help you regain your emotional balance and wellness. It can be incredibly empowering to do so. A therapist or mental health professional can offer valuable tools and coping strategies to help you manage feelings of depression, stress, or anxiety. You can also participate in support groups for retirees or those facing similar life challenges. Engaging with others who are going through similar experiences can provide a sense of comfort and feeling understood. When you make your mental well-being a priority during this transition, you set the stage for a fulfilling retirement. Embrace this journey with kindness toward yourself and know that taking proactive steps can make a positive difference. Remember, you are not alone on this journey; if you ever experience overwhelming thoughts or emotional distress, don't hesitate to call 988—The Suicide & Crisis Lifeline—for immediate support.

BUILDING A STRONG FOUNDATION FOR EMOTIONAL WELLNESS IN RETIREMENT

Voltaire's quote, "The most important decision you make is to be in a good mood," emphasizes the importance of choosing a positive mindset, which is crucial for emotional wellness during retirement. Establishing a foundation of emotional wellness during retirement is important for a balanced life. Maintaining a positive mindset and adapting to change can improve overall well-being. Developing healthy habits and focusing on emotional wellness can provide benefits such as reduced stress, improved mood, and a greater sense of purpose.

GUIDELINES FOR A POSITIVE STATE OF MIND

The following guidelines help support a positive outlook, which will maximize your experiences in your retirement years:

- **Adjust Your Attitude.** View retirement as a journey with opportunities for growth. Focus on new experiences and what you are gaining.
- **Redefine Your Identity.** Find new ways to define yourself beyond your career through activities and relationships.
- **Set Realistic Goals.** Establish achievable goals to provide purpose and excitement. Celebrate successes along the way.
- **Embrace a Sense of Purpose.** Engage in meaningful activities, volunteer work, or hobbies that add joy and enrich your life.
- **Establish a Routine.** Create a daily schedule that includes time for activities, exercise, social interactions, and relaxation.
- **Nurture Hobbies and Interests.** Pursue longstanding or new interests such as traveling, nature, sports, or the arts.

Volunteer and Contribute. Donating time to causes you care about can provide a sense of accomplishment and expand your social network.

Cultivate a Religious or Spiritual Practice. Engaging in spiritual activities, such as prayer, meditation, or attending religious or spiritual ceremonies, offers comfort and purpose during periods of transition.

- **Stay Physically Active.** Engage in regular exercise like walking, swimming, or yoga to boost mood, relieve stress, and promote relaxation. Even with mobility limitations, staying active for 30 minutes on most days is beneficial.
- **Stay Mentally Engaged.** Challenge your mind with puzzles, reading, or learning new skills.
- **Prioritize Social Connections.** Maintain and nurture relationships with family, friends, and community groups. Socializing can combat loneliness and provide emotional support.

Build Your Support Network. Open up to your partner, friends, and family about your feelings. Communication strengthens your social bonds, and surrounding yourself with a supportive network can significantly enhance your mental health. Don't hesitate to reach out; together with others, you can navigate challenges more effectively.

- **Limit Screen Time.** Be mindful of the amount of time spent looking at screens—phones, tablets, laptops, and television—particularly when on social media, which can sometimes lead to negative feelings or comparisons.
- **Look After Your Health.** Maintain a healthy lifestyle with proper sleep, diet, exercise, and routine.
- **Learn Something New.** Expand your mind with adult education classes or new skills.
- **Get a Pet.** Caring for a pet can boost mood, ease stress, and provide companionship.

Travel and Explore. Use the free time and flexibility of a retirement lifestyle to travel and discover new places.

SPIRITUALITY AND FAITH FOR A FULFILLING RETIREMENT

Embracing your spirituality as you plan for retirement, transition into this new phase, and navigate post-retirement life can provide a deep sense of meaning and feelings of wellness. To further your aim of emotional balance, reflect on and cultivate your spiritual life as you plan for and during retirement. Here are some suggestions.

Reflect on Your Beliefs. Take time to explore and clarify your spiritual beliefs and values. Journaling about your thoughts on spirituality can help you understand what is important to you and how it shapes your approach to retirement.

Engage in Spiritual Practices. Incorporate daily or weekly spiritual practices or observances into your routine, such as prayer and meditation. Spending time in nature often connects you to your spiritual self and the beauty of the world around you. These practices can inspire spiritual reflection, provide a sense of peace and serenity, and help clarify your thinking as you transition into retirement.

Cultivate Gratitude. Focus on the positive aspects of your life by keeping a gratitude journal. Writing down what you are thankful for can uplift your mood and overall outlook. Celebrate the small victories, as they can bring joy and fulfillment to your day.

Embrace Mindfulness and Relaxation Techniques. Regularly practice mindfulness to stay present in the moment. This can be as simple as taking a few minutes each day to focus on your breath, helping you to ground yourself and reduce feeling overwhelmed. This is a good practice when you are thinking about the past or experiencing anxiety about the future.

Seek Spiritual Connection with Others. Connect with like-minded individuals who share your spiritual values. Building relationships with others on similar journeys can encourage discussion, reflection, growth, and a sense of community. (Chapter Ten discusses how to find a spiritual- or faith-based community.)

By actively incorporating spirituality and faith into your life, you're taking meaningful steps toward nurturing your emotional health. Remember, prioritizing your well-being is a strength, and you deserve to thrive in all aspects of your life.

EMBRACING CULTURE TO ENHANCE EMOTIONAL WELLNESS

There are a number of ways culture can affect those in retirement. One is the broader society or culture of their environment. This culture may include media messages about aging that are not realistic or supportive. Then, there is an individual's more unique cultural background. This can significantly influence how that person's attitude toward themself and retirement.

Cultural beliefs about aging can shape an individual's perspective, whether it's one that celebrates and respects having achieved wisdom or it views aging negatively. Embrace the positive aspects of aging and any positive messages from your culture to enrich your life and learn to challenge any negative feelings or beliefs you've absorbed from your culture.

Reflect on how culture affects your emotional expression. Some cultures encourage open discussions, while others may be more reserved. Exploring open communication can enhance emotional well-being. Challenge any stigmas and seek support through therapy or groups for older adults when needed.

Cultural norms can also guide how you seek support. In many cultures, family ties are vital. Nurture your network of family, friends, and community to boost emotional health. If spirituality is important to you, let it guide and comfort you. Engaging in mindfulness or journaling can enhance resilience during retirement.

By incorporating diverse cultural perspectives, you create a supportive environment that honors your background and boosts emotional wellness. Understanding these dynamics enriches your retirement experience.

Engaging in cultural practices can strengthen your sense of belonging and purpose in retirement. Some ways doing so can enhance your emotional well-being are discussed next.

Attend Cultural Events. Take part in festivals, ceremonies, or reunions to connect with your heritage and strengthen your identity. These gatherings foster solidarity and resilience as you celebrate your shared history. Many cultures have traditional dances or practices that reflect their heritage, allowing you to connect with your roots while promoting physical health. Engaging in these activities not only boosts your mood and enhances your well-being but also celebrates cultural expressions of joy and community,

Preserve Family Rituals. Traditions such as shared meals, storytelling, and the preservation of family albums that document your family's history are meaningful approaches to incorporating cultural influences into retirement. Traditions enhance emotional well-being, commemorate a family's history, reinforce familial bonds, and provide stability by deepening someone's connection to their cultural heritage.

Engage with Your Community. Participate in local events to build friendships and support networks. Volunteer or join interest-based groups to meet new people and share passions.

Reconnect to Spiritual Traditions. This can help you connect with your cultural heritage and foster a deeper sense of identity and belonging in this new phase of life.

Pursue Creative Endeavors Rooted in Culture. Art, dancing, or music allows you to engage with and celebrate your cultural heritage in a meaningful way. By participating in creative endeavors rooted in your culture, you can experience a sense of joy and fulfillment while fostering a deeper appreciation for the rich tapestry of your background.

Utilize Mental Health Resources. Familiarize yourself with culturally responsive mental health resources. Knowing where to seek support empowers you to adapt to retirement.

Advocate For and Seek Out Culturally Competent Care. Seek health care providers who respect cultural influences on emotional health. Open communication and advocacy leads to better care.

By integrating these practices, you cultivate purpose and emotional wellness during retirement. Embrace the opportunity to shape a vibrant, fulfilling new chapter.

ENHANCING EMOTIONAL WELLNESS THROUGH GENERATIONAL INSIGHTS

Generational cohorts play a significant role in shaping emotional wellness during retirement by influencing members' values, beliefs, and approaches to life. Economic conditions, technological advancements, and cultural shifts affect how each generation views health, relationships, and personal growth. Social norms and support systems within a cohort also affect emotional wellness and the overall quality of the retirement experience.

As you age and transition into retirement, recognize how generational distinctiveness influences your emotional wellness. Each cohort—whether you identify as a Baby Boomer, Gen Xer, Millennial, or Generation Zer—has unique perspectives and values that can shape your mental health and well-being. By understanding these generational insights, you can better navigate your retirement journey, enhancing your emotional wellness and creating a more fulfilling and meaningful life during this important phase.

GENERATIONAL STRATEGIES

Baby Boomers may have grown up in a time when discussing mental health was often stigmatized. Because of this, Boomers might find it challenging to seek help or open up about emotional struggles. They can realize that acknowledging this history is the first step toward overcoming barriers to support. Boomers can also focus on nurturing their emotional wellness through personal connections and face-to-face interactions, as these tend to resonate more with their generational preferences.

If someone belongs to Generation X, they have witnessed a gradual shift in societal attitudes toward mental health. While self-reliance and financial independence are the Gen Xer hallmarks, the members of this cohort should not hesitate to participate in discussions about mental and emotional health. The members of this group will be willing to embrace both traditional support methods and modern digital tools to enrich their emotional resilience. Prioritizing building a robust financial portfolio for retirement is valid but so is recognizing the power of seeking emotional support when needed.

Millennials might feel comfortable engaging in open conversations about mental health since this generation seems to reject the stigma about it that earlier generations faced. One of their strengths is their willingness to seek help. With their affinity for technology, Millennials are already using online therapy sources, so they might consider using online communities to connect with others who share their experiences and values. As they approach retirement, Millennials could think about how they can engage in social responsibility and community involvement, which can enrich their sense of purpose and enhance emotional well-being.

Gen Zers' progressive views on mental health and their ability to seamlessly integrate technology into their lives set them apart. These individuals have what it takes to advocate for open conversations about emotional wellness and use their digital skills to connect with like-minded individuals. As they age and maintain their commitment to community involvement and mental health awareness, these principles will guide their approach to retirement.

Recognizing how these generational perspectives influence your emotional health during aging and retirement can help you navigate this life stage more effectively. Embrace the unique influences of your generation and adopt strategies that honor your background while prioritizing your emotional wellness. This approach will empower you to create a fulfilling and meaningful retirement experience that resonates with your individual values and aspirations.

ACTION STEPS FOR EMOTIONAL WELLNESS

A fulfilling retirement depends on emotional balance. As discussed, the first step is to self-reflect to understand where you stand on emotional wellness. Maybe you just need to develop a more positive state of mind. Or, it may be that connecting to your cultural community or generational cohort is the therapy you need. And sometimes, outside mental health support would serve you best.

Here are 11 actions you can take to enhance your emotional wellness:

1. **Prioritize Mental and Emotional Health.** Be proactive in supporting your mental and emotional health throughout life and retirement.

2. **Practice Self-Care.** Focus on self-care routines, especially for Generation X, who may be juggling responsibilities for both children and aging parents.

3. **Discuss Anxiety and Depression.** Foster open conversations about mental health by discussing any feelings of anxiety or depression with your doctor and loved ones.

4. **Develop Healthy Stress Management Habits.** Start cultivating effective stress management techniques early in life to prepare for the challenges that may arise in retirement.

5. **Seek Positive Role Models and Mentors.** Look for role models and mentors who can provide valuable insights and guidance for navigating retirement.

6. **Engage in Volunteer Activities.** Find volunteer opportunities that align with your values and passions, allowing you to give back while enhancing your sense of purpose.

7. **Cultivate Friendships.** Focus on building and keeping friendships to create a robust support system that nurtures your emotional well-being.

8. **Pursue Lifelong Learning.** Engage in activities that stimulate your mind and foster personal growth, such as workshops, classes, or reading.

9. **Utilize Technology.** Embrace technology to stay connected with friends and family, helping to combat feelings of isolation.

10. **Incorporate Mindfulness Practices.** Consider integrating mindfulness practices, like meditation, into your daily routine to promote emotional balance.

11. **Participate in Community Events.** Get involved in community events that foster a sense of belonging and fulfillment.

Identify any obstacles you may encounter in taking these actions and seek support if necessary. By applying these practices, you can improve your emotional wellness and create a fulfilling retirement experience that reflects your individuality and goals. Additionally, continue learning about emotional health through books, workshops, and online resources related to retirement planning and wellness. This approach will help you navigate this important stage of life.

CAROL AND GEORGE:
BUILDING THE NEXT CHAPTER TOGETHER

As an African American baby boomer and empty nester with a successful career, I faced an immense challenge with the loss of my husband of 37 years. This loss prompted me to reorganize my life and prioritize what truly mattered as I looked toward the next chapter, eventually leading me to retirement. During this time, seeking support and reflecting on my values became crucial. I acknowledged the importance of family, friends, meaningful relationships, and community to my overall well-being.

With a solid retirement savings plan, assets, and health benefits in place, I created a 10-year aspirational plan to retire by age 70. I focused on finding a location closer to my family and friends while ensuring ease of travel both internationally and throughout the United States.

Serendipitously, I met George, a like-minded African American Baby Boomer who was also navigating significant life changes. He was divorced, had adult children, and lived in another state, which initially led to a long-distance relationship. Although, at the time, retirement wasn't at the forefront of his mind, he values family, friends, and partnership just as much as I do. After rebuilding his life post-divorce, he also had a retirement savings plan and assets to support his future.

Together, we developed a plan that embraced the "century living" concept, setting realistic goals for our future as a couple. We chose to move to a state that suited both our needs, where we could pursue our hobbies and interests while fostering meaningful connections in our new community. It was vital for us to find a place that celebrated diversity and featured professional sports teams, beautiful lakes or beaches, a variety of restaurants and cuisines, and rich cultural activities.

While some family members lived nearby, others were scattered across different parts of the country. We created a welcoming home where our blended family could visit and spend extended time with us. Once we retired, we would also have more time to reconnect with family and friends across the country. By building a life together, we embraced our blended family, nurtured old friendships, formed new connections, and prepared for retirement at age 70. In doing so, we successfully integrated our lives and experiences, ensuring that this latest chapter is filled with meaning, fulfillment, and connection.

CAROL AND GEORGE'S ADVICE

As you contemplate retirement, remember to prioritize self-care and recognize that life is not linear. There will be ups and downs along the way, so be ready to navigate sudden changes to your long-term plan. Embrace resilience and understand that life comprises multiple chapters. By being open to change and seeking support, you can create a fulfilling retirement that reflects your aspirations and values.

PLANNING FOR OVERALL WELL-BEING

Now that you have read this chapter, it is time to put it to work. The Overall Well-Being Worksheet and Action Plan is designed to help you assess your current emotional state and develop strategies for improving your emotional well-being as you prepare for retirement or if you are already retired. Complete the worksheet and then review your responses.

Overall Well-Being Goal Setting and Action Plan

Name: _____

Date: _____

Part I Current Emotional Health Self-Assessment

- Current Emotional State. How would you characterize your current emotional state? (Feel free to choose from options like happy, joyful, anxious, sad, content, overwhelmed, afraid, or provide your own description).

_____
_____
_____

On a scale of 1 to 10, how would you rate your overall emotional well-being right now? (1 = very poor emotional health; 10 = excellent emotional health) _____

Identify Emotions. List the emotions you experience most often.

_____
_____

Recognize Patterns
a) What activities or situations tend to trigger negative emotions?

_____
_____

b) What activities or situations boost your positive emotions?

_____
_____

Part II Emotional Wellness Goals and Action Steps

- Emotional Wellness Goals:

  What are your top three emotional wellness goals for retirement?

  1. _____
  2. _____
  3. _____

Action Steps. Identify specific actions you can take to achieve these goals.

For 1st Goal:

_____
_____
_____

For 2nd Goal:

_____
_____
_____

For 3rd Goal:

_____
_____
_____

Part III Coping Strategies

- Coping Mechanisms:

  What are three effective strategies you can use to manage stress and anxiety in your daily life? (Think about techniques, activities, or practices that have worked for you or that you would like to try.)

  1. _____
  2. _____
  3. _____

Self-Care Activities:
What are some activities or practices that you engage in or would like to incorporate into your routine to enhance your self-care and emotional well-being?

1. _____
2. _____
3. _____

Part IV Support System

- Support Network:
Who are some individuals in your life that you can turn to for emotional support? Please list their names and a brief note on how they can help you.

a) Name: _____
How they can support you: _____
_____

b) Name: _____
How they can support you: _____
_____

c) Name: _____
How they can support you: _____
_____

- Mental Health Resources to Explore:
Reflect on whether seeking professional help, such as therapy or counseling or becoming involved with a support group or other community activities, would be beneficial in supporting your mental and emotional well-being.

Research and consider what resources are available to you, then select those that best fit your needs.

List therapists, counselors, or community organizations offering counseling that you can contact and work with to support your mental and emotional wellness.

1. _____
2. _____
3. _____

List support groups where you could share issues that are challenging you.

1. _____
2. _____
3. _____

Name community groups to become involved with.

1. _____
2. _____
3. _____

Other community activities geared toward emotional wellness you can take part in.

1. _____
2. _____
3. _____

Part V Reflection and Check-In

- Progress Check. Schedule a date to review goals and strategies (suggest every 1–2 months):

Date: _____

Notes or your observations:

_____
_____

Please note: This worksheet is designed to assist you in concentrating on your emotional well-being. Modify and update it as necessary to reflect and track your ongoing journey toward emotional wellness during retirement. If you are experiencing depression or suicidal thoughts, please contact the 988 Suicide & Crisis Lifeline for immediate support.

Action Plan

What are your next steps? What can you commit to? List them below. Be specific about the actions you will take, such as "Join a local retirement community group" or "Start a daily mindfulness practice." Periodically update this action plan.

Date _____

1. _____
2. _____
3. _____
4. _____
5. _____
6. _____

Continue adding as needed...

TAKEAWAYS FROM FOSTERING EMOTIONAL WELLNESS IN RETIREMENT

This chapter discussed the importance of managing emotional wellness in retirement and how it is possible to do so. The guidelines and recommended actions in this chapter put you in charge of your mental and emotional health, provided you keep the following in mind:

Regularly evaluate your emotional well-being and seek to maintain a positive outlook.

Practice mindfulness and meditation to manage stress and engender a sense of calm. Develop other spiritual practices or observances as coping mechanisms.

Practice self-care. Focus on physical activities like exercise and healthy eating.

Engage in meaningful activities by participating in hobbies and activities that bring joy.

Embrace cultural, community, and generational cohort connections. Stay connected to your cultural roots and support networks, using technology to keep in touch with loved ones.

Volunteer and Give Back. Engage in community service to find a sense of purpose.

Seek Professional Support. Don't hesitate to consult mental health professionals when needed, using counseling services for guidance and support.

Set Personal Goals. Establish and pursue goals that align with your values.

CHAPTER TEN

FAMILY, FRIENDS, AND COMMUNITIES: *BUILDING SOCIAL NETWORKS FOR A REWARDING RETIREMENT*

If you feel rooted in your home and family, if you're active in your community, there's nothing more empowering.
—JULIA LOUIS-DREYFUS

Count your age by friends, not years.
—JOHN LENNON

Surround yourself with only people who are going to lift you higher.
—OPRAH WINFREY

The greatness of a community is most accurately measured by the compassionate actions of its members.
— CORETTA SCOTT KING

More than at any other time of life, people depend on family, friends, and community in retirement. For one thing, there is the loss of workplace relationships, and for another, family members, friends, and community connections can offer invaluable guidance, shared experiences, and a sense of belonging. Cultivating and maintaining these relationships prevents social isolation and loneliness and enhances well-being. As you strengthen these bonds and seek new friendships, you ensure that you have people to rely on during this important new chapter of life.

Another way to become more engaged socially is to consider exploring opportunities to contribute to your community. Volunteering your time or skills can be highly rewarding, helping you to create meaningful connections while making a positive impact on others. Engaging in service contributes to you having a sense of purpose and fulfillment as it benefits others. You do not have to feel alone in retirement—others are there to help you thrive if you seek them out.

FAMILY AND FRIENDS

Regular interaction with family and friends significantly reduces social isolation and loneliness, ensuring a more connected and fulfilling life. Many long-time friends can provide a sense of shared history and understanding of one another. Family members can help with practical matters and needs, which will support their loved one in navigating challenges and coping with stressors more effectively. Additionally, family gatherings can involve meaningful interactions with loved ones. Trusted family members and friends also provide a sense of safety and overall happiness and make a difference in someone's life as they contribute to a rewarding retirement and a positive outlook on life.

STRATEGIES TO ENHANCE YOUR FAMILY AND FRIEND SUPPORT NETWORK

As people's lives are more complex, family and long-time friends may be living some distance away. Thus, nurturing these relationships requires some intention and specific care. Luckily, technology and social media can help.

In addition, depending on their life circumstances, there may be times when specific family members are unavailable while some existing friendships have changed. Therefore, those in retirement should continue to be open to cultivating new friendships and connections, which can also take a bit of intention and effort. Yet, all good things are worth fighting for. New friends can also strengthen your social network by helping with introductions to other retirees as well as by encouraging participation in new social activities. Here are some strategies to nurture family and friendship relationships:

Regularly Communicate. Keep in touch through regular phone calls, messages, or video chats. Staying connected helps maintain strong relationships and reinforces your bond. It will help you stay engaged and feel connected.

Stay Connected Through Technology. Create a family newsletter or group chat to share updates, photos, and stories. This keeps everyone in the loop and maintains those valuable connections.

Encourage Openness. Foster an environment where you and your family members and friends feel comfortable sharing their thoughts and feelings. This openness builds trust and intimacy, strengthening these connections. Don't appear to be vulnerable, and share what is really going on with you.

Celebrate Milestones. Mark important events like birthdays and achievements together. Celebrating these occasions together are shared experiences that reinforce your relationships.

Plan Gatherings. Organize regular get-togethers, such as reunions or holiday celebrations. These shared experiences create lasting memories and provide opportunities for deeper, in-person interactions.

Engage in Shared Activities. Take part in leisure activities together. Whether it's going for walks, cooking, or attending events, these activities can enrich the time spent with loved ones.

Offer and Ask for Help with Practical Tasks. Don't hesitate to ask family and friends for help with chores or errands when needed. You're giving others the opportunity to be of service, which makes them feel good. Similarly, help others where you can. It will uplift your spirits.

Include Family or Close Friends in Financial Planning. It's important that others know about your plans, decisions, budgets, investments, and location of legal documents. If you don't have a family member to inform, tell a trusted friend. And be open to their feedback since their insights can be invaluable.

Proactively Offer Support. Take the initiative to help provide emotional support and actively listen. Offer nonjudgement and acceptance. Such actions can strengthen bonds and build deeper relationships.

To cultivate new relationships:

Be Open. While nurturing existing bonds, be open to forming new friendships. Don't be too quick to judge whether someone is right for you.

Expanding your network can bring fresh perspectives, companionship, and possibly new sources of support into your life.

Be Proactive in Widening Your Social Circle. To expand your social circle, actively seek opportunities to meet new people by joining interest-based groups, volunteering, or attending local events. Set small goals like starting conversations or following up with new contacts to foster connections. Engaging openly with others can make forming new relationships easier. Attend community events, workshops, or classes to enhance your social life and create new connections.

Focus on Mutually Supportive Friendships. Look for new friends with similar health and wellness goals so you can support each other in healthy habits, such as exercising, eating well, and staying on top of medical care.

By keeping these points in mind and acting proactively, you can surround yourself with significant relationships that enhance your emotional well-being during retirement. You are not alone in this journey—embrace the connections you have and the new ones you will make.

ORGANIZATIONS AS SOCIAL NETWORKS

In addition to family and friends, community programs, services for older adults, and other organizations can serve as social support nets and provide connection, provided someone reaches out and makes themselves known to them. Many groups offer retirement-related services that help individuals navigate this new phase of life by providing access to resources and programs that reduce isolation and enhance their well-being.

Consider connecting with organizations dedicated to providing services for adults and retirees. Participating in these groups allows you to meet others and share your skills, fostering personal growth and meaningful relationships. By actively engaging in social activities, you may expand your support network, ensuring a more active and rewarding retirement. Embrace the opportunity to seek out and become involved with the appropriate organizations and programs that are there to support you. Some tips on how to connect with retirement-focused organizations are presented next.

JOIN RETIREMENT ASSOCIATIONS

Organizations like AARP, the National Council on Aging, and local senior groups provide resources, discounts, and advocacy for retirees. Also, do the following:

Attend Retirement Planning Workshops. Banks, investment firms, and nonprofit groups often offer free seminars on topics like Social Security, Medicare, and estate planning.

Explore Employer or Union Retirement Groups. If you're retiring from a company or union, check for retiree clubs or financial advisory programs tailored to former employees.

Engage with Professional Networks for Retirees. Many industries have alumni groups or retired professional associations that provide networking and social opportunities.

Chapter 10: Family, Friends, and Communities: Building Social Networks

FIND WHAT SUPPORTIVE RETIREMENT SERVICES ARE AVAILABLE

Learn what services are available to you as a member of your community. Some examples are:

Check with Local Politicians' Offices. Local government officials, such as city council members, usually have lists of resources for older citizens. Make it your business to be aware of all that is available to you, such as:

Use Government and Nonprofit Resources. Programs like Social Security offices, Medicare counseling, and veterans' services can provide financial and health care guidance.

Explore Senior Housing and Assisted Living Options. Whether looking for independent living communities or assisted care, researching options early can help with future planning.

Connect with Transportation and Meal Services. Services like Meals on Wheels and senior transportation programs can help retirees stay independent and engaged.

GET INVOLVED IN THE COMMUNITY

By actively engaging with organizations, community groups, and services, you can access services and connect with others for a fulfilling and well-supported lifestyle. Here are some ways to get involved:

Join Local Senior Centers. These hubs offer activities, classes, and social events specifically for retirees. They are also a useful source of information.

Participate in Wellness and Fitness Programs for Seniors. Many community centers and gyms offer senior-friendly exercise classes, including yoga, swimming, and walking groups.

Take Advantage of Lifelong Learning Programs. Lifelong Learning is the continuous pursuit of knowledge and skills, especially after retirement. It helps retirees stay intellectually engaged, socially connected, and fulfilled. Universities and online platforms offer free or discounted courses for retirees.

Participate in Hobby or Travel Clubs. Many communities have groups for gardening, travel, hiking, or creative arts that welcome retirees.

Volunteer for Local Causes. Schools, hospitals, libraries, and food banks often seek volunteers, offering a wonderful way to stay active and contribute to the community. Also, consider becoming more involved in your community politically through clubs and volunteering with elections or elected officials.

Engage in Faith-Based Retirement Groups. Many churches and religious organizations offer senior-focused programs, including social gatherings and support services.

Attend City or Neighborhood Meetings. Stay involved in local decision-making and community initiatives that affect retirees.

KEY ORGANIZATIONS INVOLVED IN RETIREMENT SERVICES

Listed below are service organizations and resources to look for as you plan for retirement or are retired. Many are involved in advocacy. They offer an extensive array of information and services and provide opportunities for education, engagement, volunteering, and sharing your expertise. Here are some key organizations to become familiar with:

AARP (American Association of Retired Persons). Focuses on health care, financial security, and consumer protection through legislative advocacy, voter education, community service, and member benefits (visit the website: https://www.aarp.org/).

AARP Community Connections. Offers a platform to find and create online and in-person social groups, as well as volunteer opportunities (visit the website: https://www.aarp.org/social-connections/).

National Council on Aging (NCOA). A nonprofit organization that enhances older adults' lives through advocacy for financial security, healthy aging, and social well-being. Aims to improve the lives of vulnerable older adults with programs like Benefits Enrollment Center and Senior Community Service Employment Program (visit the website: https://www.ncoa.org/).

Alliance for Retired Americans. Advocates for Social Security, Medicare, and pension benefits through grassroots activism and educational initiatives (visit the website: https://retiredamericans.org/).

Justice in Aging. Fights senior poverty by securing access to affordable health care and economic security through policy advocacy and legal assistance (visit the website: https://justiceinaging.org/).

National Senior Citizens Law Center (NSCLC). Protects low-income older adults' rights in health care and economic security through policy advocacy and litigation (visit the website: https://nsclcarchives.org/).

Senior Legal Hotlines. Many states offer hotlines providing advice on health care, housing, and consumer protection (visit the website: https://www.seniorlaw.com/senior-legal-hotlines/).

Medicare Rights Center. Helps people navigate Medicare with counseling, education, and policy advocacy (visit the website: https://www.medicarerights.org/).

Meals on Wheels. This program delivers meals to seniors, helping to combat hunger and malnutrition while also providing opportunities for social interaction through friendly visits (visit the website: https://www.mealsonwheelsamerica.org/).

HealthFinder.gov. A resource for seniors to find a range of health-related services and information tailored for older adults, focusing on preventive care and wellness resources (visit the website: https://odphp.health.gov/myhealthfinder).

Consumer Financial Protection Bureau (CFPB)—Office for Older Americans: Protects older adults from financial fraud and exploitation through education and advocacy (visit the website: https://www.consumerfinance.gov/consumer-tools/educator-tools/resources-for-older-adults/).

Local Senior Centers. These facilities provide programs, services, and activities for adults 50 and older, including social engagement, health programs, and educational opportunities. To find local centers, contact government agencies like your local Department of Aging or Parks and Recreation.

SERVICE ORGANIZATIONS

Community service organizations and support agencies are essential in delivering helpful services that improve the lives of retirees. They offer vital information, resources, and assistance to support healthy, active, and engaged living. In addition to the key organizations mentioned earlier, these service providers include:

COUNSELING AND SUPPORT SERVICES

Community organizations and other resources offer counseling, support groups, and other services to help retirees navigate the emotional aspects of retirement or other life transitions.

COUNSELING

For counseling or therapy seek out resources such as:

Licensed Therapists and Counselors. Many therapists and counselors specialize in mental health issues that affect retirees. Websites like Psychology Today enable you to search for therapists by specialty and location, making it easier for retirees to find the support they need. (Visit the Psychology Today Therapist Finder: https://www.psychologytoday.com/us/therapists).

Teletherapy services. Talkspace and BetterHelp provide remote counseling options that are accessible from home. These platforms are especially helpful for retirees who face mobility or transportation challenges. You can learn more about their services (visit the website for Talkspace; https://www.talkspace.com/ and the website for BetterHelp: https://www.betterhelp.com).

Medicare. Covers mental health services, including counseling and therapy sessions. Check eligibility and coverage details (visit the website: https://www.medicare.gov/).

Local Senior Centers. Often provide counseling services, support groups, and social activities for older adults. Contact your local senior center for available services.

MENTAL HEALTH AND PEER SUPPORT GROUPS

In addition to local resources, these organizations can point you in the right direction when seeking a support group:

Alzheimer's Association Support Groups. Provides support groups for individuals with Alzheimer's and their caregivers (visit the website: https://www.alz.org/help-support/community/support-groups).

GriefShare. Provides support groups for individuals experiencing grief and loss (visit the website: https://www.griefshare.org/).

Meetup. A platform for finding and creating groups based on interests and activities, helping older adults meet new people and stay socially active (visit the website: https://www.meetup.com/).

Other Support Groups. Some senior service and community organizations offer support groups for retirees. Talking with others who understand your experience can help reduce stress, anxiety, and isolation. Find retirement groups online or through AARP and NCOA. You can also seek information from HealthGuide.org (visit the website: https://www.helpguide.org/aging/healthy-aging/adjusting-to-retirement).

HOTLINES AND HELPLINES

These are relevant emergency support hotlines:

Friendship Line. A crisis intervention hotline and a warmline for non-emergency emotional support, designed specifically for older adults (visit the website: https://www.ioaging.org/services/friendship-line/).

988 Suicide and Crisis Line. Provides 24/7 free and confidential support for people in distress, suicide prevention, and crisis resources. Phone: 1-800-273-8255 (visit the website: https://988lifeline.org/?utm_source=google&utm_medium=web&utm_campaign=onebox).

SAMHSA's National Helpline. A free, confidential, 24/7, 365-day-a-year treatment referral and information service for individuals and families facing mental and/or substance use disorders. Phone: 1-800-662-HELP (4357) (visit the website: https://www.samhsa.gov/find-help/helplines/national-helpline).

TRANSPORTATION SERVICES

Some communities have transportation services specifically designed for older adults, ensuring they have access to essential services and can take part in community activities. Resources include:

Senior Discounts. Many cities offer discounted fares for seniors on public buses, subways, and trains. Check with your local transit authority.

Paratransit Services. Door-to-door transportation for individuals with disabilities or those unable to use regular public transit. Check your local resources.

Volunteer Driver Programs. Volunteers provide rides for older adults to medical appointments, grocery shopping, and other errands. An example is the Community Transportation Association of America (visit the website: https://ctaa.org/).

Uber and Lyft. Ride-sharing apps offer convenient transportation options. Some services have special programs for seniors, such as Lyft's "Grocery Access Program" and Uber's "Uber Health."

GoGoGrandparent. A service that connects seniors to ride-sharing services without the need for a smartphone (visit the website: https://gogograndparent.com/)

Area Agencies on Aging (AAA). These agencies often provide information and access to transportation services.

CHURCHES AND RELIGIOUS INSTITUTIONS

Many religious organizations offer pastoral counseling and support groups for retirees. Inquire with local churches or religious institutions about available support services.

CULTURAL AND RECREATIONAL SERVICES OR ACTIVITIES

Taking part in cultural, community, and recreational events is a fantastic way for retirees to stay active, engaged, and connected where they live. Community groups often organize cultural events and recreational activities that retirees can enjoy, fostering a sense of belonging in a community.

CULTURAL EVENTS

Many cities and towns have a vibrant cultural scene. Look for:

Local Theater and Performing Arts. Many theaters offer matinee performances, discounted tickets for seniors, and special programs.

Museums and Historical Societies. Volunteer as docents, tour guides, or researchers. Many museums offer free or discounted admission for retirees and host events tailored for them. Check local museum websites for programs.

Music and Concerts. Attend local concerts, symphony performances, and music festivals. Some venues offer special pricing for seniors and free events. Contact local concert halls or symphonies for senior discounts and event schedules.

Book Clubs and Literary Events. Join book clubs, author readings, and literary discussions at local libraries and bookstores. Visit your local library or bookstore for information on book clubs and events.

Cultural Festivals. Take part in cultural festivals celebrating art, music, food, and traditions from around the world. Check community event calendars for upcoming festivals.

Sports and Games. Take part in sports like golf, tennis, pickleball, and bowling. Many facilities offer leagues and groups for older adults. Contact local sports clubs and recreational centers for senior leagues and events.

Travel and Day Trips. Join travel groups or clubs that organize day trips and excursions to interesting destinations.

Eventbrite. Lists events happening in your area, including cultural festivals, classes, and workshops (visit the website: https://www.eventbrite.com/).

HOBBY AND INTEREST GROUPS

Community organizations may host clubs or groups centered around shared hobbies or interests. Participating provides retirees with the chance to connect with like-minded individuals. Resources include:

Art and Creative Skills. MasterClass Offers online classes taught by renowned experts in various fields, including arts, writing, cooking, and more (visit the website: https://www.masterclass.com/).

Sierra Club. Engage in local conservation efforts and advocacy as well as travel (visit the website: https://www.sierraclub.org/).

LIFELONG LEARNING PROGRAMS AND EDUCATION

Staying brain-healthy and engaged requires challenging yourself to learn new skills. Here is a list of organizations that offer workshops and classes:

Library Programs. Public libraries offer educational programs, workshops, book clubs, and technology training for older adults. Visit local library websites for more information.

Road Scholar Service Learning. Road Scholar offers educational travel and volunteer programs for older adults in fields like education, conservation, and community development (visit the website: https://www.roadscholar.org/).

Community Colleges and Universities. Many community colleges offer reduced tuition for seniors and a variety of courses and workshops. Check local community colleges for senior programs.

Audit University Classes. Some universities allow seniors to audit classes for free or at a reduced cost. Contact local universities for details on auditing policies.

Language Learning. Learning a new language has cognitive benefits and helps keep minds active. Resources include **Duolingo**, a free app offering language courses (visit the website: https://www.duolingo.com/); **Rosetta Stone**, which provides language learning software and online courses (visit the website: https://www.rosettastone.com/); and Memrise offers virtual study groups and an immersive language practice (visit the website: https://www.memrise.com/).

VOLUNTEER WORK OPPORTUNITIES

Retirement can be a wonderful time to give back to the community and the world. Many organizations welcome volunteers, and retirees can find fulfillment by contributing their time and skills to various causes. Resources include:

VolunteerMatch. An online platform that connects volunteers with local and virtual opportunities based on interests and skills (visit the website: https://www.volunteermatch.org/).

RSVP (Retired and Senior Volunteer Program), part of AmeriCorps Seniors, is a national volunteer program that connects people aged 55 and older with meaningful volunteer opportunities in their communities (visit the website: https://www.americorps.gov/serve/americorps-seniors/americorps-seniors-rsvp).

Big Brothers Big Sisters. Mentor young people to help them achieve their potential (visit the website: https://www.bbbs.org/).

Reading Partners. Help children improve their reading skills (visit the website: https://readingpartners.org/).

Hospitals and Clinics. Volunteer in various roles such as greeters, guides, or administrative support.

Museums. Local museums may offer volunteer opportunities, which may include supporting events, staffing the store, or serving as a docent. Docents share their knowledge and enthusiasm for a museum's collection (e.g., art, antiquities, or natural history) with visitors.

American Red Cross. Help with blood drives, disaster response, and more (visit the website: https://www.redcross.org/).

National and State Parks. Take part in trail maintenance, guided tours, and conservation projects (visit the website: https://www.nps.gov/index.htm).

Animal Shelters and Rescues. Assist with animal care, adoption events, and fundraising. Contact your local shelters and rescues.

Therapy Animal Programs. Train pets to provide comfort to hospital patients and nursing home residents. Contact local offices.

Chapter 10: Family, Friends, and Communities: Building Social Networks

VOLUNTEERING ABROAD

International volunteering offers older adults the chance to use their skills and experience to make a difference while exploring new cultures and building new social connections. Here are some organizations and opportunities for adults looking to volunteer internationally. Resources include:

Global Volunteers. Provides short-term and long-term volunteer opportunities in various countries, focusing on community development, education, health care, and more (visit the website: https://global-volunteers.org/).

Projects Abroad. Offers a range of volunteer programs worldwide, including community development, conservation, teaching, and health care. They have special programs for older volunteers (visit the website: https://www.projects-abroad.org/).

Peace Corps Response. Offers short-term, high-impact assignments for experienced professionals. Opportunities are available in various fields, including education, health, and community development (visit the website: https://www.peacecorps.gov/ways-to-serve/serve-with-us/peace-corps-response/).

Cross-Cultural Solutions (CCS). CCS offers volunteer opportunities that focus on education, health care, and community development. They have specific programs and support for older adult volunteers (visit the website: https://www.volunteerforever.com/program/cross-cultural-solutions/).

IVHQ (International Volunteer HQ). IVHQ offers affordable volunteer programs in over 40 destinations. They have a wide range of projects, including those suitable for older adults in teaching, conservation, and health care (visit the website: https://www.volunteerhq.org/destinations/).

Earthwatch Institute. Provides opportunities to join scientific research projects around the world, focusing on environmental conservation and sustainability (visit the website: https://earthwatch.org/).

Habitat for Humanity Global Village. Habitat for Humanity's Global Village program offers opportunities to build homes and improve communities in various countries. They welcome volunteers of all ages, including older adults (visit the website: https://www.habitat.org/volunteer/travel-and-build/global-village).

DRAWING UPON FAITH AND SPIRITUALITY FOR SUPPORT

As you approach retirement, consider how your spiritual practice or religion might support you. Beyond observance, participation in your spiritual- or faith-based community can offer you social connection, support your emotional well-being, and instill a strong sense of purpose in your life. Such communities not only offer essential social support but also provide opportunities for personal and spiritual growth.

Whether you are already active in your faith community, contemplating more involvement with it, or are considering joining one, know that the connections you form there can enrich your life and contribute to your overall well-being. This section will help you explore effective ways to create supportive networks and highlight various opportunities for engagement within your chosen communities. By actively taking part, you can enhance your retirement experience and cultivate a meaningful, purpose-driven life.

Chapter 10: Family, Friends, and Communities: Building Social Networks

BECOMING ACTIVELY INVOLVED IN YOUR FAITH COMMUNITY

As discussed in Chapter Nine, faith and spirituality can be important to emotional wellness and overall well-being in retirement. When individuals are already involved in a faith community or decide that spirituality should be an important aspect of their retirement life, retirement can be a time of renewed commitment to their retirement lives.

A very important aspect of spiritual life is to join with like-minded others rather than practice by yourself, which can reinforce feelings of isolation. If you already belong to a community, become more involved. Regular attendance can enrich your spirit and provide a strong sense of community, offering comfort, inspiration, and purpose during retirement.

Participate in worship or study groups, join committees, or stay for coffee after services. Be open to allowing people in the community to get to know you. In this way, you will form bonds with other members and feel a true sense of belonging.

Another way to participate more fully and benefit from having shared experiences with other members is to participate in **retreats or workshops.** Usually, these events are dedicated to personal development, mindfulness, spirituality, and faith, so not only do such experiences result in valuable insights and enhance your spiritual practice, but they usually create closeness among the people participating, which can often form strong bonds.

A powerful way to get to know community members is to **e**ngage in **outreach or service work** together that aligns with community values. Helping others can create a strong sense of shared purpose and satisfaction. Working side-by-side is an easy way to get to know others.

JOINING A FAITH COMMUNITY

If you do not yet belong to a spiritual or faith-based community, consider seeking out and joining a local religious or faith-based organization that aligns with you. Use this step-by-step guide to find the right group for you.

1. **Reflect on Your Spiritual and Social Needs.** Ask yourself:

    Do I want a community that aligns with my lifelong beliefs, or am I open to exploring?

    Am I looking for worship, social activities, or volunteer opportunities?

    Do I prefer a large, structured group or a smaller, intimate setting?

2. **Research Local Faith Communities.** The following can help:

    Use online directories—websites like FaithStreet or ChurchFinder can help find nearby places of worship.

    Google and social media—search for local churches, temples, mosques, or synagogues. Many have websites with service times, events, and missions.

    Community bulletin boards at senior centers, libraries, and local newspapers for faith-based gatherings.

3. **Visit and Experience Different Communities.** Here are some suggestions:

    Attend a service, Bible study, or meditation session to get a feel for the atmosphere.

    Speak with leaders or members to learn about their beliefs, activities, and outreach programs.

    Participate in coffee hours or social gatherings to meet people informally.

4. **Look for Senior-Friendly Activities.** Examples include:

    Retiree or senior ministries—many faith communities offer groups specifically for older adults.

    Volunteer opportunities—faith-based charities and service projects can help you stay active.

    Educational and social programs—Bible studies, book clubs, or discussion groups tailored for retirees.

5. **Seek Recommendations.** Talk to others to get ideas, for example:

    Ask friends, family, or neighbors if they belong to a welcoming faith community.

    Senior groups or assisted living centers often have partnerships with local religious organizations.

6. **Consider Online or Hybrid Communities.** Seek out the following:

    If mobility is a concern, explore virtual faith communities that offer live-streamed services and discussion groups.

    Many churches and spiritual centers have Facebook groups or Zoom study groups.

7. **Trust Your Instincts.** Find a place where you feel comfortable, valued, and spiritually fulfilled. If one community doesn't feel right for you, don't hesitate to explore other options. Your comfort and happiness are what's most important in finding the right fit.

HOW TO SEEK OUT SOCIAL SUPPORT THAT CONNECTS WITH YOU

The availability of social support networks can vary greatly for individuals with diverse racial, ethnic, and cultural backgrounds or lifestyles, such as members of the LGBTQ+ community or those living with disabilities. To foster meaningful connections that improve overall well-being in retirement, it is important for members of such groups to seek out resources tailored to their specific needs. Somewhat similarly, it is also valuable to take into account generational differences.

Finding and participating in your community's social support networks can be highly beneficial in retirement, here are some strategies tailored to your unique experiences:

- **Embrace Your Identity.** Celebrate your cultural background and experiences. Sharing your story can help others relate to you and foster deeper connections.

- **Seek Culturally Appropriate Services.** Retirement services should be culturally competent, including language accessibility, culturally relevant materials, and an understanding of cultural norms.

- **Seek Inclusive Communities.** Look for organizations and groups that prioritize diversity and inclusion. Joining multicultural or intersectional community organizations can help you connect with individuals who share similar values and experiences.

Be Proactive in Seeking Social Support That Reflects You. Don't hesitate to reach out to your community when you need help (visit website https://www.phnxman.com/embracing-change-andtransition-strategies-for-adapting-to-lifes-challenges/. Taking the initiative can reinforce your social ties. Building lasting connections may take time, but your resilience and perseverance will pay off.

- **Join Support Groups.** Consider taking part in support groups that cater to your specific identity or experiences, whether related to race, gender, sexual orientation, or disability. These groups provide understanding and connection.

- **Participate in Cultural Events.** Attend local cultural festivals, workshops, and community gatherings. See them as opportunities to meet new people who share similar traditions or backgrounds.

- **Promote Open Dialogue.** Encourage open conversations about experiences and feelings among your networks. Create a safe space for sharing that fosters mutual understanding and support.

- **Connect Across Generations.** Seek intergenerational opportunities that allow you to learn from different age groups. This can enrich your perspective and expand your support network.

- **Utilize Online Platforms.** Use social media and online forums to connect with others who share your background or interests. Online communities can serve as valuable support networks and may lead to offline connections.

- **Volunteer and Give Back.** Engage in community service or advocacy work that resonates with you. Volunteering allows you to meet like-minded individuals while making a positive impact in your community.

These strategies can be employed by anyone seeking the resources and support of groups and organizations that are geared to their specific concerns, which could include women, caregivers, and low-income individuals. By employing these strategies, it is possible to set up a dynamic social support network that acknowledges and respects your identity while promoting your overall well-being. It is important to recognize that you have the capability to cultivate meaningful connections that contribute positively to your life and empower you within your community.

DEBORAH AND SUE:
NAVIGATING RETIREMENT TOGETHER

Deborah and Sue are a married same-sex couple. Here, they share their retirement planning experience.

I'm Deborah, a Gen Xer in my late fifties. I've dedicated much of my life to academia, holding significant leadership roles that demanded my full attention and energy while focusing on formulating policies to benefit students and faculty. Retirement was always a distant thought for me. While I took part in employer-sponsored retirement plans, my primary concern has often been the possibility of falling ill post-retirement. Growing up in a multigenerational household, I witnessed family members face health challenges after retiring, which instilled a deep-seated apprehension about my future. Nevertheless, I am optimistic. I envision my retirement as a time for new opportunities—engaging in political activities, consulting, and even writing novels.

And I'm Sue, a Baby Boomer and Deborah's partner. Ten years ago, at age 53, I received a cancer diagnosis that served as a profound wake-up call. Thankfully, I'm now in good health, but that experience reshaped my outlook on life and work. Having led nonprofit organizations throughout my career, I realized there was much more to life than professional achievement, which encouraged me to step away from full-time employment and consider how to spend my time meaningfully.

Deborah's and my move to a new state and community in 2019 meant leaving behind a well-established social network. Due to the challenges of the COVID-19 pandemic, building new connections took time. However, I found a sense of belonging by joining a local online community that resonated with my beliefs, and I'm actively involved with them today. I've also embraced an eco-conscious lifestyle, focusing on recycling, conserving energy, and supporting sustainable initiatives. As I manage our household, I ensure that Deborah can concentrate on her demanding job without added worries. However, we both recognize that when Deborah retires, we'll need to renegotiate our household responsibilities.

As we've navigated this journey together, we've taken proactive steps to secure our future. We've completed our wills and estate plans and engaged in open discussions with our niece and her husband about our estate and long-term care preferences. Furthermore, we've set up advance directives to outline our medical treatment preferences should we ever be unable to communicate our decisions. These measures provide us with peace of mind, knowing that our wishes will be respected.

DEBORAH AND SUE'S ADVICE

We both want to emphasize the importance of investing time in your relationship and having open discussions about your mutual retirement goals. Honest communication about your aspirations ensures that both partners are aligned and can support one another effectively. Additionally, finding love in your life—people to cherish and who cherish you back—is vital for transitioning into this next chapter with confidence and joy.

As you reflect on your retirement journey, it's important to acknowledge the crucial role that relationships and a strong social network play in enhancing your experience—something Deborah and Sue exemplify through their proactive efforts.

GENERATIONAL COHORTS AND SOCIAL SUPPORT

Understanding the differences among generational cohorts—Baby Boomer, Gen X, Millennial, and Gen Z—can help you better understand other generations, enabling you to connect to those who are part of them. Your own cohort will be most comfortable for you, yet connections with individuals in other cohorts can provide new insights and an expanded community of friends and social support.

In terms of knowing how to reach out, here are some important insights and actionable strategies to consider.

Addressing Social Isolation & Loneliness. If you identify as a Baby Boomer, you may experience feeling more isolated due to the change in your work identity and social interactions. Remember, you have valuable relationship-building skills that can help you connect with new people. Consider creating or joining local Meetup groups or clubs that align with your interests, which can address loneliness and foster meaningful connections.

Overcoming Technology Barriers. If you're from an older generation, using online tools may feel daunting. Don't hesitate to reach out to individuals who are part of younger generations—like Millennials and Gen Zers—who thrive on virtual interactions. Join intergenerational training sessions to build your technology skills and comfort with online communities.

Navigating Changing Family Structures. With rising singlehood and more people living alone, fewer family caregivers may be available to support aging relatives. This makes it essential to establish external support networks. Look for community programs designed to connect retirees with volunteers who can provide companionship and assistance.

Addressing Mobility and Health Issues. As people live longer, the need for ongoing social and health care support becomes more important. Prioritize finding support networks that offer mental health resources, transportation options, and home-visiting programs, especially if mobility is a concern for you or someone close.

Finding Like-Minded Communities. If you are a Baby Boomer, you might find it challenging to find communities that align with your diverse interests and values. Seek tailored activities and intergenerational events that promote interaction among different age groups, allowing you to share experiences and perspectives.

Tackling Financial Insecurity. Both Baby Boomers and Gen Xers may be concerned about insufficient retirement savings, while Millennials and Gen Zers face their own economic hurdles, like student debt. Take advantage of financial literacy workshops to boost your understanding of budgeting and retirement planning, ensuring you're equipped to navigate your financial future confidently.

Embracing Change. Transitioning into new social structures can be difficult, especially for some Boomers who may resist stepping out of their comfort zones. Consider engaging in storytelling or experience-sharing sessions with peers to facilitate connection and ease this transition.

By recognizing these generationally distinct challenges and embracing the strengths each cohort brings, you can build a supportive social network that enhances your emotional wellness in retirement. Remember, a collaborative approach that fosters understanding and connection will empower you to navigate the complexities of aging and retirement with confidence and fulfillment. Take these insights to heart, and actively work on creating a rich, supportive environment in this new phase of your life.

CONSTRUCTING YOUR SOCIAL SUPPORT ACTION PLAN

To begin shaping your social network, utilize the worksheet below to create a personalized plan. Start by listing the individuals and groups that support you currently and clearly define your level of engagement with each. Next, look for community organizations and spiritual networks that resonate with your beliefs, as these connections can significantly enrich your social well-being.

While Deborah and Sue may not have used a formal worksheet, their approach to building connections and nurturing relationships embodies the essence of creating a personalized support system. As you face potential challenges in maintaining your networks, remember that retirement offers a unique opportunity to strengthen these connections. Embrace this time to cultivate meaningful relationships and engage in activities that reflect your values and interests. By taking proactive steps now, you will lay the groundwork for a fulfilling and supportive retirement, empowering you to thrive in this exciting new chapter of your life.

Use the Social Network for Retirement Worksheet to formalize your current support system and how you plan to strengthen your social network during retirement. This will help ensure you have the emotional support you need and alert you when it's time to work on building more.

Social Network for Retirement Worksheet

Family Support
Family Member _____

    Type of Support Needed
    _____

    Current Level of Engagement
    _____

    Plan to Strengthen Connection
    _____

Keep expanding the range of family support resources

Friend Support
Friend's Name _____

    Type of Support Needed
    _____

    Current Level of Engagement
    _____

    Plan to Strengthen Connection
    _____

Keep expanding the range of friend support resources

Organizational Support
Organization/Group _____

    Type of Support/Services Offered
    _____

    Current Level of Engagement
    _____

Plan to Increase Involvement
_____

Keep expanding the range of organization/group support resources

Community Programs and Services
Program/ Service _____

Type of Support Provided
_____

Current Level of Engagement
_____

Plan to Participate
_____

Keep expanding the range of community support resources

Spirituality and Faith Community Support
Faith Community _____

Type of Support Offered
_____

Current Level of Engagement
_____

Plan to Get Involved
_____

Keep expanding the range of Spirituality and Faith Community Support

Other Support Systems
Support System _____

Type of Support Provided
_____

Current Level of Engagement
_____

Plan to Utilize
_____

Keep expanding the range of supportive resources

Multicultural Considerations
Cultural Group _____

Support Opportunities
_____

Current Level of Engagement
_____

Plan to Connect
_____

Keep expanding the range of multicultural supportive resources

Generational Considerations
Generational Cohort _____

Support Opportunities
_____

Current Level of Engagement
_____

Plan to Connect
_____

Continue broadening generational support resources

REFLECTION QUESTIONS

Now that you've completed the worksheet, some thoughts and ideas about social support systems may have arisen. With these in mind, answer the following questions:

1. What types of support do you feel are missing from your current network?
2. What specific actions can you take to increase your engagement with family and friends?
3. Which community programs or organizations have you found helpful in the past, and how can you reconnect with them?
4. Are there any new groups, clubs, or classes that align with your interests that you'd like to explore?

Next, use this worksheet to keep track of your social support network and ensure you are proactively building a fulfilling retirement filled with meaningful connections.

ACTION PLAN FOR BUILDING A SOCIAL SUPPORT NETWORK

Use this worksheet to plan the steps needed to reinforce and broaden your social support network, one that is filled with meaningful connections.

1. Identify Key Individuals
List family members, friends, or colleagues who are important to you. Note their relationship to you and how they support you.

Name _____

Relationship _____

Level of Engagement *(Daily/Weekly/Monthly)*

_____

Add additional names as needed.

2. Community Groups and Organizations

Identify local clubs, groups, or organizations that align with your interests or values. How might these communities enhance your social support?

Name _____

Type *(e.g., hobby, spiritual, advocacy)*

_____

Level of Engagement *(How often do you participate?)*

_____

Add additional community groups or organizations as needed.

3. New Connections

Consider people you would like to connect with, either through networking events, workshops, or social gatherings. What steps can you take to initiate these connections?

Potential Connection

_____

How to Reach Out

_____

Follow-Up Date

_____

Add additional connections as needed.

4. Challenges and Solutions

Reflect on any potential challenges you might face in maintaining your social support network. What strategies can you employ to overcome these challenges?

Challenge
_____

Solution/Strategy
_____

Add additional challenges and solutions as needed.

5. Goals for Engagement
Set specific goals for how you would like to engage with your network. Consider activities or events you want to participate in.

Engagement Goal
_____

Timeline *(Short-Term/Long-Term)*
_____

Add additional goals as needed.

By taking the time to fill out this worksheet, you are actively shaping your social support network to enhance your retirement experience. Remember, the journey to a fulfilling retirement is about cultivating meaningful connections and embracing every opportunity for growth and joy.

Your Action Plan Goals
Short-Term Goals: Identify immediate steps you can take over the next month to enhance your social network.

1. _____
2. _____
3. _____
4. _____
5. _____

Long-Term Goals: Outline a plan for how to continue building and supporting these connections over the next year.

Chapter 10: Family, Friends, and Communities: Building Social Networks

1. _____
2. _____
3. _____
4. _____
5. _____

TAKEAWAYS FROM FAMILY, FRIENDS, AND COMMUNITIES

Social connections are just as important as financial security in retirement. Here is a summary of key points about building social support networks in retirement:

Start Early and Be Proactive. Nurturing existing friendships and family relationships while building a strong support system takes time, so start developing friendships and community ties before retirement.

Embrace technology for connection. Use social media, video calls, and online groups to support relationships, especially if loved ones live far away.

Explore apps like Meetup, Nextdoor, or Stitch (for seniors) to find like-minded individuals.

Engage in hobbies, clubs, or volunteer work that can transition into post-retirement activities.

Investigate community and faith-based organizations to

join as a way to expand your social support network and meet new people.

Volunteering, mentoring, or teaching can keep you socially connected and fulfilled. Similarly, being active in local charities, religious groups, or advocacy organizations helps maintain a strong support network.

Find culturally supportive ways to connect to others.

Diversify your social circles. Maintain a mix of friendships across different generations for varied perspectives and companionship.

Prioritize Health & Mobility.

Staying physically and mentally active ensures you can take part in social activities.

Join fitness groups, wellness retreats, or mental health support communities to stay engaged.

Widen your social support network purposefully and with a plan.

CHAPTER ELEVEN

RETIREMENT LIVING:
OPTIONS FOR EVERY LIFESTYLE

Home is where our story begins.
—ANNIE DANIELSON

Wherever you choose to land, make it a place where your heart feels at home and your spirit can roam.
—UNKNOWN

Retirement is not just about leaving work behind—it's about finding a place where you want to start your new journey.
—UNKNOWN

Collect moments, not things.
—UNKNOWN

Where will you live in the next phase of your life? Will you remain in your current residence, transition to a 55+ community, or live with friends or relatives? Will you relocate to another city, state, or country, or consider alternative options such as residing on a cruise ship? Planning future living arrangements is essential.

As you plan for retirement, it's important to explore a variety of living options tailored to your evolving needs. Being fully informed not only helps you to make decisions about where you will live when you retire but will arm you with the knowledge you need as your requirements evolve.

Someone might be thinking about moving to a different city, state, or country that better suits your retirement goals. Alternatively, you may want to age in place, making modifications to your current home for greater accessibility, or stay in your current community, only downsizing to a more manageable space. In both cases—whether moving or staying—evaluate whether that location is aging-friendly.

Another choice is to move to a retirement community designed specifically for older adults, including 55+ communities that offer amenities and services catering to your lifestyle. Cohousing is also worth considering, as these intentional communities provide a supportive environment where neighbors collaborate and share resources while supporting their own private homes. And there are more options for housing than you might think. Some move in with relatives or roommates, others choose tiny home living or even living onboard cruise ships.

Each of these choices requires careful planning, so it is essential to weigh your options thoughtfully. Let's explore these possibilities together to help you find the best fit for your retirement journey. The foremost priority is to select an aging-friendly, livable community that supports your lifestyle and well-being.

AGING-FRIENDLY LOCATIONS

The ideal retirement location considers its aging citizens, so designs to accommodate their needs are in place, with amenities and services suited for older individuals. These communities focus on promoting independence through specific features and support systems.

Living in an aging-friendly location significantly enhances the quality of life because the essential resources for healthy aging are in place. These environments foster relationships, encourage physical activity, and offer easy access to crucial services.

Chapter 11: Retirement Living: Options for Every Lifestyle

WHAT IS LIVABILITY?

Livability refers to how well a locality meets the needs of its residents, regardless of age. A livable community enhances residents' comfort and quality of life through access to health care, green spaces, such as parks and recreational areas, and social opportunities that facilitate meaningful engagement. Livability contributes to a fulfilling retirement experience that allows retired individuals to engage meaningfully with the world around them.

It is strongly advised that when evaluating where to live, you think about whether the location is both aging-friendly and livable.

WHAT DOES AN AGING-FRIENDLY, LIVEABLE LOCALE LOOK LIKE?

While many facing retirement might be more focused on the housing options before them—staying in their homes, cohousing, or moving to a 55+ or assisted living community—it is critical to take a hard look at the locales where those options are located. For example, a 55+ community in a beautiful location might be great, but if the area where it is located doesn't have enough doctors or a hospital, that could prove to be a problem. The same holds for where they live now.

Evaluating whether a location is livable and aging-friendly can help you make informed decisions about the best place to live and consider relocating if your current town no longer suits you. Just don't consider a move to a new location without evaluating if it is aging-friendly and livable.

As you assess where you want to live in retirement, it's important to figure out how well it supports your overall well-being and accommodates your needs for aging in place. A valuable resource for evaluating community livability is the AARP Public Policy Institute's Livability

Index: Great Neighborhoods for All Ages. This interactive tool assesses the quality of life across essential dimensions, including housing, transportation, neighborhood features, environment, health, opportunity, and civic engagement, making it easy for you to compare different communities. This and other resources can be found on AARP's website (visit https://livabilityindex.aarp.org).

As you evaluate your community, consider the World Health Organization's (WHO) criteria for Age-friendly Cities and Communities (World Health Organization, 2007). Look for features such as:

- **Outdoor Spaces and Buildings.** Access to parks and recreational facilities enhances your quality of life.
- **Safe and Affordable Transportation.** Various transportation options and pedestrian safety measures are crucial for mobility.
- **Affordable and Accessible Housing.** Seek diverse housing options that accommodate various needs and are near public transit.
- **Social Participation Opportunities.** Check for cultural organizations and programs that encourage engagement.
- **Respect and Social Inclusion.** Communities that support multigenerational interactions and caregiver assistance help combat isolation.
- **Civic Participation and Employment.** Opportunities for volunteering and continued learning enhance your sense of purpose.
- **Communication and Information.** Access to technology that connects you with your community and family is essential, as is clear, accessible information.
- **Community Support and Health Services.** Look for wellness programs and proximity to health care facilities, along with access to nutritious food.

By using the resources provided and understanding what constitutes an age-friendly and livable community, you can make informed decisions about your retirement location and make sure that it aligns with your goals for a vibrant and fulfilling future.

IDENTIFY YOUR PERSONAL PREFERENCES AND NEEDS

In addition to livability and age-friendliness, personal preferences regarding where you live factor in. Remember David? He and his wife decided to move to a warmer climate in search of a location where they could be nearer to friends and establish a vibrant social network. They aimed to build a foundation for new connections in their new community. Patricia, on the other hand, planned to age in place, anticipating making some modifications to her home to ensure it remained comfortable and accessible as she embraced this chapter of her life.

Here are some important suggestions to guide your journey:

- **Understand Your Unique Needs.** Take time to reflect on what truly matters to you. If you're single or child-free, you may prioritize social connections and a strong sense of community. Consider environments that foster friendships, cultural and other activities, and support networks to fill familial voids.
- **Accessibility Is Essential.** If you have a disability, seek out a community that caters to your specific needs. Look for inclusive transportation options and services.
- **Cultural Relevance.** Finding a community that honors and respects your cultural background is vital. Explore places that offer diverse dining options, cultural activities, and an inclusive environment, allowing you to feel accepted and valued.
- **Consider Affordability.** If finances are a concern, research retirement locations that provide affordable living arrangements and access to supportive services. Choosing a city or town with a less-expensive standard of living or within your budget can significantly reduce stress and enhance your quality of life.
- **Engagement and Connection.** Seek out areas that encourage social interaction and participation in various activities, for example,

by sponsoring events so that they are free. Building relationships and engaging in community events can substantially improve your emotional well-being and help you feel more at home.

Meeting Cultural and Generational Needs. As you plan your retirement living arrangements, it's essential to recognize the diversity of perspectives that influence what will work best for you. Whether you identify as part of a diverse demographic, are a member of the LGBTQ+ community, are living with disabilities, or are single or child-free, your unique background and situation will shape your choices. Our cities, towns, and communities are becoming increasingly diverse, and this dynamic is something to embrace when considering where you want to live during retirement.

By considering these factors and what's important to you, you can create a retirement experience that is not only comfortable but also enriching. Remember, you deserve a fulfilling retirement that celebrates who you are—regardless of your background—and enhances your overall well-being.

POINTS FOR EVALUATING LIVING ENVIRONMENTS

As individuals plan for retirement, they had best consider how their home environment—or the one they hope to move to—will support them in the long term. Is the space safe, comfortable, and adaptable to their evolving needs? Among key features to consider are the number of steps to access entryways and whether there are internal stairways, bathrooms are safe and accessible, and doors are wide enough to accommodate mobility aids.

This section will give you a foundation of what to look for as those facing retirement evaluate their housing options. It may be that someone can modify or redesign their home for aging-in-place, or it may be better for them to move.

WHAT IS UNIVERSAL DESIGN?

As you plan for your retirement, consider how the layout of your home can support your independence as you age. Universal Design principles mean the end users of a product, building, or environment can be as broad and diverse a population as possible, ensuring that living spaces are adaptable and accessible for all ages and abilities. Universal Design enhances retirement quality of life while helping maintain independence.

Universal design principles ensure:

- **Adaptable Living Spaces.** Homes that can be easily modified for various individual needs.
- **Accessibility for All Ages and Abilities.** Features that cater to a wide range of physical abilities and disabilities.

These principles can also be applied to how cities and towns are designed. When looking at locations, ask if the locality has put Universal Design in place so, for example, there are ramps in public spaces and public transport is accessible to those with disabilities.

VISITABILITY: HOMES THAT WELCOME EVERYONE

While there are no federal standards for the design of single-family homes, the concept of "Visitability" provides essential accessibility guidelines for new construction. Visitability aims to make the main level of a home accessible to everyone—both those living there or visiting. Originally introduced by Eleanor Smith, the founder of Concrete Change, Visitability incorporates key requirements such as zero-step entrances, first-floor bathrooms, and wheelchair-accessible doorways.

Over time, additional features—like accessible outdoor pathways, first-floor bedrooms, and easily reachable light switches—have been recognized as vital components of Visitability. Not only does it provide for ease-of-access housing, but it enables social visiting by individuals with mobility constraints, creating spaces that promote social interaction. Visitability design also facilitates easy movement of strollers or large objects. Many 55+ communities have embraced this design philosophy, ensuring welcoming environments.

Incorporating Universal Design and Visitablity into your living arrangements will result in a supportive environment that meets your current needs, can be adapted to support you as you age gracefully, and facilitates social involvement that enriches your retirement experience. Take inspiration from individuals like Patricia, whose story was in Chapter Eight. By looking into installing an elevator or stair lift to address her mobility issue, she addressed her unique challenges actively, thereby ensuring she could remain engaged in her daily life.

These principles can also be applied to how cities and towns are designed. When looking at possible locations to live, study whether the locality has put Universal Design and Livability principles in place so, for example, there are ramps in public spaces and public transport is accessible to those with disabilities.

LIVING ENVIRONMENTS— MORE OPTIONS THAN SOME MIGHT THINK

Whether you're exploring and assessing different living arrangements and lifestyle choices or requesting extra services, advocating for yourself is essential to finding a living situation that genuinely meets your needs and supports your well-being.

Chapter 11: Retirement Living: Options for Every Lifestyle

AGING IN PLACE IN YOUR COMMUNITY

As you enter retirement, your family dynamics, interests, and abilities will evolve. You might choose to age in place and stay where you have been living, perhaps realizing that you may require home modifications for accessibility to do so. Alternatively, you may opt to move to a smaller, more manageable home to avoid the upkeep of a larger property. Downsizing could be practical when children have become independent or if keeping a larger home becomes financially challenging with reduced retirement income.

Numerous studies and surveys have consistently shown that a considerable proportion of older adults prefer to age in place, meaning they wish to continue living in their current homes for as long as possible. According to AARP's Home and Community Preferences survey (2021), approximately 77% of adults aged 50 and older express the desire to remain in their existing home and community as they grow older, emphasizing the importance of keeping their independence. Research conducted by The Joint Center for Housing Studies of Harvard University (2023) corroborates these findings, showing that the aging population places considerable value on their homes and communities, with a substantial percentage of older homeowners intending to stay in their residences indefinitely.

These preferences are influenced by several factors, including familiarity with the home and neighborhood, social relationships with nearby friends and neighbors, and the accumulated memories and life experiences associated with their home. Even when individuals decide to move, they often choose to remain within or close to the same community. Consequently, many communities have evolved into Naturally Occurring Retirement Communities (NORC). Additionally, there is a growing interest in forming or living in Village Model Communities or various forms of Cohousing.

NATURALLY OCCURRING RETIREMENT COMMUNITIES (NORC)

Naturally Occurring Retirement Communities (NORC), sometimes known as NORC-SSP (Supportive Services Program), represent a unique type of community. While the terms NORC and NORC-SSP are often used interchangeably, they denote different concepts. Such communities emerge as individuals move in at a younger age and remain over time, eventually forming a long-established community of older adults. The origins of the NORC movement can be traced to New York City, where population density in high-rise apartment buildings or complexes helped the early development of many NORCs.

NORC may exist in a block of apartments or neighborhood that consists of older single-family homes. It may be characterized as a housing-based NORC, featuring a single building or housing development such as multi-age apartment buildings or condominiums with a high concentration of older adults. Additionally, there are neighborhood-based NORCs, which consist of single-family or multi-family homes within a multi-age neighborhood inhabited by older adults. Residents of NORCs typically contribute annual membership fees to access the NORC program's services.

NORCs offer an array of benefits or services. Some offer basic benefits such as visiting nurses and doctors, on-site case management, wellness activities, on-site dances, clubs or groups or organized outings, help with benefits and entitlement programs (i.e., social security), and educational activities. Some NORCs provide added services such as walkability and mobility-device accessible pathways, public transportation, parks, and safety features. They may encourage a high level of community participation and interaction as they advocate for senior-friendly local government policies and encourage private sector companies to be responsive to the needs of older adults.

NORC-SSP refers to a program that builds collaboration between residents and local health and social service providers to help older adults aging in a NORC area. They may also provide care or case management, meals, and housekeeping services. NORC-SSP programs are funded jointly by government agencies and private organizations. NORCs are more prevalent in urban areas. The best way to find a NORC near you is to contact your local area agency on aging, which you can find using the government's "Eldercare Locator" tool online. Some examples of NORCs are located in Bay Ridge, Brooklyn, Co-Op City, Rochdale Village, Boulevard Gardens, Woodside in New York City, and the Community Options in Cleveland, Ohio. Fees vary by location, the NORC, and the number of adults enrolling (an individual or a couple). NORCs are often funded by public and private entities; fees are typically affordable and lower than those for assisted living facilities.

VILLAGE MOVEMENT

The Village Movement began in Boston with Beacon Hill Village, which promoted a cost-efficient model for aging. These "age-friendly villages" help older adults to stay in their homes and communities by forming networks that encourage independence and social engagement. They offer social interaction, reduce isolation, and provide various resources like community support, health services, transportation, and outdoor spaces. Residents pay membership fees for access to village services and programs, which are managed by volunteers and staff who coordinate activities and connect members with free or discounted services. Villages offer practical support, social connections, and a range of activities, including educational programs, health and wellness activities, and volunteer help with tasks like transportation and home maintenance.

"Village Characteristics: While each Village is different and reflects the needs of its members and community, Villages share many common characteristics. They:

Provide a strong, inclusive community that offers members new opportunities to age successfully

Are membership-driven, self-governing, grassroots, nonprofit organizations

Are run by volunteers and may have paid staff

Coordinate access to affordable services, including transportation, health and wellness programs, technology support, home repairs, social and educational activities

Offer access to vetted service providers (e.g., plumbers, electricians, painters)

Positively affect isolation, interdependence, health, and purpose, reducing their members' overall cost of care

Serve as one-stop-shopping for the services members need to age safely and successfully in their own homes

Form linkages with community partners to help address the challenges of aging

To find a village near you or to start one, visit the Village to Village Network website.

BLENDING LIVES WHILE PRESERVING INDIVIDUAL RESIDENCES

If someone is single, living alone, yet is in a relationship, it may be that blending lives with the partner while keeping separate households is a fulfilling arrangement. This approach allows the couple to enjoy companionship and mutual support without living together on a regular basis or giving up their own homes and independence. Here are some key considerations and strategies to help you navigate such a partnership successfully:

Open Communication. Set up clear and honest communication from the outset. Discuss your needs, preferences, and boundaries openly to ensure both you and your partner feel comfortable and understood.

Define Shared and Private Spaces. While you may keep separate households, it's important to agree on where and how you will spend time together. Consider choosing specific times to visit each other's homes or take part in shared activities while still preserving your own spaces for personal comfort.

Establish a Routine. Create a routine that allows for both shared moments and separate personal time. Whether it's enjoying meals together and engaging in hobbies as a duo balanced by individual time at your separate homes, a regular routine can foster a harmonious relationship.

Engage in Joint Activities. Find shared interests that you both enjoy strengthening your connection, such as cooking, gardening, or attending community events. Participating in activities together can nurture your relationship and create quality time.

Support Each Other's Independence. Encourage one another to keep personal interests, friendships, and activities outside of the relationship. Supporting each other's independence can enhance your bond and enrich your lives significantly.

Embrace Flexible Living Arrangements. Be open to adapting your living situations as circumstances evolve. This might include reevaluating how you spend time together or considering added support services if needed.

Set Boundaries. Clearly discuss and set up boundaries about finances, responsibilities, and social commitments. This clarity will help prevent misunderstandings and ensure that both partners are aligned in their expectations.

Plan for Future Care Needs. As you both age, consider how your partnership and living arrangements will support each person's changing needs. Discuss each other's care preferences and create legal documents like living wills, advance directives, and appoint a healthcare proxy to ensure your wishes are known. Working with an elder law attorney can help you navigate these steps, and storing all documents in a safe, accessible place ensures they can be easily found when needed.

Create a Supportive Environment. Foster a welcoming, accepting, and encouraging atmosphere. Celebrate each other's achievements and be there for one another during challenging times to further strengthen your bond.

Prioritize Enjoyment. Remember to infuse fun and leisure into your relationship. Schedule outings, travel opportunities, or relaxed evenings together to keep the spark alive and create lasting memories.

By pursuing these strategies, you can successfully blend your life with a partner while each of you keeps your own home. Such a partnership allows for intimacy and closeness while respecting your need for independence. Embrace the journey ahead, knowing that thoughtful planning and open communication will help you create a fulfilling relationship that works for both of you.

MOVE IN WITH RELATIVES

Moving in with a relative during retirement can be a practical and supportive possibility for many individuals. This arrangement can provide emotional, physical, and financial benefits, allowing retirees to enjoy companionship and help as they age, such as:

Companionship and Emotional Support. Living with a relative can reduce feelings of loneliness and isolation, offering daily companionship and emotional support.

Shared Responsibilities. Sharing a household can help distribute responsibilities such as cooking, cleaning, and home maintenance, making day-to-day life more manageable.

- **Cost Savings.** This arrangement can help reduce living expenses. Costs for housing, utilities, and groceries can be shared, providing financial relief for both parties.
- **Increased Security and Safety.** Having a relative nearby can enhance safety and security, providing peace of mind for both the retiree and their family.
- **Health and Wellness Monitoring.** Living together means someone else is there to assist in monitoring health and wellness, ensuring that the retiree receives support when needed.

Here are some considerations and strategies to make this transition smooth and beneficial when moving in with relatives:

Open Communication. Discuss the decision to move in openly to ensure both parties are truly in agreement on the arrangement. Establish clear expectations and boundaries from the outset. Talk about daily routines, preferences, and any concerns related to living together.

Establish Boundaries. Respect each other's privacy and personal space. Create boundaries about shared spaces and individual time. Discuss roles and responsibilities to avoid misunderstandings and ensure that both parties contribute to household chores and management.

Financial Arrangements. Address financial contributions upfront. Clarify how expenses such as rent, utilities, groceries, and maintenance will be shared. Consider drafting a written agreement detailing financial responsibilities and conditions under which arrangements may change in the future.

Adapt the Living Space. Assess and modify the living space to meet the retiree's needs, ensuring safety and accessibility. This may include removing tripping hazards, adding grab bars, or clearing out to make more space so the living area is comfortable for both parties.

Support Network. Maintain social connections and activities outside the household. Encourage each other to pursue relationships, hobbies, and interests independently to avoid codependency.

Health Care Considerations. Discuss any health care needs and how they will be managed. Share contact information on individuals' health care providers. Keep communication open about any health issues and the need for help.

Plan for the Future. Talk about long-term plans and what might happen as health care needs change. Be open about discussing potential future scenarios, such as the possibility of engaging in-home care services or requiring alternative living arrangements.

Moving in with a relative during retirement can provide a nurturing and supportive environment and foster stronger family bonds while offering practical benefits. By prioritizing open communication, setting clear expectations, and addressing personal needs, both parties can enjoy a harmonious and fulfilling living arrangement that enhances their quality of life.

CASITAS

Casitas, also known as guest houses, can be a wonderful choice for retirement living. These small, detached spaces offer privacy and independence while keeping you close to your family and nurturing those connections. This arrangement shares many of the same benefits as living near relatives or friends, allowing you to enjoy the support and companionship of loved ones while keeping your own space. The difference is that living in a casita means being near the main house, which could affect the retiree's privacy.

Still, it often proves to be a cost-effective choice that requires fewer resources. Downsizing to a casita is also an excellent way to save on expenses and reduce clutter. Casitas can also be customized to suit the inhabitant's personal preferences and needs. Living close to family and friends can mean that caregiving and support is more available during retirement.

By applying the strategies presented in "Moving In With a Relative," such as open communication, setting clear boundaries, and discussing financial arrangements, someone in retirement can ensure a harmonious and fulfilling living environment that meets everyone's needs. Embrace the opportunity to enjoy both your independence and your family's presence.

COHOUSING

Cohousing is an intentional community of private homes and shared spaces to encourage social interaction and resource sharing. Residents have their own units but share areas like kitchens, dining rooms, gardens, and recreational spaces, promoting both community and privacy. This setup reduces isolation and builds social networks, helping older adults socially and economically.

Cohousing targets adults 50+ with accessible designs and often focuses on sustainability, using shared resources, energy-efficient buildings, and eco-friendly landscaping. Typically, pedestrian-friendly, they encourage walking, communal activities, and integration into the larger neighborhood.

Facilitating a successful cohousing arrangement requires careful planning, collaboration, and clear communication among participants. Here are several key recommendations to help set up an effective cohousing community:

Define Shared Values and Goals. Gather potential members to discuss and set up common values, goals, and visions for the cohousing community as a foundation for guiding future decisions and to help ensure alignment among members.

Establish Governance and Decision-Making Processes. Decide on a governance structure and how decisions will be made within the community, such as regular meetings, consensus-based decision-making, or forming committees to handle specific tasks.

Create a Cohousing Design. Work with architects or professionals experienced in cohousing to design the physical layout of the community. Ensure the design incorporates private living units as well as shared common spaces, such as gardens, community rooms, and kitchens, to foster social interaction.

Develop Financial Arrangements. Establish a clear financial plan that outlines costs associated with housing, maintenance, and shared resources. This might include shared expenses, individual contributions, and funding mechanisms to ensure long-term sustainability.

Encourage Open Communication. Encourage transparency and open lines of communication among members by establishing regular meetings, communication platforms (like group chats or forums), and informal gatherings to build trust and strengthen relationships.

Promote Community Engagement. Organize social events, collaborative projects, and communal activities that encourage engagement among members to help create a sense of belonging and strengthen community bonds.

Develop Conflict Resolution Strategies. Establish guidelines for addressing conflicts that may arise within the community. Effective strategies could include mediation processes, open dialogue, or designated conflict resolution members to help in discussions.

Be Inclusive and Diverse. Aim for diversity within the cohousing community by welcoming individuals from various backgrounds, ages, and experiences. A diverse community can enrich interactions and enhance mutual support.

Consider Accessibility and Usability. Incorporate universal design principles to ensure that the living environment is accessible and accommodating for all residents, including those with disabilities or mobility challenges.

Establish Maintenance and Responsibilities. Clearly outline shared responsibilities for maintenance, cleaning, and management of communal spaces. Regularly scheduled chores and a system for supporting shared areas can help keep the environment pleasant for all members.

Provide Resources and Support. Offer information and resources related to cohousing, including best practices, successful models, and educational opportunities. Encourage members to take part in workshops or training sessions on community living, conflict resolution, and cooperative governance.

Evaluate and Adapt. Regularly assess the community dynamics and processes, gathering feedback from members to find areas for improvement. Flexibility and a willingness to adapt to changing needs are essential for a thriving cohousing arrangement.

By implementing these recommendations, you can create a cohesive, supportive, and thriving cohousing community that promotes strong relationships and enhances the quality of life for all its members.

55+ RETIREMENT COMMUNITIES

Considering moving to a 55+ community? Contrary to the stereotypes of senior living establishments, 55+ communities often have vibrant social calendars with events such as yoga classes, book clubs, and community gardening projects. Residents must be at least 55 years of age but do not have to be retired. In fact, many residents are in the peak earning years of their careers in their mid-fifties. Others are choosing to ease into retirement by phasing into a part-time work schedule. Most residents are still leading active, productive, fully mobile lives.

Also referred to as Age Restricted, Active Adult, or Independent Living Communities, 55+ Communities are residential housing where at least one household member must be 55 years of age or older. Typically, other adult residents must be over 40 years old, and children must be over 18 years old. A community qualifies if at least 80% of its residents are aged 55+ or all residents are over 62. Individuals in these communities can buy, rent, or lease homes, which may include individual houses, condominiums, or apartments. These communities are designed to accommodate aging with features such as livability and universal design.

Here are some common amenities found in 55+ communities:

Homes are usually on a single level to avoid staircases. Standard models have 2-3 bedrooms and two bathrooms.

Some communities are gated and restrict access, while others do not. Gated 55+ communities provide an added element of safety for residents and visitors. They usually also prevent anyone from soliciting, which puts residents at a lower risk of scams.

In apartment-style 55+ communities, garage space or designated parking may be available, depending on the community. Visitor parking is also provided.

These communities provide maintenance services, freeing residents from chores like mowing, shoveling snow, or cleaning gutters.
- Communities are typically built at locations that are central and convenient to local points of interest and services. "It is important to consider easy access to nearby services."

- Each 55+ Community typically features a central clubhouse designated for communal use, serving as a central meeting place for various community clubs and activities. This facility generally includes a fitness center. Pool exercise is low impact, which makes it ideal for older adults. Most active adult communities provide either an indoor or outdoor pool and spa.
- These communities are designed to anticipate the needs of aging residents and incorporate Universal Design in consideration of potential mobility issues.
- Amenities in 55+ Communities vary by location and price. Common features include walking paths, fitness centers, and activity clubs. Some communities also offer added amenities such as golf courses, tennis courts, or equestrian facilities.

In 55+ communities, you'll find opportunities to enhance your social life and stimulate your mind. These communities also allow you to spend more time on meaningful activities, such as visiting family, exercising, or volunteering. Living among peers your own age can create a strong sense of community and shared experience, making it easier to address common concerns. However, be mindful that this homogeneity may limit diversity and exposure to younger perspectives, which could reinforce narrow viewpoints among residents. Embrace the benefits of active living while staying open to new ideas and experiences.

There are many 55+ communities available in every state, with warm weather locations often offering a wide variety of options. To help you explore whether a 55+ community is right for you and find a community that suits your needs and lifestyle, here are some valuable online resources to help you gather essential information:

- **55places.com**. This website is specifically dedicated to active adult communities, providing comprehensive listings, articles, and reviews. You can search by state or community type and filter results based on amenities, price range, and other criteria.

- **Realtor.com.** You can search for properties specifically listed for the 55+ market by using filters and advanced search options when looking for homes in active adult communities.
- **Zillow.com.** Like Realtor.com, Zillow allows you to filter searches for properties in 55+ communities. You can set criteria for price, location, and home type.
- **Local Real Estate Websites.** Many real estate websites specific to a region or local agent websites offer listings for 55+ communities and can provide insights into market trends and communities in specific areas.

These databases can help you find a variety of 55+ communities across the United States, compare options, and gather essential information for your search.

TINY HOMES COMMUNITIES

Tiny home communities present an exciting and attractive choice for retirees looking for a simpler, more sustainable lifestyle. The number of these communities across the country is growing because they afford the chance to live more affordably alongside like-minded individuals who share your values.

One of the main advantages of tiny homes is their lower construction and maintenance costs, making them a financially appealing choice, especially for those on a fixed income. In addition, many tiny home communities foster a strong sense of belonging and social interaction, allowing you to build close relationships with your neighbors. Transitioning to a tiny home encourages a minimalist lifestyle, helping you reduce clutter and focus on what truly matters in your life. Many of these communities also offer shared amenities, such as communal gardens, recreational areas, and maintenance services, enhancing your living experience.

If you are contemplating relocating to a tiny home community, there are several critical factors to consider in order to be sure that it aligns with your retirement goals.

Following are the essential considerations when deciding whether this distinctive and rewarding housing option is suitable for you:

- **Lifestyle Fit**. Figure out if a minimalist lifestyle suits you by carefully considering your belongings versus available space.
- **Community Culture**. Research the community's culture and values; engage with neighbors and visit to assess compatibility.
- **Amenities and Services**. Check for amenities like shared laundry facilities, social activities, and maintenance services.
- **Zoning and Regulations**. Verify local laws and regulations regarding tiny homes to be sure a community is in legal compliance.
- **Accessibility**. Check that the community and any possible tiny home you purchase, or rent can accommodate mobility and health needs as you age.
- **Future Plans**. Consider how the tiny home will work in the long term, including whether home modifications or other changes will be necessary.
- **Finances**. Compare costs, including purchase price, fees, utilities, and taxes, to current housing. Research if there are any fees or expenses that may not be obvious.
- **Social Engagement**. Seek opportunities for social interaction to make new friends and avoid isolation.
- **Climatic Considerations**. Choose a location with a climate that fits your comfort preferences.

Tiny home communities offer an alternative living arrangement that can support a simplified lifestyle while providing a strong sense of community among retirees. By carefully considering personal preferences, community culture, finances, and future needs, retirees can figure out if a tiny home lifestyle aligns with their goals for retirement living.

UNIVERSITY-BASED RETIREMENT COMMUNITIES

University-based retirement communities (UBRCs) are most appealing to those interested in academic learning and campus life. University-Based Retirement Communities (UBRCs) are residential communities designed for older adults who have a connection to universities or colleges. These communities typically capitalize on the resources, educational opportunities, and cultural amenities provided by the institution, such as offering lifelong learning opportunities and access to university-affiliated hospitals or recreational facilities. Some common criteria for UBRCs:

Location. University-Based Retirement Communities (UBRCs) are strategically situated close to the university's main campus, allowing residents convenient access to lectures, seminars, workshops, and library resources. This proximity also facilitates easy transportation options, including university shuttles and public transit.

Intergenerational Interaction. UBRCs promote interaction between older adults and university students, fostering mentorship, collaboration, and social engagement that helps both groups. These programs effectively integrate community residents with students, faculty, and staff.

Housing Options. UBRCs offer a variety of housing choices, including independent living, assisted living, skilled nursing, and memory care. They may also be organized as villages, Naturally Occurring Retirement Communities (NORCs), or cohousing communities.

Lifelong Learning. Residents commonly have access to educational programs, workshops, lectures, and courses provided by the university, promoting an environment of lifelong learning and intellectual stimulation.

Health and Wellness Services. Many UBRCs provide comprehensive health and wellness programs, fitness facilities, and other resources aimed at enhancing the well-being of residents. Universities often offer health resources, wellness initiatives, and physical fitness programs, including fitness centers, medical facilities, and wellness workshops.

Community Support. Residents typically receive help from community support services such as transportation, social activities, and daily living help, ensuring a high quality of life.

Cultural and Recreational Opportunities. The proximity to a university allows residents to take part in a wide range of cultural activities, including theater productions, art exhibitions, and sporting events, enriching their social and recreational experiences.

RETIRE ON A CRUISE SHIP

Retiring on a cruise ship is becoming a popular choice for those seeking a unique lifestyle in their retirement years. All-inclusive services cover meals, accommodations, and entertainment, simplifying daily living and reducing the stress of maintaining a traditional home. The benefits of cruise ship living also include various amenities, social opportunities, and predictable costs. This lifestyle allows retirees to explore interesting destinations and cultures without packing and unpacking. Many cruise lines are equipped with medical facilities and staff, but it is important to research health care options and understand onboard medical care limitations.

Among the amenities cruise ships offer are a variety of dining options, entertainment events, fitness centers, swimming pools, and wellness programs. They also provide educational opportunities through lectures and workshops. A close-knit community and friendships often form among residents as the result of onboard social activities and on-land touring.

Retiring on a cruise ship can take several forms, each offering a unique experience. There are three types.

RESIDENTIAL CRUISES

Residential cruises allow individuals to live onboard a cruise ship for extended periods and often cater specifically to retirees. Some of the features of these cruises include:

Ships that are equipped with residential-style accommodations, amenities, and services.

A lump sum or monthly fee that includes housing, meals, and access to onboard programs and activities.

A sense of community develops from living onboard a residential cruise ship as residents take part in social events, fitness classes, and entertainment together.

BACK-TO-BACK CRUISES

Booking consecutive cruise itineraries back-to-back without returning home in between is the equivalent of living onboard in that this allows retirees to enjoy extended travel without interruption. The difference from residential cruising is that by switching ships and itineraries, the community of fellow passengers changes, and a greater variety of destinations can be enjoyed.

It's essential to verify availability and arrangements when booking back-to-back cruises with the cruise operator. Do the same regarding travel and accommodations between cruises, which are generally handled by the cruise line also.

WORLD CRUISES

These are long, comprehensive voyages that circumnavigate the globe, typically lasting three months or longer. These cruises offer a unique opportunity to visit multiple continents and many countries while enjoying the amenities of a cruise ship. World cruises often feature enriching programs, guest speakers, and excursions designed to provide deeper cultural experiences at each port. This choice is ideal for those looking to immerse themselves in diverse cultures, scenic landscapes, and global experiences without the hassle of extensive travel planning. Costs for world cruises tend to be higher due to their length and the number of destinations included. Planning and booking early can help secure the best rates.

CRUISING CONSIDERATIONS

Before embarking on a retirement journey at sea, conduct thorough research and consider your personal preferences, health considerations, and financial situation. While retiring on a cruise ship may appear cost-effective, long-term cruising can entail substantial expenses. The costs vary based on factors such as the chosen cruise line, cabin type, and the frequency of cruises.

Access to quality health care is an important concern, as medical facilities on cruise ships may have limitations. Therefore, it is vital to secure comprehensive health insurance that provides coverage both on board and at various ports of call.

Additionally, it is advisable to explore cruise lines that offer long-term cruising options, each giving unique opportunities to retirees wanting a lifestyle of travel and adventure. Whether you favor the communal environment of residential cruises, the flexibility of consecutive voyages, or the extensive exploration provided by world cruises, thoughtful consideration of your preferences, budget, and travel goals will help you select the most suitable choice for your retirement lifestyle.

International Retirement Living

According to a recent study by International Living (visit the website https://internationalliving.com/), Americans could retire 10 years earlier—and enjoy a higher standard of living—by moving beyond our country's borders. "*International Living* magazine publishes an annual global retirement index that ranks the World's Best Places to Retire (visit the website https://internationalliving.com/the-best-places-to-retire/). Also, (search on the website "Working and Living Abroad After Retirement—AARP"). Twenty-three countries were identified as top destinations for retirement, which include Panama, Ecuador, Mexico, Costa Rica, Spain, and Portugal. The cost of living, health care, housing, Internet access, infrastructure factors such as international airports, and, of course, weather were considered. An added resource is ExpatExchange.com (visit the website https://www.expatexchange.com/), a popular website on living abroad.

If you are thinking about retiring in another country, do your research. The attitudes toward retirement vary significantly from one country to another, as cultural, economic, and social factors influence them. Moving abroad for retirement is a weighty decision that requires careful planning. Consult experts and relocation specialists. Consider the cost of living, unexpected expenses, health care quality, visa requirements, language, culture, social networks, and safety. International retirement can provide new experiences and cultural enrichment. It can be rewarding but needs thorough planning.

Planning for international living during retirement involves several key steps to ensure a smooth transition and a fulfilling experience abroad. Here's a guide to help you navigate the process:

1. Research Destinations.

2. Find countries that are known for being retirement-friendly. Consider factors such as climate, cost of living, health care quality, and cultural opportunities. Popular options often include countries in Central America, Southeast Asia, and Europe.

3. Utilize resources like international living websites, expat forums, and travel blogs to gather information about potential destinations.

4. Visit potential locations.
    a. Before committing, visit your top choices to experience the area first-hand. Spend time exploring neighborhoods, local amenities, and lifestyle options.
    b. Engage with local expat communities to gather insights and tips about living there.

5. Evaluate the Cost of Living.
    a. Evaluate the overall cost of living, which includes housing, groceries, health care, transportation, and entertainment. Compare these costs to your current living situation to assess financial feasibility.
    b. Consider the effect of exchange rate fluctuations on your retirement income.

6. Understand visa and residency requirements.
    a. Research the visa options available for retirees in your chosen destination. Many countries offer specific retiree visas with varying requirements.
    b. Familiarize yourself with residency permits and the process for obtaining them; requirements may differ significantly by country.

7. Consider health care accessibility.
    a. Investigate the health care system in your prospective country, including the availability of medical facilities and services. Check if expats are eligible for local health care or if you will rely on private insurance.
    b. Review health insurance options for international coverage, ensuring it meets your needs while abroad.

8. Plan for Housing.
    a. Decide whether you want to rent or buy property. Start by looking into short-term rentals to give a try-out period and to settle in.
    b. Consider factors like proximity to amenities, safety, and local culture when selecting a neighborhood.

9. Develop a Financial Plan.
    a. Assess how your retirement income will translate in your chosen country, including pensions, Social Security, savings, and investments.
    b. Consult a financial advisor or planner familiar with international finance to set up how to manage your assets and currency exchanges efficiently.

10. Prepare for Cultural Adjustment.
    a. Learn about the local culture, customs, and language to ease your transition. Taking language classes can significantly enhance your experience and integration into the community.
    b. Stay open-minded and patient as you adapt to a new way of life.

11. Connect with the Expat Community.
    a. Join local expat groups or forums to connect with others who share similar experiences. This can provide support, resources, and advice.

b. Participate in community events to help set up local connections and friendships.

12. Plan for Logistics.
    a. Organize important documents, including passports, health records, legal documents, and travel insurance.
    b. Consider the logistics of relocating, such as shipping belongings, banking, and notifying relevant institutions of your change in address.

By following these steps and planning thoroughly, you can create an enjoyable and fulfilling international retirement living arrangement that meets your lifestyle and personal preferences.

CONTINUING CARE RETIREMENT COMMUNITY

Are you considering a Continuing Care Retirement Community (CCRC)? These communities are tailored to provide a continuum of care for older adults so that someone can transition from one level of care to another as their health needs change. An individual may start with independent living and eventually require long-term care. CCRCs are designed so that residents receive support and services at every stage of their aging process.

These are the levels of care offered in CCRCs:

- **Independent Living.** Designed for active older adults who can live on their own but prefer a community lifestyle with amenities and social activities. Services often include daily meals, housekeeping, laundry, beauty salons, fitness centers, spas, and swimming pools.

- **Assisted Living.** When a resident can no longer live independently, they move to assisted living. This choice offers care for daily activities like dressing, bathing, and medication management without 24-hour nursing. Assisted living supports residents with personal care and health maintenance while promoting independence.

- **Skilled Nursing Care.** Provides comprehensive specialized medical care and support for those who need 24-hour nursing care and medical attention due to chronic or acute health conditions or requiring rehabilitation services. Skilled nursing facilities are staffed with licensed medical professionals.

- **Memory Care.** Specialized services for residents with Alzheimer's disease or other forms of dementia. These units focus on creating a safe and supportive environment tailored to the unique needs of individuals with cognitive impairments.

- **Rehabilitation Services.** Many CCRCs offer post-acute rehabilitation services, including physical therapy, occupational therapy, and speech therapy, helping residents recover from surgery or illness.

- **Long-Term Care.** CCRCs offer long-term supportive services for individuals with chronic illnesses or disabilities, providing assistance with daily activities such as bathing, dressing, and medication management. These services ensure a supportive environment for residents as their needs evolve.

CCRCs allow residents to age in place, meaning they can access the necessary level of care without needing to move to a different location. In addition, they allow couples or long-time partners who may have distinct care needs to remain in the same community. This approach can provide peace of mind for both residents and their families, knowing that proper care options are available as needs change over time.

Finding a Continuing Care Retirement Community (CCRC) involves researching various options available in your preferred area. Here are some steps to help you in your search:

1. **Online Directories.** Use online resources and directories specifically designed for senior living, such as:
    - **A Place for Mom.** This website provides personalized help in finding CCRCs and other senior living options.
    - **SeniorHousingNet.com.** Offers a comprehensive listing of CCRCs across the country, with detailed descriptions and contact information.
    - **Caring.com.** Provides listings, reviews, and articles related to CCRCs and senior living communities.

2. **State and Local Agency Resources.** Check with your state's Department of Aging or local Area Agencies on Aging for information about licensed CCRCs in your area.

3. **AARP Resources.** AARP offers a wealth of information on various senior living options, including CCRCs, and may have tools to help you search for communities.

4. **Personal Recommendations.** Ask friends, family, or health care professionals if they know of any reputable CCRCs based on personal experience or feedback.

LONG-TERM CARE

Long-term care facilities include assisted living and skilled nursing facilities and strive to enhance overall well-being by fostering independence and addressing the physical, emotional, and social needs of aging persons. The level of care needed distinguishes the two, as discussed in the next sections. Both support individuals needing help and provide a secure, safe environment in which to live with others.

ASSISTED LIVING FACILITIES

Assisted living communities offer a supportive environment where residents can keep their independence while receiving help with daily tasks. These communities can be freestanding or part of a larger Continuing Care Retirement Community, and they may be integrated with nursing homes or hospitals. If you find that you need help with activities of daily living (ADLs), such as bathing, dressing, or meal preparation, assisted living may be the right choice for you. This option doesn't include skilled nursing care, which is reserved for individuals needing specialized medical attention from licensed nurses.

In assisted living facilities, residents typically have their own apartment or room, giving them privacy while still being part of a community. These communities offer a range of services that enhance residents' quality of life, including meals, housekeeping, and a variety of activities designed to engage and enrich their day-to-day experience, such as trips to local stores and cultural activities. They also provide the security that assistance is available 24/7 if needed, ensuring an individual's safety while maximizing their dignity and independence.

Many assisted living facilities may include memory care units for individuals living with Alzheimer's disease or other forms of dementia but may not yet need skilled nursing. Memory care units have specific safeguards to prevent residents from going astray or wandering off, which is common in those with dementia.

Additionally, many assisted living facilities offer short-term respite care for those who may need temporary help or want to try out the community before making a long-term commitment. This flexibility allows someone to explore their options in a supportive environment.

If you're considering assisted living, know that you have choices that can cater to your needs while helping you keep your sense of autonomy.

SKILLED NURSING FACILITY

This type of long-term care is designed for individuals who require more extensive ongoing medical help than what is typically offered in assisted living or independent living settings. It is especially valuable for retirees dealing with chronic illnesses or disabilities.

In addition to receiving daily support with bathing, dressing, and eating in skilled nursing facilities, individuals receive continuous medical care from licensed health care professionals, including registered nurses, nurse practitioners, and certified nursing assistants. They are dedicated to ensuring that patients' health needs are met and emergencies are addressed promptly. Each resident receives care based on a personalized plan tailored by their doctors and the medical staff to their specific health requirements, which is regularly assessed and adjusted as needed, including various medical services and rehabilitation and recreational therapies.

In addition to medical care, these homes often organize social activities, programs, and events that encourage interaction and engagement with staff and other residents. Many skilled nursing homes offer rehabilitative services to help residents recover from surgery, illness, or injury, focusing on restoring their strength, mobility, and functionality. Also, dietary professionals work diligently to create nutritious meal plans that cater to resident's food needs and preferences, including any special restrictions they may have. Moreover, skilled nursing facilities are committed to supporting the families of those under their care as well. They provide valuable resources, including education on managing chronic conditions and guidance on how to offer emotional support.

If you're considering skilled nursing care for yourself or for a loved one, you are not alone in this journey; there are many resources available to support you every step of the way. Take some time to reflect on the following steps to help you select the right facility for your needs:

1. Assess your or the individual's specific care needs, ensuring they align with the services offered.

2. Verify that the facility is properly licensed and accredited, checking for quality assessments from organizations such as Medicare and Medicaid.

3. Evaluate the facility's location in relation to family and friends ("Assisted Living in My Area—seniorsinfo.org").

4. Tour and evaluate potential facilities. If possible, engage with current residents and their families to gain insight.

5. Understand financing, including what costs Medicare, Medicaid, or long-term care insurance may cover.

6. Inquire about specialized services such as rehabilitation or memory care.

7. Ask about the facility's emergency protocols for handling medical emergencies and unforeseen health changes.

DETERMINING THE IDEAL RETIREMENT HOUSING

Where someone chooses to live forms an integral part of their overall retirement vision and plan. The initial choice made upon retirement may then be followed by other decisions based on changing needs and longevity.

These choices are highly significant and personal, as they can profoundly influence an individual's quality of life during their later years. Both the location and type of housing selected can affect their access to health care services, social connections, recreational activities, and overall well-being.

This section assists you in examining your preferences about retirement living—where you want to live and what type of living arrangement would work best for you.

EXAMINE YOUR LIVING AND LIFESTYLE PREFERENCES

The questionnaire below will help guide you in selecting a retirement living arrangement that best suits your needs and desires. As you answer the questions, understand that it's okay to have several options under consideration and that how you feel about them may change as you move closer toward retirement, your next chapter. Take the time to reflect on what matters to you most as you plan for this exciting new chapter in your life.

Living Arrangement Preferences Questionnaire

Part One—Current Living Arrangement

Where is your current place of residence? (Please specify the community, city/town, state, and country.)

_____

Do you currently live in a city, suburban, or rural area?

_____

What type of climate do you live in *(warm, cold, or seasonal)*?

_____

How would you describe your access to high-quality health care providers and facilities?

_____

Are public transportation options and general walkability available where you live?

_____

Chapter 11: Retirement Living: Options for Every Lifestyle

Do you currently engage in social clubs, recreation centers, volunteer work, or other community activities?

___

Describe what you appreciate about your neighborhood/community.

___

What type of housing do you currently live in (*house, townhouse, condominium, apartment*)?

___

How long have you lived in your current residence?

___

Who do you currently live with?

___

Do you prefer living near loved ones?

___

What activities do you typically engage in at home?

___

What's your favorite part of your home?

___

Do you plan to stay in your current home long-term, including after retirement?

___

Would you consider making any modifications to your home for retirement? *(Please explain your reasoning.)*

___

Part Two—Retirement Living

Take your time to reflect on the questions below.

1. Where to live: What are the top possibilities you are considering for retirement housing *(number your top 3 from the list below)*?
    a. __Aging in place—staying in your community (including blending lives)
    b. __Moving in with family or a casita arrangement
    c. __Cohousing
    d. __55+ Retirement Community
    e. __A tiny home community
    f. __University-Based Retirement Community
    g. __Cruise Ship
    h. __International Living
    i. __Continuing Care Retirement Community
    j. __Assisted Living Facility
2. Evaluate the cost and affordability of the options you have selected:
    a. **Housing Costs.** What is the average rent in your target area? For homeowners, what mortgage or downsizing options do you have? Include HOA fees if applicable. Include a budget for repairs if you own your home.
    b. **Property Taxes.** What are the property taxes in the chosen location?
    c. **Utilities.** What are your estimated monthly utility costs *(electricity, water, gas, Internet, cable, trash collection)*?
    d. **General Living Expenses.** Will you own a vehicle or use public transportation? What are the costs for gas, maintenance, insurance, or transit passes? Do not forget to budget for potential unexpected expenses, such as medical emergencies.
3. Do you prefer a warmer or cooler climate? How do you feel about seasonal variations and extreme weather conditions? Share your thoughts.

Chapter 11: Retirement Living: Options for Every Lifestyle

4. How accessible will your social support system be in the retirement living arrangement you have selected? *(Consider the proximity to family and friends for emotional and practical support.)*

   _____

5. Evaluate the ease of traveling to visit loved ones and their travel to visit you.

   _____

6. Check if there are quality health care facilities near the retirement living options you selected. If you have specific health conditions, are specialists and treatment options available in the area?

   _____

7. Evaluate the availability of public transportation and the convenience of getting around.

   _____

8. Check how walkable the area is, especially if you prefer not to drive. Share your results.

   _____

9. Do your options offer activities you enjoy, such as hiking, golfing, or cultural events? Consider the availability of social clubs, volunteer opportunities, community centers, and lifelong learning programs.

   _____

10. Does the cultural and social environment of the area align with your values and interests?

    _____

11. Check crime rates and safety in areas you are considering for retirement. Share the results.

    _____

12. Visit neighborhoods to get a feel for the community atmosphere and security. What did you find?

    _____

13. Explore the cost of living as well as the level of state income taxes, property taxes, and any tax benefits for retirees.
_____

14. Will the housing options you have selected be suitable for your needs as you age, including having accessibility features?
_____

As you answer the questions and review your responses, your preferences will begin to come into focus. Maybe you really do want to age in place, if possible. Or perhaps another location closer to family would be better for you. You don't have to decide right now; you can weigh how you feel and let it sink in.

SELECTING THE IDEAL RETIREMENT LIVING ARRANGEMENT

Now that you've collected your thoughts, the "Retirement Living Arrangement Comparison" worksheet provided in this section will allow you to organize them. It helps you to compare your housing options based on criteria that assess location, affordability, long-term suitability, and availability of support.

How to use the worksheet:

1. Living Arrangement. Fill out the spaces for the retirement living choices you are considering.

2. Aging-Friendly. Answer yes or no about the city, town, or village in which the option is located.

3. Livability. Answer yes or no about the location in which the option is located. You may have a second answer regarding the housing option itself. Are they livable?

4. Sufficient Retirement Income. After evaluating what it will cost you to live in the option, answer yes or no about whether your income is sufficient to support you there. If not, you may want to add other options to the table for evaluation.

5. Later-Life Support System. Think through what later-life support systems you will have access to if you are living in that option (such as those provided by a community) and note any considerations related to emotional and practical support (e.g., proximity to family and friends).

6. Long-Term Suitability. Evaluate how well an option will meet your needs in the future, considering how the housing and/or community may adapt to changes in your circumstances.

7. Safety and Comfort for Aging. Rate how safe and comfortable you will feel with the option, including as you age, consider factors such as crime rates, proximity of supporters, physical accessibility (Universal Design), and overall livability.

Retirement Living Arrangement Comparison

Please evaluate each living arrangement by considering its suitability, safety, support system, and your preferences. Use the space to note your thoughts or responses.

Aging in Place (stay in your current home or community)
Aging-Friendly (Yes / No): _____
Livability (Yes / No): _____
Support System (Assess): _____
Long-Term Suitability (Assess): _____
Comments/Notes: _____

Naturally Occurring Retirement Community (NORC)
Aging-Friendly (Yes / No): _____
Livability (Yes / No): _____
Support System (Assess): _____
Long-Term Suitability (Assess): _____
Comments/Notes: _____

Village Community
Aging-Friendly (Yes / No): _____
Livability (Yes / No): _____
Support System (Assess): _____
Long-Term Suitability (Assess): _____
Comments/Notes: _____

Move in with Relatives (e.g., Casita)
Aging-Friendly (Yes / No): _____
Livability (Yes / No): _____
Support System (Assess): _____
Long-Term Suitability (Assess): _____
Comments/Notes: _____

Cohousing (shared living community)
Aging-Friendly (Yes / No): _____
Livability (Yes / No): _____
Support System (Assess): _____
Long-Term Suitability (Assess): _____
Comments/Notes: _____

55+ and Retirement Communities
Aging-Friendly (Yes / No): _____
Livability (Yes / No): _____
Long-Term Suitability (Assess): _____
Comments/Notes: _____

Tiny Home Communities
Aging-Friendly (Yes / No): _____
Livability (Yes / No): _____

Support System (Assess): _____
Long-Term Suitability (Assess): _____
Comments/Notes: _____

University-Based Retirement Community
Aging-Friendly (Yes / No): _____
Livability (Yes / No): _____
Support System (Assess): _____
Long-Term Suitability (Assess): _____
Comments/Notes: _____

Cruise Ship Living
Aging-Friendly (Yes / No): _____
Livability (Yes / No): _____
Support System (Assess): _____
Long-Term Suitability (Assess): _____
Comments/Notes: _____

International Living
Aging-Friendly (Yes / No): _____
Livability (Yes / No): _____
Support System (Assess): _____
Long-Term Suitability (Assess): _____
Comments/Notes: _____

Continuing Care Retirement Community (CCRC)
Aging-Friendly (Yes / No): _____
Livability (Yes / No): _____
Support System (Assess): _____
Long-Term Suitability (Assess): _____
Comments/Notes: _____

Assisted Living Facility
Aging-Friendly (Yes / No): _____
Livability (Yes / No): _____
Support System (Assess): _____
Long-Term Suitability (Assess): _____
Comments/Notes: _____

Living Preferences

Did the table further clarify your thoughts? Based on the evaluation, please list your three preferred options for retirement living.

1. _____
2. _____
3. _____

TAKEAWAYS FROM RETIREMENT LIVING

By considering what type of lifestyle is important to you, you can decide upon a location and type of housing arrangement that fits your vision of retirement living to a T. Consider these takeaways:

Assess your needs by evaluating your health, mobility, social connections, and daily activities to determine the best living situation.

Evaluate locations based on aging-friendliness: Ensure your choice has accessibility features, safety measures, and support services for aging.

Pick a location for its livability, i.e., the availability of activities and green space to keep you engaged and thriving.

Prioritize social support, if possible, and choose to be near family and friends.

Understand your housing options by exploring different retirement living arrangements like aging in place, 55+ communities, and assisted living.

With increasing longevity, long-term options may need to be considered, including a Continuing Care Retirement Community.

Your financial situation determines your options. Analyze what different housing choices will cost so you can choose what is affordable for you.

Opt for living arrangements with features that promote ease of mobility and security.

Before making any decision, research thoroughly by visiting cities, towns, neighborhoods, communities, and facilities.

Be your own advocate. Communicate your needs and preferences to find the right living arrangement.

Use these takeaways as a guide to navigate your retirement living choices, ensuring that you find a solution that fits your lifestyle and enhances your well-being. Your retirement should be a time of comfort, joy, and connection, and careful planning will help you achieve that.

PART

IV

YOUR HOLISTIC RETIREMENT PLAN

CHAPTER TWELVE

PUTTING IT ALL TOGETHER: ACTION PLAN FOR THRIVING IN RETIREMENT

The biggest adventure you can ever take is to live the life of your dreams.
—OPRAH WINFREY

Plan for the life you want, and make it happen.
—ANONYMOUS

Life is your artwork. Create it! No one else can do it for you. You create it by seeing life, and living it to its fullest.
—MAX EHRMANN

Without goals, and plans to reach them, you are like a ship that has set sail with no destination.
—FITZHUGH DODSON

Welcome to the chapter that brings everything together. Here, you will create a comprehensive retirement plan that reflects your unique vision for the future. We'll start by revisiting what truly matters to you—your purpose, your aspirations, and your vision statements.

Next, you'll be guided through the process of merging all the worksheets you've completed throughout this book. This includes your vision for retirement and thoughtful assessments of your financial needs, health considerations, emotional wellness, social support systems, and housing options for retirement.

YOUR HOLISTIC RETIREMENT PLAN

By the end of this chapter, your Holistic Retirement Plan will be complete and you'll have a clear and cohesive plan that supports your desires and empowers you to step confidently into the next exciting chapter of your life by ensuring that every aspect of your retirement aligns with your dreams and goals.

As demonstrated in the previous chapters, holistic retirement planning encompasses all aspects of your life and extends beyond just financial considerations. It also addresses your health, lifestyle choices, emotional well-being, social connections, and living arrangements. By integrating all these elements, you can develop a comprehensive retirement plan that ensures you thrive throughout retirement.

Your Holistic Retirement Plan serves as your roadmap since it includes the outline you created of your goals and priorities. With this comprehensive plan, you can navigate the complexities of retirement with peace of mind and a clear sense of direction.

HOLISTIC PLANNING: ALIGNING WITH YOUR VISION

As you define your ideal retirement, refining your vision statement is a crucial step. Earlier in this book, you created a statement that captured your life themes, goals, and values. Perhaps this statement from Chapter Three is still the one for you. Or, now that you've explored the holistic planning process and reflected on what truly matters to you, you might want to update your vision statement to better reflect the retirement you aspire to.

Think about how you want to spend your days. Do you see yourself traveling, exploring interests, volunteering, or strengthening connections with your community or loved ones? Your vision statement should paint a clear picture of your desired lifestyle, where you want to live, and what is most important to you.

This statement serves as more than just a set of goals. It's your personal guide, keeping you focused on what brings you joy and fulfillment. Allow yourself to dream big. Be honest about what excites and motivates you. Your updated vision will empower you to stay aligned with your priorities and make choices that support the life you want in retirement. Embrace this opportunity to shape your future. Your vision statement will be a powerful tool in creating a retirement that's truly meaningful to you.

Personal Vision Statement for Retirement

_____
_____
_____
_____

BUILDING A LIFE WITH PURPOSE AND MEANING

In Chapter Seven, "Anchoring Retirement in Purpose and Meaning," you considered what is meaningful to you and developed a life purpose statement. Earlier in this book, you took the time to create a life purpose statement that reflected your motivations, aspirations, and goals. Now, after exploring the comprehensive retirement planning steps in the earlier chapters and reflecting on your vision, it's time to revisit and update that statement to align with your renewed sense of purpose in retirement.

Your revised life purpose statement should reflect your core motivations and how you plan to contribute to retirement. Whether your emphasis is on engaging in meaningful work, fostering relationships, contributing to the community, or pursuing passions that inspire you, this purpose will serve to guide your actions and decisions. Take this opportunity to think deeply about what truly resonates with you and how you envision making a difference in your own life and the lives of others.

A well-defined life purpose statement will not only enhance your fulfillment but also provide you with a clear direction as you embark on the vibrant journey of retirement.

Life Purpose Statement

_____
_____
_____
_____

Now that you have clear and updated Vision and Purpose Statements, the next step is to develop specific action plans for each important life area. Combine the key insights and strategies you have learned throughout this book. They will not only guide you in making informed plans but also empower you to embrace your new phase of life with confidence and purpose.

FINANCIAL STRATEGIES AND ACTION PLAN

When planning for retirement, your finances are the foundation of achieving a fulfilling retirement. Your financial health lays the groundwork for living your vision and purpose. Use the Retirement Financial Action Plan worksheet below to assess what actions you need to take vis a vis retirement

Chapter 12: *Putting It All Together: Action Plan for Thriving in Retirement*

planning considerations and give yourself a period or deadline in which to complete it. Begin by reviewing the list of possible financial issues, such as savings, health care costs, or income sources. Then, outline specific strategies to address each need, whether it's increasing your savings rate, exploring investment options, or seeking professional guidance. Next, write down your actionable steps and set realistic time frames for when you plan to implement them. Remember, this plan is your roadmap to financial security in retirement, and taking these steps will empower you to navigate this transition with confidence. You've got this.

How to Use This Tool

Here is a brief description of what to do to complete the worksheet:

1. **Review and Reflect on Each Financial Issue/Need:** Assess your financial situation and identify any concerns or needs as you near retirement. Include any other issues or needs not listed above.
2. **Outline the Strategy:** Consider effective strategies to address each identified issue. Feel free to add your own ideas in the space provided. Think through specific actions you can take to implement each strategy.
3. **My Action Plan:** Write down your personalized action steps, including specific goals to hold yourself accountable.
4. **Timeframe:** Set a time for when you plan to carry out each action step, helping you stay organized and on track.

Retirement Financial Action Plan

Take charge of your financial future by thoroughly evaluating your financial needs, exploring various strategies, and crafting a robust action plan. Empower yourself to make informed decisions and achieve your financial goals with confidence.

Retirement Savings:

Strategy: Review and adjust your savings strategy to meet your retirement goals.
Other strategies: _____
_____

Action Plan: Calculate how much you need to save by retirement.
Set a monthly savings goal and automate contributions to your retirement accounts.
Other actions: _____
_____

Time Frame:_____

Rising Healthcare Costs:

Strategy: Explore health care options and plan for potential expenses.
Other strategies: _____
_____

Action Plan: Research Medicare and supplemental insurance options.
Set aside a dedicated health savings fund.
Other actions: _____
_____

Time Frame:_____

Managing Debt:

Strategy: Create a plan to pay down existing debts before retirement.
Other strategies: _____
_____

Action Plan: Assess your current debt situation and prioritize repayment.
Create a budget that allows for extra payments on high-interest debts.
Other actions: _____
_____

Time Frame:_____

Chapter 12: Putting It All Together: Action Plan for Thriving in Retirement

Income Diversification:

Strategy: Identify other income streams to supplement retirement savings.
Other strategies: _____
_____

Action Plan: Consider part-time work, consulting, or freelance opportunities. Explore investments that generate passive income, such as rental properties.
Other actions: _____
Time Frame: _____

Budgeting for a Fixed Income:

Strategy: Develop a realistic budget that reflects your retirement income.
Other strategies: _____
_____

Action Plan: Calculate your expected post-retirement income, including Social Security and pensions. Track your expenses and create a monthly budget that aligns with your income.
Other actions: _____
_____

Time Frame: _____

Estate Planning:

Strategy: Create or update your estate plan to ensure your wishes are met.
Other strategies: _____
Action Plan: Consult with an estate planning attorney to draft or revise your will and trusts. Discuss your plans with family members to ensure clarity.
Other actions: _____
Time Frame: _____

Understanding Taxes in Retirement:
Strategy: Research how taxes may affect your retirement income and take steps to minimize them.
Other strategies: _____
Action Plan: Meet with a tax advisor to understand the implications of your retirement withdrawals. Consider converting a part of your traditional IRA to a Roth IRA if it helps your tax situation.
Other actions: _____
Time Frame: _____

Limited Knowledge of Investment Options:
Strategy: Educate yourself about different investment vehicles to enhance your retirement portfolio.
Other strategies: _____
Action Plan: Attend workshops or seminars on retirement investing. Consult with a financial advisor to develop an investment strategy that suits your risk tolerance.
Other actions: _____
Time Frame: _____

Adjusting Lifestyle Expectations:
Strategy: Assess and adjust your expectations for your retirement lifestyle based on your financial situation.
Other strategies: _____
Action Plan: Make a list of your desired lifestyle elements and evaluate their costs. Prioritize your goals and adjust your plans accordingly to ensure financial stability.
Other actions: _____
Time Frame: _____

Social Security Optimization:

Strategy: Understand how to maximize your Social Security benefits.
Other strategies: _____
Action Plan: Evaluate different claiming strategies based on your circumstances. Use online calculators to estimate the best time to claim your benefits.
Other actions: _____
Time Frame: _____

Inflation Planning:

Strategy: Develop a strategy to account for inflation in your retirement budget.
Other strategies: _____
Action Plan: Research historical inflation rates and project future costs. Consider investments that have the potential to outpace inflation, such as stocks or real estate.
Other actions: _____
Time Frame: _____

Financial Literacy Improvement:

Strategy: Increase your understanding of personal finance and retirement planning.
Other strategies: _____
Action Plan: Take online courses or read books on retirement finance. Join local workshops or seminars for hands-on knowledge and networking.
Other actions: _____
Time Frame: _____

Other Financial Needs or Issues:

_____
_____
_____
_____

By proactively addressing your financial needs, you can establish a solid foundation for your retirement. Take your time to work through each area and remember that you are not alone—support is available as you navigate your path toward a secure and fulfilling retirement. Once your financial strategies are in place, it's equally important to shift your focus to health and wellness, ensuring you're physically and mentally equipped to enjoy the rewarding experiences ahead. With that in mind, let's now turn our attention to the vital aspects of supporting your health and wellness in retirement.

STRATEGIES AND ACTION PLAN TO PROMOTE GOOD HEALTH

Your health and wellness are vital components of a fulfilling retirement. As you transition into this new phase of life, prioritizing your physical and emotional well-being will enable you to enjoy the experiences that await you fully. The Retirement Health and Wellness Action Plan worksheet is designed to help you assess your current health needs and commit to actions that promote good health.

Use the worksheet as a tool to identify any health planning issues you may be facing, outline effective strategies to address those concerns, and develop actionable steps to enhance your overall well-being. By taking a proactive approach to your health, you can create a solid foundation for a lively and rewarding retirement. Let's get started on building a healthier future.

Chapter 12: Putting It All Together: Action Plan for Thriving in Retirement

How to Use This Tool
Here is a brief description of what to do to complete the worksheet:
1. **Review and Reflect on Each Health Planning Item:** Reflect on each area of your health and wellness as you approach retirement.
2. **Outline What Needs to Change:** Define specific changes you want to make to improve your health and wellness. Set specific, measurable goals.
3. **Develop Your Retirement Plan:** Think about how each area will look in your retirement. Develop measures for your goals and explain in those terms how you will reach them.
4. **Set a Time Frame:** Set a realistic period or date for implementing changes and achieving your health goals.

Retirement Health and Wellness Action Plan
Develop a well-rounded plan to optimize your health and well-being in retirement. This planning guide highlights key health planning items, areas for improvement, what it might look like in retirement, and your timeline. Use this tool to create a personalized strategy that supports your wellness today and throughout your retirement.

Health Literacy

Communicate effectively with health care providers
Areas for Improvement: Improve my ability to ask questions and express concerns with healthcare providers.
What it may look like in retirement: I actively participate in my health care decisions by: _____
_____
Time Frame: _____

Understand Health-Related Materials

Areas for Improvement: Learn to interpret medication labels, test results, and health risks.

What it may look like in retirement:

I confidently manage my own health information by_____

_____

Time Frame: _____

Evaluate Health Information Sources

Areas for Improvement: Build skills to identify trustworthy information.

What it may look like in retirement: I rely on credible sources for health decisions as shown by_____

Time Frame: _____

Make Informed Health Decisions

Areas for Improvement: Obtain and use information to choose treatments and lifestyle options.

What it may look like in retirement: I prioritize preventive measures and healthy choices by: _____

Time Frame: _____

Access Healthcare Services

Areas for Improvement: Learn how to navigate scheduling, transportation, and insurance.

What it may look like in retirement: I will efficiently use healthcare services as needed by: _____

Time Frame: _____

Use Electronic Health Records (EHR/EMR)

Areas for Improvement: Familiarize myself with systems and online portals.

What it may look like in retirement: I access my health records easily by _____

Time Frame: _____

Utilize Community Resources
Areas for Improvement: Identify local programs, health events, and literacy resources.
What it may look like in retirement:
I engage with community health resources and events by:_____
_____

Time Frame: _____

Healthy Lifestyle

Assess overall wellness
Areas for Improvement: Assess overall wellness and current health management strategies.
What it may look like in retirement: I maintain a well-rounded wellness plan.
Time Frame: _____

Assess emotional and cognitive health:
Areas for Improvement: Develop strategies to enhance mental and emotional well-being.
What it may look like in retirement: I actively engage in activities that promote well-being.
Time Frame: _____

Maintain healthy routines:
Name resources that support my healthy aging plan.
_____

What it may look like in retirement: I adopt and sustain healthy habits and routines.
Time Frame:_____

Health Insurance

Comprehensive health coverage
Areas for Improvement: Review my insurance needs for retirement to ensure coverage.
What it may look like in retirement: I ensure I have adequate health insurance coverage.
Time Frame:_____

Research Medicare: Learn when and how to enroll in Parts A, B, C, and D.
Make informed Medicare decisions: Decide on supplemental and prescription plans.
Time Frame: _____

Long-term Care
Assess long-term care needs
Areas for Improvement: Assess long-term care needs and explore insurance options.
What it may look like in retirement: Create a comprehensive long-term care plan with professionals and family.
Time Frame:_____

Advance Care Planning
Review advance care preferences
Areas for Improvement: Secure necessary documents and clarify my wishes.
What it may look like in retirement: I will ensure my advance care documents are prepared and accessible.
Time Frame: _____

Chapter 12: Putting It All Together: Action Plan for Thriving in Retirement

Challenges and Opportunities

Explore health-related challenges:
Areas for Improvement: Identify potential issues or challenges and prepare strategies.
Explore health-related opportunities: I will have strategies in place to address health challenges in retirement.
Time Frame: _____

CULTIVATING EMOTIONAL WELLNESS: STRATEGIES AND ACTION PLAN

Emotional wellness is an ongoing journey that involves developing skills and strategies to manage your emotions effectively. As you transition into retirement, it's crucial to maintain a strong foundation for your emotional well-being. As seen in Chapter Eight, begin by evaluating your current emotional state and naming areas that may need attention. Explore ways to enhance your well-being by adopting healthy coping mechanisms and nurturing positive relationships. Doing so will facilitate a smooth transition into this new phase of life. Use the tool below to create strategies that will support your emotional wellness during retirement, ensuring you thrive in this exciting chapter.

Action Plan to Enhance Emotional Wellness During Retirement

1. Support Network

Find individuals in your life who can provide emotional support. Consider how they can assist you in achieving emotional wellness:

Name: _____
How they can support you: _____
Name: _____

How they can support you: _____

Name: _____

How they can support you: _____

2. Mental Health Resources to Explore

Action: Consider seeking professional support to enhance your emotional well-being. Reflect on how and why therapy or counseling might help you.

_____

Potential therapists, counselors, or organizations that provide counseling services:

_____

3. Building a Strong Foundation of Emotional Wellness

Action: Think about how you will achieve emotional wellness in retirement. Consider the key issues you need to address.

_____

Routine Emotional Assessment

Action: Regularly evaluate your mental and emotional states through journaling or self-reflection. Schedule monthly check-ins with yourself.

Time Frame. I have set reminders for these evaluations (how many times per week/month or on what dates): _____

_____

Follow-Up Notes: _____

_____

4. Engage in Meaningful Activities

Action: Find hobbies you want to pursue or groups you'd like to join. Plan to dedicate time each week to these activities.

Time Frame. List specific days or times to engage: _____

_____

Chapter 12: Putting It All Together: Action Plan for Thriving in Retirement

Follow-Up Notes: _____

_____

5. Incorporate Self-Care Practices

Action: Develop a routine that includes exercise, healthy eating, and relaxation techniques like meditation or yoga.

Time Frame. Create a weekly schedule for these activities:

_____

_____

Follow-Up Notes: _____

_____

6. Embrace Lifelong Learning

Action: Research workshops or classes of interest and register for at least one course every few months.

Time Frame. Set a timeline for when you'll enroll: _____

_____

_____

Follow-Up Notes: _____

_____

7. Maintain Cultural and Community Connections

Action: Plan regular visits with family or friends and connect with cultural organizations or community events.

Time Frame. Plan these check-ins ahead of time: _____

_____

Follow-Up Notes: _____

_____

8. Practice Mindfulness and Coping Techniques

Action: Integrate mindfulness practices into your daily routine, such as meditation or deep-breathing exercises.

Time Frame. Ensure consistent practice by dedicating time daily or several times a week: _____

_____

Follow-Up Notes: _____

_____

_____

Seek Professional Support:

Action Steps: Find a therapist or counselor and reach out for an initial consultation as needed.

Time Frame. Plan to implement this within one month if necessary:

_____

Follow-Up Notes: _____

_____

_____

Volunteer and Give Back

Action: Research local volunteer opportunities that align with your interests and schedule time to take part.

Time Frame. Schedule your first volunteering experience in the next few weeks:

_____

Follow-Up Notes: _____

_____

_____

Set Personal Goals

Action: Write down specific emotional wellness goals that align with your values. Make them SMART (Specific, Measurable, Achievable, Relevant, Time-bound).

Time Frame. Review and adjust these goals every few months:

_____

_____

Follow-Up Notes: _____
_____

9. Community Support and Groups to Explore

Support Groups

Select the types of support and community groups that may be helpful to your emotional wellness. Look for local or online groups that focus on specific life transitions, such as retirement, grief, or caregiving. Sharing experiences with others can foster a sense of belonging.

Potential group(s) to connect with: _____
_____
_____
_____

Social Clubs

Join clubs that align with your interests, such as book clubs, gardening groups, or art classes. These communities provide social interaction and opportunities for engagement.

Potential group(s) to connect with: _____
_____
_____
_____

Exercise and Wellness Classes

Take part in yoga, tai chi, or fitness classes that promote physical health and emotional well-being. Group settings can also enhance social connections.

Potential group(s) to connect with: _____
_____
_____
_____

Lifelong Learning Programs

Seek out local community colleges or libraries that offer classes and workshops for older adults. Engaging in learning fosters a sense of fulfillment and cognitive engagement.

Potential group(s) to connect with:_____
_____
_____
_____

Volunteer Organizations

Engage with local non-profits that match your interests. Volunteering helps your community and can improve your sense of purpose and connection.

Potential group(s) to connect with: _____
_____
_____
_____

10. Action Plan

What are your next steps? List them below, and be specific about the actions you will take:

1. _____
2. _____
3. _____
4. _____
5. _____
6. _____

Chapter 12: Putting It All Together: Action Plan for Thriving in Retirement

STRATEGIES AND ACTION PLAN FOR BUILDING SOCIAL SUPPORT

This worksheet is designed to help you assess your current support system, name areas that may need strengthening, and outline actionable steps to ensure you have the emotional support you need as you transition into retirement. Establishing a solid social support plan is vital, as strong connections with family, friends, and the community can enhance your well-being, reduce feelings of isolation, and provide a sense of belonging during this new chapter in your life. By actively engaging in building your social network, you're setting the stage for a more fulfilling and connected retirement experience.

Social Support Networks in Retirement Plan
1. Reflection Questions
- What types of support do you feel are missing from your current network?
- What specific activities can you take to increase your engagement with family and friends?
- Which community programs or organizations have you found helpful in the past, and how can you reconnect with them?
- Are there any new groups, clubs, or classes that align with your interests that you'd like to explore?

2. Plan To Strengthen Family Support (Pre and Post Retirement)
Identify Essential Family Support

_____

Current Level of Support and Challenges

_____

List Specific Activities and the Strategies to Overcome Challenges

_____

3. **Plan for Organizational Support** (For example, AARP, National Council on Aging)
   Organization/ Group
   _____

   Type of Support or Services Needed
   _____

   Current Level of Involvement
   _____

   Plan to Initiate or Increase Use or Involvement
   _____

4. **Plan for Engagement with Community Programs and Services** (For example, YMCA, volunteer opportunities, travel clubs, arts and crafts workshops)
   Program/Service
   _____

   Type of Support Provided and Needed
   _____

   Current Level of Engagement
   _____

   Plan to Participate
   _____

5. **Spirituality and Faith Community Support**
   Faith and Spiritual Communities
   _____

   Type of Support Provided
   _____

   Current Level of Engagement
   _____

Plan to Get Involved
_____

6. **Plan to Engage Other Support Systems**
   Other Needed Support System
   _____

   Type of Support Provided _____

   Current Level of Engagement
   _____

   Plan to Utilize
   _____

7. **Diversity Considerations in Strengthening Social Support**
   (Consider inclusivity factors, such as accessibility for individuals with disabilities, reliable transportation options, language support for non-English speakers, access to culturally responsive health care, celebration of cultural heritage, guidance in navigating financial resources, diverse housing solutions, and support for caregiving responsibilities.)
   Social Support Needed
   _____

   Current Level of Engagement
   _____

   Plan To Access and Use This Resource
   _____

8. **Social Support System Needs by Generation**
   (For example, Baby Boomers = financial planning and health care access. Gen Xers = work-life balance and financial literacy resources. Millennials = affordable housing solutions. Gen Zers = career guidance, including resources to aid their transition into the workforce and retirement planning.)

Support Needed
_____

Opportunities
_____

Current Level of Engagement
_____

Plan to Connect
_____

Now, state your action plans in the form of short-term and long-term goals. Identify immediate steps you can take over the next month to enhance your social network as well as in the longer term. Plan for how to continue building and supporting these connections over the next year.

Action Plan

_____
_____
_____
_____
_____
_____

This worksheet serves as a supportive tool to help you thoughtfully build your social network for a fulfilling retirement. Prioritize connecting with others and take proactive steps toward strengthening your emotional support systems.

Chapter 12: Putting It All Together: Action Plan for Thriving in Retirement

YOUR ACTION PLAN FOR OPTIMAL AGING-FRIENDLY LIVING

Use the worksheet below to assess your preferences and plan for a living situation that aligns with your vision and needs as you transition into retirement. This tool is designed to help you identify the most suitable options, evaluate associated costs, and set up actionable steps for each living arrangement. By taking the time to complete this assessment, you'll be empowered to create an aging-friendly environment that supports your independence and enhances your quality of life in retirement.

Preferences for Living Arrangements
1. **Aging in Place (i.e., aging in your community)**
   - Preference/Suitability (rate on a scale of 1–5):
   - Considerations *(aging-friendly/visitability/universal design)*:
   - Action Steps:
   - Time Frame:
2. **Naturally Occurring Retirement Communities (NORC)**
   - Preference/Suitability (rate on a scale of 1–5):
   - Considerations *(aging-friendly/visitability/universal design)*:
   - Action Steps:
   - Time Frame:
3. **Village Community**
   - Preference/Suitability (rate on a scale of 1–5):
   - Considerations *(aging-friendly/visitability/universal design)*:
   - Action Steps:
   - Time Frame:
4. **Blending Lives While Living Separately**
   - Preference/Suitability (rate on a scale of 1–5):
   - Considerations *(aging-friendly/visitability/universal design)*:
   - Action Steps:
   - Time Frame:

5. **Move in with Relatives**
   - Preference/Suitability (rate on a scale of 1–5):
   - Considerations *(aging-friendly/visitability/universal design)*:
   - Action Steps:
   - Time Frame:
6. **Casitas**
   - Preference/Suitability (rate on a scale of 1–5):
   - Considerations *(aging-friendly/visitability/universal design)*:
   - Action Steps:
   - Time Frame:
7. **Cohousing**
   - Preference/Suitability (rate on a scale of 1–5):
   - Considerations *(aging-friendly/visitability/universal design)*:
   - Action Steps:
   - Time Frame:
8. **55+ and Retirement Communities**
   - Preference/Suitability (rate on a scale of 1–5):
   - Considerations *(aging-friendly/visitability/universal design)*:
   - Action Steps:
   - Time Frame:
9. **Tiny Homes Communities**
   - Preference/Suitability (rate on a scale of 1–5):
   - Considerations *(aging-friendly/visitability/universal design)*:
   - Action Steps:
   - Time Frame:
10. **University-Based Retirement Communities**
    - Preference/Suitability (rate on a scale of 1–5):
    - Considerations *(aging-friendly/visitability/universal design)*:
    - Action Steps:
    - Time Frame:

11. **Retire on a Cruise Ship**
    - Preference/Suitability (rate on a scale of 1–5):
    - Considerations *(aging-friendly/visitability/universal design)*:
    - Action Steps:
    - Time Frame:

12. **International Retirement Living Arrangements**
    - Preference/Suitability (rate on a scale of 1–5):
    - Considerations *(aging-friendly/visitability/universal design)*:
    - Action Steps:
    - Time Frame:

13. **Continuing Care Retirement Community** (CCRC)
    - Preference/Suitability (rate on a scale of 1–5):
    - Considerations *(aging-friendly/visitability/universal design)*:
    - Action Steps:
    - Time Frame:

Action Plan
Select Your Top Three Housing Options

- _____
- _____
- _____

Evaluate the Cost and Affordability of Your Selections

Housing Costs. What is the average rent in your target area? For homeowners, what mortgage or downsizing options do you have? Include HOA fees, if applicable.

- _____
- _____
- _____

Property Taxes. What are the property tax rates in your chosen location?

- _____
- _____
- _____

Utilities. What are your estimated monthly utility costs? (Electricity, water, gas, Internet, trash collection)

- _____
- _____
- _____

General Living Expenses

What will your grocery costs be? Will you own a vehicle or use public transportation? If you own a home, what are the possible unexpected expenses? Budget a monthly and yearly cost for the general living expenses below.

Monthly-Yearly

Food	_____ - _____
Car Costs (gas, insurance, repairs)	_____ - _____
Home repairs	_____ - _____
Transportation (mass transit and air travel)	_____ - _____
Medical and Dental Premiums and Deductibles	_____ - _____
Extraordinary Medical and Dental (uncovered, e.g., a dental implant)	

_____

Climate Preferences

Do you prefer a warmer or cooler climate? How do you feel about seasonal variations and extreme weather conditions?

- _____
- _____

Home Modification and or Support Needed

Home Accessibility Improvements
Assess how to make your current or future home more accessible and aging-friendly.

Action

_____

_____

Time Frame

_____

_____

Transportation Options
Find available options for getting around, whether in your community or when traveling.

Action

_____

_____

Time Frame

_____

_____

Assisted Care Options
Research local services for in-home care or assistance.

Action

_____

_____

Time Frame

_____

_____

Social Networks and Support

Determine how to stay connected with family, friends, and community resources.

Action

_____

_____

Time Frame

_____

_____

Reflect and Plan
Questions to Think About

- Which living option resonates most with your lifestyle and needs?
- What modifications will you prioritize to enhance your living environment for optimal aging?
- How will you ensure that you stay connected socially within your chosen living arrangement?

Immediate Actions

List specific steps you can take in the next month to assess and prepare for your chosen living situation.

_____

_____

_____

_____

Long-Term Goals

Outline a plan for how you will continue to assess and refine your living situation over the next year.

_____

_____

_____

_____

Chapter 12: Putting It All Together: Action Plan for Thriving in Retirement

By using this assessment and planning tool, you can thoughtfully design a retirement living arrangement that supports your aging-friendly goals. Take proactive steps to ensure your home and community fit your needs, allowing you to age gracefully and enjoy this exciting new chapter of your life.

LIFE AFTER RETIREMENT: *INSPIRING STORIES AND ADVICE*

Let us examine two notable examples of individuals who have successfully incorporated these planning elements into their retirement plans: Alexa, who has already integrated them, and Jewel, who is in the process of formulating her retirement plan.

ALEXA'S TRANSITION TO A CREATIVE LIFE— RENEWED, REVITALIZED, AND REALIGNED

After a fulfilling career in corporate financial services, I made the bold decision to take early retirement at 55, equipped with a pension and retirement package that provided me with financial stability. Inheriting my childhood home only added to that stability and allowed me to take the next steps in my life with confidence.

As a divorced single woman, I relocated to another state to be closer to my family, purchased a new home, and later remarried. Upon moving, I found myself returning to work while also nurturing my artistic passions. It was during an entrepreneurship class that I met a wonderful couple of artists, which sparked my connection to the local artist community. I began volunteering at their artist collective, where they had studio space, and took another class aimed at unlocking creativity. This experience reignited my passion for painting and helped me develop my artistic talents.

Eventually, I left my corporate job to embrace retirement fully and dive headfirst into my artistic journey. Now, I'm proud to say I am an established artist, enjoying a balanced life filled with painting, family, daily yoga, and walks. I feel fulfilled, doing what I love in my own way and on my own time. All is good.

ALEXA'S ADVICE

In the same way that I found joy in reconnecting with my creative side, I encourage you to seek out interests or hobbies that bring you happiness. My transition into this next chapter involved embracing my artistic talents and becoming an established artist, all while connecting with the local art community.

You have the power to make a difference in your community by volunteering. My journey shows that pursuing your passions and contributing to the world around you can lead to a fulfilling and balanced life. Whether it's through art, volunteering, or whatever sparks your interest, you can renew, revitalize, refresh, and realign your life. Go for it!

JEWEL STEPPING OUT OF MY COMFORT ZONE AND EMBRACING NEW EXPERIENCES

For 34 years, nursing was more than just my profession—it was a defining part of my identity. As a nurse practitioner, I took immense pride in my commitment to helping others and making a tangible difference. Being regarded as the expert in the room provided me with a sense of fulfillment. My patients relied on me, my department depended on my expertise, and I felt deeply needed in a career that was both meaningful and essential.

Retirement was a distant concept, one I hadn't seriously contemplated until a few years ago. Immersed in the daily rhythms of work, I

Chapter 12: Putting It All Together: Action Plan for Thriving in Retirement

found comfort in routine, which perhaps shielded me from considering what lay beyond my professional life. When thoughts of retirement did surface, financial apprehensions loomed large.

Despite having a pension, a 403(b), and solid benefits, I questioned whether I had saved enough to sustain a comfortable retirement. Consulting with a financial planner and other professional advisors provided much-needed clarity and reassurance. Additionally, familial responsibilities weighed heavily on my mind—I was the primary caregiver for my 90-year-old mother and felt a duty to be present to support my adult children. Complicating matters further, my partner and I were contemplating significant decisions about our future residence and lifestyle.

A pivotal shift in my perspective occurred during the past two years. The end of the COVID-19 pandemic prompted many of my colleagues and friends to retire, especially those who had the means to do so. Observing this exodus, coupled with the evolving nature of health care delivery, compelled me to reflect on my own future. I came to understand that waiting for the "perfect" moment to retire was futile. Witnessing peers transition into retirement, some opting for per diem nursing work to maintain a connection to the field while enjoying greater control over their schedules, illuminated a path forward. This realization transformed my fear of leaving my job into a fear of remaining stagnant. The pendulum had swung, and I am now eager to explore the possibilities that lay ahead.

With excitement and anticipation, I am preparing to retire this year. I am organizing various aspects of the transition, including ensuring financial stability, maintaining health and social connections, and relocating from the Northeast to a warmer climate in the South near a network of friends. Open discussions with my partner and family have been instrumental in crafting a plan that aligns with our collective aspirations. I have come to trust that my children will navigate their paths successfully, and I am ready to dedicate the next chapter of my life to personal fulfillment. Over the past year, I pursued and obtained a coaching certificate, equipping me to guide others in health and wellness at a pace that suits me. I am granting myself the freedom to explore and embrace a life marked by peace and simplicity.

Jewel's Advice

As I reflect on my experience, I recognize the importance of early financial planning. In my younger years, I didn't fully grasp the significance of maximizing contributions to my 403(b) plan. As a divorced mother of two, my focus was on my family's immediate economic needs rather than long-term savings. If given the chance to redo this aspect of my life, I would prioritize saving more aggressively and taking full advantage of retirement accounts.

Financial literacy wasn't emphasized during my upbringing, and I had to learn its value over time. Women must be encouraged to budget wisely and manage their finances proactively. Moreover, it's important not to become overly tethered to one's workplace. While our professions are significant, they should not define our entire existence. A balanced perspective allows for a more fulfilling transition into the enriching opportunities that retirement can offer.

The Road Ahead: Putting It All Together

As you wrap up your exploration of retirement planning, it's time to bring together all the insights and strategies you've gathered into a cohesive, holistic retirement action plan. This plan will serve as your roadmap, guiding you through the various aspects of your life as you transition into retirement. By encompassing key areas such as financial security, emotional wellness, health considerations, social connections, and living arrangements, you'll create a comprehensive strategy that supports your journey ahead.

Remember, this plan is a powerful tool that will help you navigate this exciting transition with confidence and clarity. Embrace the opportunity to shape your future, knowing you have the knowledge and resources to create a fulfilling and rewarding retirement. You can do this!

You've spent time reflecting on your vision for retirement, defining your goals, and exploring how to achieve financial security, support your health, and nurture your emotional well-being. You've also considered how to build meaningful social connections and shape the lifestyle that will bring you joy. Now, it's time to pull everything together into a comprehensive action plan.

This plan serves as your personalized roadmap for retirement, reflecting the life you truly want to lead. It will help you stay focused, motivated, and adaptable as your circumstances and priorities evolve. Think of it as a living document — one you can revisit and adjust as you continue to grow and experience new opportunities.

Your Holistic Retirement Plan

Your Vision for Retirement
Reaffirm your overall vision for this next chapter of life. What does a fulfilling retirement look like to you? Keep this vision at the heart of your plan.
Your Vision

_____
_____
_____

Purpose and Goals
Clarify your goals—both big and small. Whether it's traveling the world, volunteering, learning new skills, or spending more time with loved ones, write them down. Define actionable steps to pursue these goals.

Your Purpose and Goals

_____
_____
_____

Financial Security and Satisfaction

Align your financial plan with your lifestyle goals. Ensure your income, savings, and expenses are balanced, and explore ways to sustain financial well-being throughout retirement.

Short-term goals and timelines:

_____
_____
_____

Long-term goals and timelines:

_____
_____
_____

Health for a Vibrant Future

Commit to practices that promote physical and mental well-being. From regular exercise and healthy eating to preventive care and wellness routines, include steps that will help you stay active and energized.

Short-term goals and timelines:

_____
_____
_____

Chapter 12: Putting It All Together: Action Plan for Thriving in Retirement

Long-term goals and timelines:

_____
_____
_____

Emotional Wellness

Recognize the importance of emotional well-being. Consider the practices, support networks, and professional resources that will help you manage life's transitions with resilience and joy.

Short-term goals and timelines:

_____
_____
_____

Long-term goals and timelines:

_____
_____
_____

Building Social Connections

Nurture relationships that bring you happiness and purpose. Identify opportunities to engage with your community, reconnect with old friends, or form new bonds through hobbies, volunteer work, or social events.

Short-term goals and timelines:

_____
_____
_____

Long-term goals and timelines:

_____
_____
_____

Retirement Living and Lifestyle

Think about where and how you want to live. Whether you plan to downsize, relocate, or stay in your current home, make choices that reflect your desired lifestyle. Consider your proximity to family, health care, leisure activities, and cultural experiences.

Short-term goals and timelines:

_____
_____
_____

Long-term goals and timelines:

_____
_____
_____

Chapter 12: Putting It All Together: Action Plan for Thriving in Retirement

PUTTING YOUR PLAN INTO ACTION

Congratulations, you now have a holistic plan for a retirement that is fulfilling and reflects your deepest desires. With your plan in hand, don't just sit back. Yes, there is more to do because your plan has to be as an evolving part of your life. As you grow, it must reflect that. This is why, you must stay connected to your plan and periodically:

1. **Review and Prioritize.** Take a step back and look at all the elements of your plan. Prioritize what's most important to you.

2. **Set Milestones.** Break larger goals into smaller, manageable steps with clear timelines.

3. **Stay Flexible.** Life can be unpredictable. Be open to adjusting your plan as circumstances and preferences shift.

4. **Seek Support.** Lean on family, friends, and professionals when needed. You don't have to navigate retirement alone.

5. **Celebrate Progress.** Acknowledge and celebrate your achievements along the way. Every step forward is a testament to your commitment to living a fulfilling retirement.

Your holistic retirement action plan is more than a checklist—it's a reflection of your hopes, dreams, and aspirations. By taking this thoughtful approach, you're setting yourself up for a purposeful, satisfying, and joyful retirement. You deserve nothing less. Now, move forward with confidence and excitement for what's to come!

CONCLUDING THOUGHTS

As you wrap up your exploration of retirement planning, it's time to bring together all the insights and strategies you've gathered into a cohesive, holistic retirement action plan. This plan will serve as your roadmap, guiding you through the various aspects of your life as you transition into retirement. By encompassing key areas such as financial security, emotional wellness, health considerations, social connections, and living arrangements, you'll create a comprehensive strategy that supports your journey ahead.

Remember, this plan is a powerful tool that will help you navigate this exciting transition with confidence and clarity. Embrace the opportunity to shape your future, knowing you have the knowledge and resources to create a fulfilling and rewarding retirement. You can do this!

You've spent time reflecting on your vision for retirement, defining your goals, and exploring how to achieve financial security, support your health, and nurture your emotional well-being. You've also considered how to build meaningful social connections and shape the lifestyle that will bring you joy. Now, it's time to pull everything together into a comprehensive action plan.

This plan serves as your personalized roadmap for retirement, reflecting the life you truly want to lead. It will help you stay focused, motivated, and adaptable as your circumstances and priorities evolve. Think of it as a living document — one you can revisit and adjust as you continue to grow and experience new opportunities.

Concrete Steps to Execute Your Holistic Retirement Plan:

Address Your Fears and Concerns: Begin by acknowledging and addressing any fears or concerns you have about retirement. This will help you approach this new chapter with a clear and positive mindset.

Create A Vision for Retirement: Reaffirm your overall vision for this next chapter of life. What does a fulfilling retirement look like to you? Keep this vision at the heart of your plan.

Financial Security and Satisfaction: Align your financial plan with your lifestyle goals. Ensure your income, savings, and expenses are balanced, and explore ways to sustain financial well-being throughout retirement.

Thrive Through Purpose and Meaning: Clarify your purpose and the activities that bring meaning to your life. Whether it's traveling the world, volunteering, learning new skills, or spending more time with loved ones, write them down. Define actionable steps to pursue these meaningful activities.

Cultivate Good Health for a Vibrant Future: Commit to practices that promote physical and mental well-being and take advantage of preventive services and wellness programs. From regular exercise and healthy eating to preventive care and wellness routines, include steps that will help you stay active and energized.

Maximize Health Insurance Coverage: Understand your policy including Medicare thoroughly. Prepare for long-term care by considering insurance options and planning ahead. Ensure you have essential legal documents like a living will and health care proxy. Work with your health care providers to create a comprehensive care plan that addresses your current and future health needs.

Foster Emotional Wellness: Recognize the importance of emotional well-being. Consider the practices, support networks, and professional resources that will help you manage life's transitions with resilience and joy.

Build Social Connections: Nurture relationships that bring you happiness and purpose. Identify opportunities to engage with your community, reconnect with old friends, or form new bonds through hobbies, volunteer work, or social events.

Retirement Living and Lifestyle: Think about where and how you want to live. Whether you plan to downsize, relocate, or stay in your current home, make choices that reflect your desired lifestyle. Consider your proximity to family, health care, leisure activities, and cultural experiences.

Putting Your Plan into Action:
Congratulations, you now have a holistic plan for a retirement that is fulfilling and reflects your deepest desires. With your plan in hand, don't just sit back. Yes, there is more to do because your plan has to be as an evolving part of your life. As you grow, it must reflect that. This is why, you must stay connected to your plan and periodically:

1. Review and Prioritize. Take a step back and look at all the elements of your plan. Prioritize what's most important to you.

2. Set Milestones. Break larger goals into smaller, manageable steps with clear timelines.

3. Stay Flexible. Life can be unpredictable. Be open to adjusting your plan as circumstances and preferences shift.

4. Seek Support. Lean on family, friends, and professionals when needed. You don't have to navigate retirement alone.

5. Celebrate Progress. Acknowledge and celebrate your achievements along the way. Every step forward is a testament to your commitment to living a fulfilling retirement.

Your holistic retirement action plan is more than a checklist—it's a reflection of your hopes, dreams, and aspirations. By taking this thoughtful approach, you're setting yourself up for a purposeful, satisfying, and joyful retirement. You deserve nothing less. Now, move forward with confidence and excitement for what's to come!

RESOURCES

Explore a wealth of resources by visiting our website at
EverythingRetirement.org

ABOUT THE AUTHORS

DR. CHERYL WAITES SPELLMAN

Dr. Cheryl Waites Spellman, a retired college professor and administrator, holds an Ed.D. in Counselor Education from North Carolina State University, an MSW from Fordham University, and a BA in Sociology from CUNY-Hunter College. As a respected scholar and fellow of prestigious gerontology and research organizations, she has made significant contributions to her field and is a widely published expert. Passionate about empowering the next generation, she believes in inspiring others to pursue their dreams, embrace lifelong learning, and live with purpose and fulfillment at every stage of life. Married with adult children and grandchildren, she delights in this enriching stage of life—traveling, engaging in ceramics, fostering community and intergenerational connections, and cherishing quality time with family and friends. Her life's mission is to uplift and motivate others to create meaningful, impactful lives now and in the future.

LESTER SPELLMAN

Lester G. Spellman Jr., a retired professional, holds an MBA from Columbia University with specializations in marketing and finance, bringing extensive expertise in strategic planning, business development, and logistics. With a proven track record in project management, marketing, and logistics, he has demonstrated exceptional leadership in media production, sales, distribution, and economic development, consistently driving growth and operational excellence. A dedicated family person with adult children and grandchildren, Lester enjoys traveling, boating, and golfing, and values nurturing strong relationships. Passionate about empowering others, he is a resilient, savvy, and highly organized well-being planner who excels at following through, inspiring others, and helping people live their best lives.

DEDICATION

Dedication to Cheryl's Mother:

To my mother, Bernice Ellegor, whose unwavering love, resilience, and dedication to service inspire me every day. Her strength, faith, courage, and joy exemplify a life driven by purpose. Her legacy of compassion and perseverance encourages me to live with meaning and to uplift others. I am forever grateful for her example and the lessons she has instilled in me to pursue a life of true fulfillment.

Dedication to Lester's Parents:

To Lester and Berenice Spellman, whose lifelong commitment to coaching, educating, and uplifting those around them has touched countless lives. Their passion for service and desire to help others live their best lives motivates me every day. Their legacy drives me to lead others toward discovering their purpose and experiencing lifelong satisfaction.

www.ingramcontent.com/pod-product-compliance
Lightning Source LLC
Chambersburg PA
CBHW080539030426
42337CB00024B/4798